ePublishing For Dummies®

W9-CFJ-009

File Extensions for Popular eBook Readers

Extension	Type of File
IMP	SoftBook Reader file
LIT	Microsoft Reader file
NKS	netLibrary document file
OPF	Package file for an OEB-compliant eBook
PDB	Peanut Press file
PDF	Adobe Acrobat file
RB	Rocket eBook file
TK3	Night Kitchen TK3 Reader

Valuable Web Sites for ePublishing

Site Name and URL	Description
AAP www.publishers.org/home/index.htm	The Association of American Publishers is the principal trade association of the book-publishing industry. The Web site is a fantastic resource for researching what's getting published and how the industry is adapting to the challenges of ePublishing.
Authorlink www.authorlink.com/	With something for everyone, this award-winning Web site is designed to serve the needs of authors, agents, editors, and publishers. In addition to many links of valuable information resources, Authorlink lets authors submit manuscripts to the ManuScript Showcase.
eBookNet.com www.ebooknet.com/	A Web site that helps build and support the eBook community. This site is a place for eBook advocates to exchange news information, ideas, and writing samples.
NetRead www.netread.com/	NetRead is a business hub for the book-publishing industry. The site provides marketing tools, a publishing job board, business listings, news, and information.
PublishersWeekly.com www.publishersweekly.com/	*Publisher's Weekly* is the Bible of the publishing industry. Each week, it covers publishing industry news, bestseller lists, top author interviews, and early reviews of adult and children's books. Of special note is the biweekly column on ePublishing issues.
Simba Information, Inc. www.simbanet.com/	Simba Information, Inc. is a research firm that collects and compiles market intelligence and forecasts for the media industry. Although most of their content is packaged and sold to large corporations, you can often find interesting statistics by reading the press releases (see www.simbanet.com/press/index.html).
Web-Source.net www.web-source.net/	A Web site devoted to providing information on eBooks, Web developer resources, Web design techniques, eMarketing, and promotional information. It takes a bit of patience to navigate this site, but you can gain some useful information if you persevere.

For Dummies®: Bestselling Book Series for Beginners

ePublishing For Dummies®

Cheat Sheet

A sample OEB Package (.opf) File

```xml
<?xml version="1.0"?>
<!DOCTYPE package
  PUBLIC "+//ISBN 0-9673008-1-9//DTD OEB 1.0 Package//EN"
  "http://openebook.org/dtds/oeb-1.0/oebpkg1.dtd">
<package unique-identifier="wonderlandebook">
  <metadata xmlns:dc="http://purl.org/dc/elements/1.0/" xmlns:
          oebpackage="http://openebook.org/namespaces/oeb-package/1.0/">
    <dc-metadata>
      <dc:Identifier id="wonderlandebook" scheme="adhoc">
          wonderland0627</dc:Identifier>
      <dc:Title>Alice in Wonderland</dc:Title>
      <dc:Creator role="aut" file-as="Carroll, Lewis">Lewis
          Carroll</dc:Creator>
    </dc-metadata>
  </metadata>
  <manifest>
    <item id="doc" href="Hello Wonderland.htm" media-type="text/
          x-oeb1-document" />
    <item id="ALice_Image" href="Hello%20Wonderland_image002.jpg"
          media-type="image/jpg" />
  </manifest>
  <spine>
    <itemref idref="doc"/>
  </spine>
</package>
```

For Dummies®: Bestselling Book Series for Beginners

ePublishing FOR DUMMIES®

by Victoria Rosenborg

IDG Books Worldwide, Inc.
An International Data Group Company

Foster City, CA ◆ Chicago, IL ◆ Indianapolis, IN ◆ New York, NY

ePublishing For Dummies®

Published by
IDG Books Worldwide, Inc.
An International Data Group Company
919 E. Hillsdale Blvd.
Suite 300
Foster City, CA 94404
www.idgbooks.com (IDG Books Worldwide Web Site)
www.dummies.com (Dummies Press Web Site)

Library of Congress Control Number: 00-108206

ISBN: 0-7645-0781-8

Printed in the United States of America

10 9 8 7 6 5 4 3 2 1

1B/RT/RS/QQ/IN

Distributed in the United States by IDG Books Worldwide, Inc.

Distributed by CDG Books Canada Inc. for Canada; by Transworld Publishers Limited in the United Kingdom; by IDG Norge Books for Norway; by IDG Sweden Books for Sweden; by IDG Books Australia Publishing Corporation Pty. Ltd. for Australia and New Zealand; by TransQuest Publishers Pte Ltd. for Singapore, Malaysia, Thailand, Indonesia, and Hong Kong; by Gotop Information Inc. for Taiwan; by ICG Muse, Inc. for Japan; by Intersoft for South Africa; by Eyrolles for France; by International Thomson Publishing for Germany, Austria and Switzerland; by Distribuidora Cuspide for Argentina; by LR International for Brazil; by Galileo Libros for Chile; by Ediciones ZETA S.C.R. Ltda. for Peru; by WS Computer Publishing Corporation, Inc., for the Philippines; by Contemporanea de Ediciones for Venezuela; by Express Computer Distributors for the Caribbean and West Indies; by Micronesia Media Distributor, Inc. for Micronesia; by Chips Computadoras S.A. de C.V. for Mexico; by Editorial Norma de Panama S.A. for Panama; by American Bookshops for Finland.

For general information on IDG Books Worldwide's books in the U.S., please call our Consumer Customer Service department at 800-762-2974. For reseller information, including discounts and premium sales, please call our Reseller Customer Service department at 800-434-3422.

For information on where to purchase IDG Books Worldwide's books outside the U.S., please contact our International Sales department at 317-572-3993 or fax 317-572-4002.

For consumer information on foreign language translations, please contact our Customer Service department at 1-800-434-3422, fax 317-572-4002, or e-mail rights@idgbooks.com.

For information on licensing foreign or domestic rights, please phone +1-650-653-7098.

For sales inquiries and special prices for bulk quantities, please contact our Order Services department at 800-434-3422 or write to the address above.

For information on using IDG Books Worldwide's books in the classroom or for ordering examination copies, please contact our Educational Sales department at 800-434-2086 or fax 317-572-4005.

For press review copies, author interviews, or other publicity information, please contact our Public Relations department at 650-653-7000 or fax 650-653-7500.

For authorization to photocopy items for corporate, personal, or educational use, please contact Copyright Clearance Center, 222 Rosewood Drive, Danvers, MA 01923, or fax 978-750-4470.

About the Author

Victoria Rosenborg is the Director of Technology for iPublish.com, Time Warner Trade Publishing's new eBook publishing venture. She also worked in the publishing industry, helping HarperCollins and R.R. Donnelley build interactive content based on bestselling books. A recognized expert in new media, Victoria is also the author of *A Guide to Multimedia*.

Victoria worked at Microsoft Corporation for six years. She started as a technical evangelist, helping executives in the publishing and television industries incorporate Microsoft technologies into their Web sites. Part of the launch team for MSNBC, Victoria managed the developers that created Web sites for *Dateline*, *Nightly News with Tom Brokaw*, the *Today Show* and *Meet the Press*. Victoria managed the development teams for the Microsoft Windows 98 Web site and the Microsoft BackOffice Web site. As a Senior Program Manager, Victoria also worked on Microsoft Publisher and on bCentral.com, Microsoft's small business portal. Victoria is married with two children, and lives in the New York City area.

ABOUT IDG BOOKS WORLDWIDE

Welcome to the world of IDG Books Worldwide.

IDG Books Worldwide, Inc., is a subsidiary of International Data Group, the world's largest publisher of computer-related information and the leading global provider of information services on information technology. IDG was founded more than 30 years ago by Patrick J. McGovern and now employs more than 9,000 people worldwide. IDG publishes more than 290 computer publications in over 75 countries. More than 90 million people read one or more IDG publications each month.

Launched in 1990, IDG Books Worldwide is today the #1 publisher of best-selling computer books in the United States. We are proud to have received eight awards from the Computer Press Association in recognition of editorial excellence and three from Computer Currents' First Annual Readers' Choice Awards. Our best-selling ...*For Dummies*® series has more than 50 million copies in print with translations in 31 languages. IDG Books Worldwide, through a joint venture with IDG's Hi-Tech Beijing, became the first U.S. publisher to publish a computer book in the People's Republic of China. In record time, IDG Books Worldwide has become the first choice for millions of readers around the world who want to learn how to better manage their businesses.

Our mission is simple: Every one of our books is designed to bring extra value and skill-building instructions to the reader. Our books are written by experts who understand and care about our readers. The knowledge base of our editorial staff comes from years of experience in publishing, education, and journalism — experience we use to produce books to carry us into the new millennium. In short, we care about books, so we attract the best people. We devote special attention to details such as audience, interior design, use of icons, and illustrations. And because we use an efficient process of authoring, editing, and desktop publishing our books electronically, we can spend more time ensuring superior content and less time on the technicalities of making books.

You can count on our commitment to deliver high-quality books at competitive prices on topics you want to read about. At IDG Books Worldwide, we continue in the IDG tradition of delivering quality for more than 30 years. You'll find no better book on a subject than one from IDG Books Worldwide.

John Kilcullen
Chairman and CEO
IDG Books Worldwide, Inc.

Eighth Annual Computer Press Awards ≥1992

Ninth Annual Computer Press Awards ≥1993

Tenth Annual Computer Press Awards ≥1994

Eleventh Annual Computer Press Awards ≥1995

IDG is the world's leading IT media, research and exposition company. Founded in 1964, IDG had 1997 revenues of $2.05 billion and has more than 9,000 employees worldwide. IDG offers the widest range of media options that reach IT buyers in 75 countries representing 95% of worldwide IT spending. IDG's diverse product and services portfolio spans six key areas including print publishing, online publishing, expositions and conferences, market research, education and training, and global marketing services. More than 90 million people read one or more of IDG's 290 magazines and newspapers, including IDG's leading global brands — Computerworld, PC World, Network World, Macworld and the Channel World family of publications. IDG Books Worldwide is one of the fastest-growing computer book publishers in the world, with more than 700 titles in 36 languages. The "...For Dummies®" series alone has more than 50 million copies in print. IDG offers online users the largest network of technology-specific Web sites around the world through IDG.net (http://www.idg.net), which comprises more than 225 targeted Web sites in 55 countries worldwide. International Data Corporation (IDC) is the world's largest provider of information technology data, analysis and consulting, with research centers in over 41 countries and more than 400 research analysts worldwide. IDG World Expo is a leading producer of more than 168 globally branded conferences and expositions in 35 countries including E3 (Electronic Entertainment Expo), Macworld Expo, ComNet, Windows World Expo, ICE (Internet Commerce Expo), Agenda, DEMO, and Spotlight. IDG's training subsidiary, ExecuTrain, is the world's largest computer training company, with more than 230 locations worldwide and 785 training courses. IDG Marketing Services helps industry-leading IT companies build international brand recognition by developing global integrated marketing programs via IDG's print, online and exposition products worldwide. Further information about the company can be found at www.idg.com.   1/26/00

Dedication

To my long-suffering husband and children, your patience and understanding deserves a family vacation. (My husband made me write this dedication . . .)

Author's Acknowledgments

Because this book wasn't ePublished, I have a lot of people to thank for the role they played in its production. Carole McClendon deserves thanks for being my agent. Because of her, I had the opportunity to write a *...For Dummies* book. Thank you to Laura Moss, the acquisitions editor who agreed to publish the book. Thank you to Steve Hayes, who took over for Laura, and helped me out during a major deadline crunch. A big thank you goes to William Barton and Rebekah Mancilla, who copy edited this book. Kim Blagg deserves thanks for her role as the technical editor. Thank you to Richard Graves and the entire IDG media team. Most of all, I'd like to thank Sheri Replin. As the project editor for this book, she has been totally wonderful to work with!

Publisher's Acknowledgments

We're proud of this book; please register your comments through our IDG Books Worldwide Online Registration Form located at www.dummies.com.

Some of the people who helped bring this book to market include the following:

Acquisitions, Editorial, and Media Development

Project Editor: Sheri Replin

Acquisitions Editors: Steven H. Hayes, Laura Moss

Copy Editors: Rebekah Mancilla, William A. Barton

Proof Editor: Mary SeRine

Technical Editor: Kim Blagg

Senior Permissions Editor: Carmen Krikorian

Associate Media Development Specialist: Megan Decraene

Media Development Coordinator: Marisa E. Pearman

Editorial Managers: Jeanne S. Criswell, Kyle Looper

Media Development Manager: Laura Carpenter

Media Development Supervisor: Richard Graves

Editorial Assistant: Candace Nicholson

Production

Project Coordinator: Nancee Reeves

Layout and Graphics: Amy Adrian, Beth Brooks, Brian Drumm, Brian Torwelle, Julie Trippetti, Jacque Schneider, Jeremey Unger, Erin Zeltner

Proofreaders: Corey Bowen, Susan Moritz, Carl Pierce, York Production Services, Inc.

Indexer: York Production Services, Inc.

General and Administrative

IDG Books Worldwide, Inc.: John Kilcullen, CEO; Bill Barry, President and COO; John Ball, Executive VP, Operations & Administration; John Harris, CFO

IDG Books Technology Publishing Group: Richard Swadley, Senior Vice President and Publisher; Mary Bednarek, Vice President and Publisher; Walter R. Bruce III, Vice President and Publisher; Joseph Wikert, Vice President and Publisher; Mary C. Corder, Editorial Director; Andy Cummings, Publishing Director, General User Group; Barry Pruett, Publishing Director

IDG Books Manufacturing: Ivor Parker, Vice President, Manufacturing

IDG Books Marketing: John Helmus, Assistant Vice President, Director of Marketing

IDG Books Online Management: Brenda McLaughlin, Executive Vice President, Chief Internet Officer; Gary Millrood, Executive Vice President of Business Development, Sales and Marketing

IDG Books Packaging: Marc J. Mikulich, Vice President, Brand Strategy and Research

IDG Books Production for Branded Press: Debbie Stailey, Production Director

IDG Books Sales: Roland Elgey, Senior Vice President, Sales and Marketing; Michael Violano, Vice President, International Sales and Sub Rights

◆

The publisher would like to give special thanks to Patrick J. McGovern, without whom this book would not have been possible.

◆

Contents at a Glance

Cartoons at a Glance

By Rich Tennant

page 7

"You show a lot of promise in ePublishing. Your first novel was rich with gripping XHTML, breathtaking in its hyperlinks, and visionary in it's cross-browser platform."

page 233

page 61

"Exactly whose idea was it to try and download all of the Harry Potter books?"

page 321

page 137

page 289

Fax: 978-546-7747
E-mail: richtennant@the5thwave.com
World Wide Web: www.the5thwave.com

Table of Contents

Introduction

● ●

So you wanna be a writer? Before the eBook revolution, becoming a writer meant making some sacrifices. It often meant years of working soulless jobs to pay the rent while churning out thousands of pages in your spare time, knowing that no one would ever read most of your work. Being a writer meant collecting dozens of rejection letters for your Magnum Opus and waiting for the rare agent or editor who could recognize your special gift. Your hope was that, perhaps one day, if you were lucky, someone might actually publish your work.

Fast-forward to a new millennium, where things are now much improved for writers. Instead of waiting for someone to take a chance on you, you can publish your own work and build a market for it. If you build enough of a market, an established publisher may even ask to produce a print-version of your eBook. If you build a large enough market, you may decide to reject the publisher because publishing eBooks makes you a bigger profit than working with an established publishing house does!

About This Book

If you want to publish original material in an eBook format but need to find out exactly how to do it, this book's for you. In these pages, I show you how to do the following:

- ✓ Become an expert on eBooks.
- ✓ Find a good topic to write about.
- ✓ Organize your content.
- ✓ Write effectively for your chosen audience.
- ✓ Package your work for multiple audiences.
- ✓ Make your content work for the medium by adding links, interactivity, and other media (such as sound and animation).
- ✓ Structure your document for digital presentation by organizing your text into easily digestible chunks.
- ✓ Provide your readers with navigational tools such as a content map.
- ✓ Use color, images, and fonts in an effective, professional manner.

✔ Build a simple eBook by adding HTML and XML tags to a document that you create in Microsoft Word 2000.

✔ Use different authoring tools to create different eBook formats: OverDrive's ReaderWorks Software, RocketWriter Software, SoftBook Personal Publisher, and Adobe Acrobat 4.0.

✔ Test your eBook document on different eBook readers.

✔ Build a Web site to sell your eBooks.

✔ Distribute your eBook through an ePublisher.

✔ Lock the content of your eBook.

✔ Become an eBook publisher.

✔ Market your eBook.

✔ Get publicity for your eBook.

✔ Avoid common blunders.

Conventions Used in This Book

The following information explains how I structure the content of this book. IDG Books calls these tidbits the book's *conventions*. (I promise to restrain myself from making election-year jokes. . . .)

Following are this book's conventions:

✔ Actions that I ask you, the reader, to perform appear in **bold** text.

✔ New terms appear in *italics*.

✔ In some sections of this book, I ask you to put content into an eBook format by using HTML and XML tags. (Relax . . . it's easier than it sounds!) These tags provide formatting information that tell a browser or eBook reader how to display the elements of a page. In this book, tags appear in a special typeface. An example of a formatting tag is `<TITLE>`.

✔ In giving the *URLs (Uniform Resource Locators)* for Web pages, I use the same special typeface as for tags. (URLs are the addresses that you use to specify the online location of a particular Web site or page.) An example of how a URL looks in this book is `www.dummies.com`.

✔ If I tell you to open a menu and choose a specific command from that menu, I use a special arrow symbol (⇨) to connect the name of the command with the menu on which it appears. If I tell you to "Choose File⇨ Save," therefore, you simply click the File menu up on the menu bar to open it, read down the menu until you find the Save command, and then click the Save command.

Foolish Assumptions

In writing this book, I make certain assumptions that I know aren't correct. I pretend that you never attended Miss Clump's Fifth Grade class or know anything about sentence structure. I act as if you've never written a memo or an e-mail. I assume that you don't know much about how to write. (In reality, most people have a great deal of experience as writers long before they attempt their first book-length work.)

I'm also assuming that you're working on a Windows PC and using Microsoft Word 2000. Although you don't really need to upgrade if you're using an earlier version of Word, the latest version enables you to more easily build some of the eBook formats that I discuss. If you need to use specialized software, such as Adobe Acrobat, I give the version numbers that I use to create the samples in the book.

Note: Macintosh users can adapt many of the concepts in this book to the Mac. You won't be able to follow the detailed instructions that I give in this book, but you can still benefit from a general understanding of eBook formats.

How This Book Is Organized

I organize this book into five different sections; each section focuses on a particular set of skills to show you how to create, format, publish, market, and sell eBooks. Reading each section (or even each chapter, for that matter!) isn't necessary. Take what you like from the following sections and leave the rest.

Part 1: Filling Up the Blank Screen

Nothing's scarier than a blank screen if you want to write something (and especially if you need to meet a deadline). If you have no idea how to begin, Part I gets you over the hump. These three chapters calm your nerves and get you ready to write.

Before you can run, you gotta know how to walk. Before you can write an eBook, you need to know what an eBook is. Chapter 1 turns you into the neighborhood eBook expert; it covers everything that you can ever want to know about eBooks but are afraid to ask. Chapter 2 guides you in deciding your topic. By the time that you finish reading it, you get a pretty good idea how to pick a topic that people want to read. Chapter 3 rounds out your initial work by showing you effective ways to research your topic online. I show you how to determine whether anyone else has written about the same topic and, if so, ways to differentiate yourself from the competition.

Part II: Starting to Write

Part II gets you writing and teaches you how to create content that works in an eBook format. Chapter 4 helps you jumpstart your creative process by giving you tools to help you organize your content. Chapter 5 shows you how to communicate effectively, how to quickly get a first draft down on paper, and how to copy edit your work. Because most current eBooks are just linear books that you "print" to an eBook format, Chapter 6 gets you thinking beyond the linear structure of your document and shows you how to add links, interactivity, and other media to make your eBook a rich digital experience for your audience. If you want even more information about how to add interactivity to eBooks, Chapter 7 tells you what works (and what doesn't) for specific types of books, including fiction, nonfiction, children's literature, general interest, how-to books, and technical books.

Part III: Packaging Your Content

Writing an eBook is just the beginning. After you finish writing the content, you need to put on your production hat and get your eBook ready for distribution. Part III shows you how to structure your document, package it for different audiences, and format it for a variety of eBook readers. Chapter 8 explains how the structure of an eBook is similar to that of a well-designed Web site and shows you how to provide a navigation map for your readers. Chapter 9 tells how to get the most out of a single document by packaging the same material as an article, a booklet, a manual, and an eBook to meet the needs of different audiences. In Chapter 10, you find out how to roll your own eBook from scratch by adding formatting tags to a simple text document. If that's too much work for you, Chapter 11 covers the various authoring tools you can use that automatically add the formatting tags to your document.

Part IV: Profiting from All That Work

As if the process of writing, packaging, and formatting your work isn't rewarding enough, Part IV shows you how to actually make money by distributing your eBook. (Isn't getting your work in front of an audience the reason that you wanted to become a writer in the first place?) You can follow the instructions in Chapter 12 and build an e-commerce–enabled Web site in less than a half-hour to sell your work. Chapter 12 also shows you how to submit your work for sale on a Web site, such as MightyWords.com (www.mightywords.com), and how to sell your eBook on BN.com (www.bn.com) or Amazon.com (www.amazon.com). Chapter 13 tells you how to work with one of the new eBook publishing houses if you decide self-publishing isn't for you. If you decide to become an eBook publisher, Chapter 14 helps you get going.

Part V: The Part of Tens

Part V is full of helpful tips that I want to pass on before waving you on your way down the road of literary fame. Each chapter covers some of the important do's and don'ts of eBook publishing. Chapter 15 lists ten great ways to market your work by using the Web as a resource. Chapter 16 identifies ten ways to publicize and promote your work. Chapter 17 gives examples of ten different forms of ePublishing (everything from digital storytelling to selling your expertise on www.ePinions.com). Chapter 18 lists ten common eBook blunders to avoid to make sure that your work doesn't look like an amateur's. In Chapter 19, I explain ways that eBooks are changing ten types of printed books (from biographies to textbooks).

The Online Directory and CD-ROM

The Online Directory lists dozens of resources on the Web to help you with your ePublishing efforts. This directory includes Web sites to help you find an agent, conduct book-related research, view examples of existing eBooks, read interactive fiction, identify eBook Publishers, find an editor, get help with your public-relations efforts, and locate places where you can sell your work.

In addition to giving you links to all the Web sites in the Online Directory, the book's CD-ROM contains forms and templates to help you jumpstart your creativity and organize your content. The CD-ROM also includes copies of Chapter 1 of this book in a variety of eBook formats, including the Adobe PDF format and the Microsoft Reader eBook format. Additionally, the CD repackages the first chapter as an article, a booklet, a manual, and an eBook to show you examples of how you can reuse material to meet the needs of different audiences and markets.

Icons Used in This Book

Throughout the book, you find funny little pictures sitting in the margins next to certain paragraphs. These pictures are known as *icons,* and they mark text to which you may (or may not) want to pay special attention. You find the following icons in this book:

This icon contains a personal anecdote that applies to a particular concept I discuss.

A paragraph displaying this icon tells you what's on the CD-ROM that comes with this book.

A Remember icon flags the information that you need to remember as you work.

If you see this icon, you can take a breather, as it points to the information that may interest you if you like to know all the technical details but that you don't necessarily need to know otherwise.

Good-to-know information that helps you in the creation, formatting, marketing, or distribution of eBooks displays this little icon.

Watch out for this icon; it identifies things that may cause you problems.

Where to Go from Here

Now you know the stuff that you need to understand to read this book. Just flip through the Table of Contents, find something that interests you, and start ePublishing!

Good luck!

Part I

Filling Up the Blank Screen

In this part . . .

Authoring a book is a big undertaking. Before you sit in front of a blank screen and write the Great American eNovel, you need to do a few things: First, find out what eBooks are and how to read them. Next, you need to decide on a topic and do a little research. Part I helps you take these steps before you type your first sentence.

Chapter 1 is a primer on how to use eBooks. This chapter describes the differences between all the different eBook readers and explains how to download, install, and use each one.

Chapter 2 helps you find a topic by determining what you hope to achieve by becoming an author. This chapter helps identify the audience for your work and shows you how to figure out your audience's needs.

Chapter 3 explains how to conduct research online to find other authors that have written about your topic. This chapter gives efficient research techniques and shows you how to analyze online reviews.

Chapter 1

Making Yourself an eBook Expert

*B*efore you can run, you have to walk, and before you write your first eBook, you need to know something about eBooks in general. After you read this chapter, you can amaze your friends and family with the depth and breadth of your eBook knowledge (okay, not really . . . but you'll know just enough to be dangerous). I know you're eager to start writing, but do yourself a favor and review this chapter before you begin. That way, you'll have an understanding of the different readers and platforms that you can write for.

Getting the Skinny on eBooks

The term *eBook* can mean a number of different things. Sometimes, it refers to hardware (like the *Franklin eBookMan* or the *Rocket eBook*) that looks like a cross between a PC and a hardcover book. These devices enable you to download and read digital texts on the screen. You can also annotate and highlight passages of text, just like you can with a printed book (if you're the type of person who doesn't mind marking up the pages).

eBook also means electronic text that's formatted specifically for people to read on a screen. (However, people often print the text for easier reading, especially if the text is more than a handful of pages.) eBooks can be delivered on a CD-ROM or floppy disk, but most of the time, they're delivered online as a file attached to an e-mail or downloaded from a Web site.

eBook readers are software applications that enable you to read eBooks that are formatted a certain way. If you want to read a document that has been saved in Adobe PDF format, for example, you need to download and install the Adobe Acrobat Reader before you can open and view the file. Or, if you want to read LIT files, you need to install the Microsoft Reader. PDF and LIT files are just two competing formats; many other formats are available.

Confused yet? You're not alone. Although the concept of electronic text has been around for many years, the term *eBook* is still relatively new, and eBooks are just starting to become more popular.

Table 1-1 contrasts the different types of eBook readers.

Table 1-1	Popular eBook Readers
Reader Type	*Products*
eBook readers	Rocket eBook, SoftBook Reader, Everybook Reader, Franklin eBookMan
Readers for PDAs (software)	Peanut Press Reader, Microsoft Reader, Adobe Acrobat (with the Ansyr Reader)
Readers for PCs (software)	Adobe Acrobat, Microsoft Reader, NetLibrary Reader, Glassbook Reader, Night Kitchen TK3 Reader

Learning to eRead Before You eWrite

Okay, eBooks are either digital books, or they are the software and hardware that help you read digital books. So why should you, as an author (or an aspiring one), care? You should care because digital books can be read on a screen — they don't need to be printed or bound. Instead of being delivered to bookstores, they can be sold over the Internet. This makes eBooks much cheaper to produce and distribute. In fact, eBooks are so inexpensive to manufacture (as compared to printed books, or *pBooks*) that authors can publish eBooks themselves.

Because authors can publish eBooks inexpensively, eBooks are getting a lot of attention from authors and from publishing houses that are trying to figure out their role in the new production and distribution models.

Appreciating eBooks

Some people claim that eBooks will never become popular because printed books are more visually pleasing, and that reading onscreen isn't as satisfying.

These people are missing the point: Printed books will never be obsolete, but eBooks offer certain advantages that pBooks can't give.

I'll be honest with you — I'm a closet Harry Potter fan. I don't even pretend to buy the books for my children . . . I bought all four to read myself. Unfortunately, when my family and I traveled during the summer, my husband vetoed bringing *Harry Potter and the Goblet of Fire* on our trip because it weighed over 2½ pounds, according to our trusty postage meter. With two children, four bags, a diaper bag, and a booster seat in the car, no one can accuse us of traveling light. But we try to cut back where we can, and Harry was just too heavy. So I packed a paperback instead.

If good ol' Harry was available as an eBook, however, I could've brought it along, plus a few magazines, and several other books. All of them would have fit on my Rocket eBook. According to the postage meter, it weighs only 1¾ pounds, plus it's smaller in size than the Harry Potter book, so it's easier to shove into a carry-on bag.

The ability to carry multiple books on a single device is only one of the advantages to eBooks. You can look up an unknown word in the device's dictionary, or you can "bookmark" pages easily, search for a string of text, or annotate and highlight passages.

Another advantage, at least with an eBook reader, is that the screen has a backlight. My husband wakes up earlier than I do, so he wants to go to sleep earlier. I stay up all night, reading in bed. With an eBook, I can see the words on the screen with the backlight, and not disturb him by leaving a light on.

Deciding what type of eBook reader you need

Before you rush out the door and buy the first eBook reader that you see, you need to know what type of content that you want to read, and whether you want to read that content on something other than your computer. Unfortunately, content that's formatted for one device doesn't work on another, so it can be hard to determine which device to use. (This situation is similar to the way it was hard to choose between VHS and Beta when videotapes first became popular.)

Currently, the Rocket eBook is emerging as the market leader in eBook readers, but devices that can read documents formatted for the Microsoft Reader (LIT files) are also becoming prevalent. The Adobe Acrobat Reader works on the largest number of platforms, but because Acrobat was created to duplicate the look of a printed page, documents formatted in the PDF format don't *scale* well (they don't resize to fit the document on different screen sizes).

Table 1-2 lists some of the most popular eBook reader file formats.

Table 1-2	Common eBook Reader Formats	
Reader Name	*File Format*	*Supported Platforms*
Adobe Acrobat	PDF	Windows PC, Macintosh, Everybook Reader, Unix, Palm, Windows CE, or PocketPC (with Ansyr PDF Reader Helper App), Glassbook Reader
Microsoft Reader	LIT	Windows PC, PocketPC, eBookMan
NetLibrary	NKS	Windows PC
Peanut Press Reader	PDB	Palm Pilot, Handspring Visor or any other Palm OS device, Pocket PC, or Windows CE
Rocket eBook	RB	Rocket eBook Reader

Some corporations are beginning to distribute internal documents formatted as Adobe Acrobat eBooks. If you need to read work-related documents in this format, you can download and install eBook reader software. If you own a laptop computer, you can choose software that lets you view a document in *portrait mode* or *landscape mode*. In portrait mode, you can open your laptop as if it were a book, and view a "page" with vertical orientation. In landscape mode, you can view a document with the long side of the paper displayed horizontally instead of vertically.

Most eBook readers for PCs are free, but you may have to pay for the software that enables you to author documents that can be opened by the audience. To find out how you can get free eBook readers, skip to the section "Picking the Right eBook Reader for Your Needs" in this chapter.

If you plan on reading long documents like novels, you may prefer to read eBooks on your Personal Digital Assistant (PDA), such as a Palm or PocketPC, or to get an eBook reader. This allows you to take your eBook on the road, or carry it to places where you can't normally bring your PC — like the bathroom!

Reading on a screen isn't always a comfortable experience. Even the best monitors can cause eyestrain if you stare at them too long. Because of the possible discomfort, you may prefer to use the Microsoft Reader. The Microsoft Reader incorporates Microsoft's *ClearType technology,* which makes fonts look as crisp as they do on printed pages. ClearType is a big advancement in making onscreen reading a more comfortable experience. The technology, however, works best on LCD monitors (monitors that are commonly used with flat-screen displays, laptops, and PDA devices).

Table 1-3 helps you to determine the eBook reader that works best for you.

Table 1-3	eBook Reader Selection Guide
If You Need To . . .	*Check Out These eBook Readers*
Transfer documents between different hardware platforms	Adobe Acrobat, Microsoft Reader
Read long documents without eyestrain	Microsoft Reader
Create eBooks using Microsoft Word	Microsoft Reader, Adobe Acrobat, SoftBook Personal Publisher, Peanut Press Reader (which reads DOC files)
Get a free eBook reader	Glassbook, Acrobat Reader, Microsoft Reader, NetLibrary Reader
Create eBooks with multimedia elements	Adobe Acrobat, Night Kitchen TK3 Reader
Read documents on your PDA	Adobe Acrobat, Peanut Press, Microsoft Reader
Feel like you're reading a printed book	Rocket eBook, SoftBook Reader, Franklin eBookMan, Everybook Reader

Organizing all of your eBooks

Although the experience of reading eBooks differs from reading pBooks, eBooks offer some advantages that pBooks can't. You can store multiple eBooks on a laptop or an eBook reader, and you can organize them into a library. Some readers, like the Microsoft Reader or the Glassbook Reader, organize the files automatically and show you the list of available eBooks when you open the eBook reader. Depending on your reader software, you can search for a string of text in a specific title or across a group of titles. This function is useful when you want to research professional journals or reference works.

eBook reading software lets you attach notes to a specific passage of text. When you get to that passage, you can click an icon to see your notes. You can also search through your notes.

Sure, you can bookmark pBooks, but unless you use a bookmark or something similar, your pages get dog-eared pretty quickly. (My husband gets annoyed because I'm constantly folding the corners of pages to save my place. After I finish reading a book, it looks pretty ratty!) With eBook readers (depending on the type of reader that you have), you can create a digital bookmark whenever you want to mark the place that you were reading. You can look at a page of the bookmarks that you've created and then click one to go back to that section in the text.

 If your eBook reader software doesn't catalog eBooks for you, you can do the job yourself by organizing your eBooks into folders that are separated according to document type. For example, you can create a folder called *eBooks* (original, right?). In your eBooks folder, you can create subfolders for PDF files, RB files (which need to be transferred to your Rocket eBook), LIT files (to be copied to your Microsoft Reader if you don't read these files on your computer), and so on. You can give these subfolders names, such as *PDF*, *RB*, and *LIT*. This way, you're able to find the files that you need quickly and easily, without having to search through your entire hard drive.

Getting an eBook Reader

Unless you have a laptop, the problem with reading eBooks on a PC is that you can't take the book with you to the beach or on the train. Because of this limitation, a number of manufacturers have built eBook readers (which are also called *dedicated reading devices*). These devices feature a screen, a means of navigating around the screen, and reading software that usually lets you search through the content, bookmark pages, highlight passages of text, and annotate pages.

I discuss the details of the most popular readers a bit later in this chapter, but the following list summarizes their main functions:

- **Franklin eBookMan:** (Price: $130) A cross between an eBook reader and a PDA. Not only can it read eBooks with the Microsoft Reader, this unit can also play MP3 audio files, record messages using the built-in microphone, and take notes in your handwriting. In addition, the unit offers a calendar, to-do list, contact list, and calculator. Three different models are available, priced at $129.95, $179.95, and $229.95.

- **Rocket eBook:** (Price: $199) This 22-ounce eBook holds the content of about ten paperback novels. In addition to reading, you can make notes onscreen, underline special passages, bookmark pages, and search the contents of text. The Rocket eBook reads only the files that are formatted specifically for the reader.

- **Rocket eBook Pro:** (Price: $269) Includes everything that the Rocket eBook offers, but the Pro version has 16MB of memory, updated Librarian software, handwriting recognition, a larger dictionary, and three one-year newspaper and magazine subscriptions formatted for your eBook reader.

- **SoftBook Reader:** (Price: $600) Comes with a built-in 33Kbps modem that enables you to download approximately 100 pages per minute. At almost three pounds, it's heavier than the Rocket eBook, but the SoftBook Reader comes with a much larger screen. The reader lets you search, bookmark, hyperlink, and mark-up text. It also comes with a stylus for marking and highlighting. To buy the reader, you can pay a one-time fee of $599.95, or you can pay $299.95 with an agreement to purchase books and magazines (totaling at least U.S. $19.95 per month) for 24 months from the SoftBook online store. The SoftBook Reader only reads eBooks that are formatted according to its proprietary format.

- **Everybook Reader:** (Price: $2,000) The Rolls Royce of readers. With two portrait-oriented color screens, the device looks more like a pBook because it can be opened to display two pages at a time. Because the price is too high to compete with the other readers on the market, Everybook Inc., has decided to focus their efforts on the business-to-business marketplace. The device is being redesigned to compete with laptop computers — it offers PC-like functionality, including e-mail and Web-browsing. Everybook Readers read Adobe PDF files.

The following sections give you more detailed information about each eBook reader. By the time you read this book, however, new readers may have come onto the market or the prices may have changed. For this reason, I include the Web site of each of the manufacturers in the Online Directory section of this book. If a specific eBook reader interests you, I recommend that you go to the Web site for the most current information.

Most of these devices include authoring software that can be downloaded from the company's Web site. This software lets you create files that can be opened and read on the reader. I haven't included information about the authoring software in Chapter 1, but if you're interested in how to create eBooks for these readers, jump ahead to Chapter 11.

The Rocket eBook

I fell in love with my Rocket eBook the first time I turned it on, and I can't explain why (but I'll give it a try). When I worked for Microsoft, my co-workers and I used to talk about *form factor* (size) and how it relates to people's enjoyment when using hardware. There's just something about the Rocket eBook's size . . . it just feels right when you use it.

Building a better eBook reader

In January of 2000, Gemstar International Group Limited announced plans to purchase two of the leading eBook reader manufacturers, NuvoMedia, Inc. (maker of the Rocket eBook) and SoftBook Press (maker of the SoftBook Reader). As a result of this acquisition, you can expect future eBook readers to be lighter in weight, have more features, and include color displays. (The first new eBook readers will be marketed under the RCA brand.)

The screen isn't as large as the screens on other eBook readers, but the size is just right for reading — it's slightly larger and heavier than a paperback book. The text on the screen, which has a backlight, is crisp and easy to read. You can use the buttons on the side of the device to move forward and backward through the pages. You can tap the screen to go to links that connect the Table of Contents to pages within a document. If a sound clip is included in a document, you can tap the speaker icon to play the sound file. The speaker is a bit tinny-sounding, but the clip was understandable in the sample file that I played.

Your computer needs to be able to download eBooks in order to read them on the Rocket eBook. The Rocket eBook comes with a cradle that attaches to your computer through the serial port. After you attach the cradle and install the Rocket eBook software on your computer's hard drive, you insert the eBook reader into the cradle to register the unit, and then you can download new eBooks.

The SoftBook Reader

Although it's heavier than the Rocket eBook, the SoftBook Reader has a larger display area, which makes it easy to read and annotate text. Although I don't like the size and weight of the SoftBook Reader as much as I like the more compact Rocket eBook, the user interface is highly intuitive, and I didn't need to refer to the documentation to figure out how the reader worked.

The SoftBook Reader comes bound in a soft leather cover, which helps to reinforce the idea that you're reading a book instead of using a computer. One of the nice features of this reader is that you can close the cover — even if you're in the middle of reading — because it turns itself off. When you open the cover again, you start reading at the page where you left off.

After purchasing the SoftBook Reader, you can visit the SoftBookStore (by plugging a phone line into the reader's built-in modem) to purchase more than a thousand titles (including periodicals like *Time* and *Newsweek*). The built-in modem is convenient because you don't need a computer (unlike the Rocket eBook) to download new titles to the reader.

The Franklin eBookMan

Although Franklin announced plans to make the eBookMan available by Christmas, 2000, at the writing of this text, they are not available for sale yet.

The Franklin eBookMan is a cross between a PDA and an eBook reader. Franklin calls the eBookMan a "multimedia reader and content player."

The eBookMan gets widespread acceptance in the market for several reasons:

✔ With a price of $129.95 for the most basic unit, it's less expensive than the competition.

✔ It features a screen larger than the screens on Palm or PocketPC devices.

✔ It comes bundled with the Microsoft Reader.

✔ Besides reading eBooks, you can also download and listen to audio books from Audible, Inc.

The basic model of eBookMan comes with a 240 x 200 pixel LCD display and 8MB of RAM. The intermediate model features an enhanced, backlit LCD display. The top-line model comes with 16MB of RAM and the purchaser is entitled to download additional content from the Franklin Web site. All three models feature Franklin's proprietary ASIC design that allows the microprocessor to process data two to three times faster than most other handheld devices.

The eBookMan lets you do much more than just read eBooks. You can also use its calendar, calculator, to-do list, and contact-management capabilities. It can even be synchronized with Microsoft Outlook, and Franklin has plans to offer synchronization with other such personal information managers in the future. The device comes with a cradle and USB cable for transferring files between your personal computer and the eBookMan. And if that isn't enough, the eBookMan plays MP3 audio files. You can also take notes using the device — the eBookMan's software includes natural handwriting recognition.

The Everybook Reader

Everybook Inc., is currently developing a high-end eBook reader that will offer an unusual two-color, hinged-screen display, which looks more like a physical book (as compared to the tablet shape of the Rocket eBook and SoftBook Reader). Users of the device will be able to read on both screens, or read on one screen while taking notes on the second screen. Because of the reader's high-quality display (450 dots per inch, or dpi), it'll be able to show images at the same quality of a computer monitor, as shown in Figure 1-1. With this superior screen quality, the Everybook Reader will make a great vehicle for displaying business directories and catalogs. The eBook reader will come with Linux OS installed on the device and will display files formatted as PDF documents.

Because the price of the Everybook Reader is high compared to other eBook readers, the company has decided to compete with the laptop computer market instead of the eBook reader market. When the product is released, it will offer the ability to store eBooks on *PCMCIA* cards (cards that are currently used for data storage and other functions on laptop computers). A single PCMCIA card is capable of storing hundreds of documents. Additional features will be offered with the devices, including the ability to browse the Web and send e-mail.

Reading on a PC, Palm, or PocketPC

If the idea of an eBook reader isn't appealing because you already carry a laptop or a Personal Digital Assistant (PDA) everywhere you go, you can use your current computer to download and read eBooks. In this section, I discuss how to read eBooks on the hardware that you already own.

Reading on a Palm

If you're one of the millions of people who own a Palm device to help organize your life, then I have some good news for you: You can now read eBooks on your Palm. Although you may not want to read *War and Peace* on it, the Palm is perfectly suited for reading reference works. Both Franklin

Electronics and Peanut Press make readers that work on the Palm. Ansyr Technology Corporation offers a product called Primer, which lets you convert Adobe Acrobat files for reading on PDAs (including Palm, Win CE, and PocketPC devices).

Franklin Reader

Franklin Electronics, the same company that makes the eBookMan, also distributes software that enables you to read Franklin titles on your Palm PDA (this requires Palm OS 3.0 or higher). The software can be downloaded for free from `www.franklin.com/estore/download/FEPreader.asp`. If you download the software, you receive a free eBook, *The Return of Sherlock Holmes.*

After you download and install the reader, you can purchase Franklin eBook titles, including the 2000 edition of the *Physician's Desk Reference,* Harrison's *Principles of Internal Medicine Companion Handbook,* or the King James Version of the Bible.

The search technology of Franklin's eBook Reader offers multilevel prioritized searching, which is useful when you're trying to find an article in a reference title. The search engine also includes phonetic spell correction, which knows you mean *knowledge* when you type *nolij.* If you spell as poorly as I do, this can be a very useful feature.

Peanut Press Reader

The Peanut Reader for PDAs can be downloaded from `www.peanutpress.com`. Two different versions of the software are available; one works with Palm OS, and the other version works with Win CE or PocketPC devices.

The software for the Peanut Reader has been compressed in a zip file. After you download the file to your PC, you need to *unzip* (uncompress) the files. If you have WinZip software (which can be downloaded from `www.winzip.com`), you can unzip the file by double-clicking it, and then following the instructions.

After you unzip the file, and if you have the Palm Desktop software installed on your computer, you can follow these instructions to install and read Peanut Press eBook titles on your Palm OS device:

1. **Start the Palm Desktop application.**

2. **Click the word *Install,* which is located on the left side of the screen.**

3. **Click Add in the dialog box that appears.**

4. **Browse to the directory where you unzipped the file that you downloaded. Double-click the PeanutReader.prc file.**

5. **Click Done and then click OK.**

6. **After you install the PRC file, click Install again and then click Add.**

   Some of the files in the directory that you unzip have a PDB file extension; these files contain the eBook's content.

7. **Double-click one of the PDB files.**

8. **Click Done and then click OK.**

   This action installs your first eBook.

9. **Repeat Steps 7 and 8 to install all the books that you downloaded.**

10. **HotSync your Palm OS device to your computer.**

11. **When you launch the Peanut Reader software on your Palm, you're prompted to open one of the books that you just installed.**

    After you select the eBook that you want to open, you need to unlock it. (This only needs to be done the first time you try to open a specific eBook.)

12. **Enter your name (as it appears on your credit card), and enter the credit card number that you used to purchase the eBook as the unlock code.**

    Your file unlocks.

In addition to reading eBooks, the latest version of the Peanut Reader can also read DOC files that are created in Microsoft Word. This feature is useful if you want to copy and view your personal documents on your Palm device.

Reading on a PC

I have to be honest. Except for reading PDF files that I download off the Web, I don't enjoy reading eBooks on personal computers. I have a desktop with a 21-inch monitor, but I still find that reading on it too much really strains my eyes. Because I read so much e-mail during the day, I don't want to sit at my desk to read for enjoyment. I prefer the experience of reading eBooks on an eBook reader or on my PocketPC.

I'm one of the many people who downloaded Stephen King's eBook, *Riding the Bullet,* but I never bothered to read it because I didn't want to spend any more time reading in front of my monitor. That's just not how I like to read. It's embarrassing . . . I'm supposed to be an authority on eBooks and I haven't read the first eBook bestseller. I *promise* I'll get around to reading it on my Rocket eBook.

But if you don't have an eBook reader or a PDA, and if buying one isn't in the budget this year, then you should experiment with reading eBooks on your PC. See the section, "Picking the Right eBook Reader for Your Needs," and then select reading software to install. If you find that you enjoy reading onscreen, you can start saving the documents that you write in the same eBook format.

Reading on a PocketPC or Win CE device

I once had a Windows CE device (the Vader CIO which looks like a baby note-book computer), but I never bothered reading eBooks on it. Then I got my HP Jornada (a PocketPC that comes bundled with Microsoft's eBook Reader), and I got hooked.

Because of Microsoft's ClearType technology, reading a document is easy on the eyes — even on the small screen — and the Microsoft Word Print-to-Lit add-in makes it easy for me to save my documents to the PocketPC, so I can read them while I commute. Plus, as more books are made available in the LIT file format, I can take them with me wherever I go. All this, plus every-thing that I use the Jornada for regularly (calendar, contact information, and to-do lists), makes the PocketPC my favorite reader.

Picking the Right eBook Reader for Your Needs

Plan to read eBooks on your personal computer? Then you need to download and install reader software. Each reader has certain benefits. Because most readers described in the following section are available for free (not counting the time you'll be connected to your ISP to download each file), you should download and install each reader (as long as room on your hard drive isn't an issue).

Downloading and using Adobe Acrobat Reader

If you're like millions of users, you've probably already installed the Adobe Acrobat Reader, which allows you to read PDF files. If you haven't installed the Acrobat Reader yet, follow these instructions to get the latest version. (Even if you've installed the reader, it's worthwhile to get the latest version so you can open files authored with the latest copy of Acrobat.)

1. **Go to** www.adobe.com/products/acrobat/readermain.html.

2. **Click the <u>Download Now</u> link.**

   The Welcome page appears.

3. **Click the <u>Get Acrobat Reader</u> link at the bottom of the page.**

   The Download Adobe Acrobat Reader page appears with a form that you need to fill out.

4. **In the Step 1 column, select the language, platform, and location nearest you.**

   If you want, you can select the option to download the reader that allows for searching through PDF files (this option requires a longer download time).

5. **In the Step 2 column, provide your name and e-mail address.**

6. **Click the Download button in the Step 3 column.**

7. **When you see the File Download dialog box, select the Save this Program to Disk option; click OK.**

8. **In the Save As dialog box, leave the default filename, but select the folder in which you want to save the file.**

   The file downloads to the folder that you select.

9. **Double-click the file you've just downloaded to start the Reader installation program.**

10. **Follow the instructions given by the installation program to install the reader on your computer.**

11. **You can launch the Acrobat Reader program by choosing Start⇨Programs⇨Adobe Acrobat⇨Adobe Reader.**

    You can also launch the Acrobat Reader by clicking any PDF file. The reader opens to the selected file.

Going to the netLibrary

netLibrary (www.netlibrary.com) is trying to create a digital version of your local library, where you can check out eBooks for a period of time to read and enjoy. After you find an eBook you want to read, you have the option to view or borrow the eBook. After you borrow an eBook, you have exclusive access to that eBook — netLibrary's patented technology ensures that only one person can use one eBook copy at a time. When an eBook is checked out, other readers who try to access the eBook are told that it's unavailable and are shown a date when the eBook will be made available again. When the check-out period expires, you will no longer be able to read the eBook; it's then checked back into netLibrary automatically.

netLibrary offers a wide selection of scholarly, reference, and professional titles from top commercial publishers and university presses. netLibrary also has a large number of public-domain titles that can be checked out by users. The netLibrary Public Collection features over 4,000 eBooks, including fiction, speeches, government reports, and other electronic texts.

You can sign up for a netLibrary account by going to this Web site: www.netlibrary.com/signup.asp. After you create an account, you need to download and install the netLibrary reader software (this requires Windows 95/98/NT 4.0 or greater, a Pentium processor (or compatible processor), 32MB of RAM, and 20MB of free disk space).

The Acrobat Reader was designed to duplicate the exact look of a printed page. Documents formatted as PDF files retain the fonts, images, and layout of the original document. This has benefits, such as great readability, but it also has drawbacks. For example, when you view the document on a small screen, the text doesn't re-flow to fit the screen size; you need to scroll from left to right, and up and down to read the entire page. Adobe is working on a version of the reader that scales the document to the size of the display screen, but this version isn't available yet.

Many eBooks are available in PDF format. MightyWords.com (`www.mightywords.com`) is a distributor of eBook titles and *eMatter* (documents that are longer than an article, but not quite as long as a book). All documents sold through MightyWords are formatted as PDF files, so this site can be a treasure trove of content.

Now you can take your PDF files with you, no matter where you go. With your handheld computer, you can install the Primer Reader. You can download it from the Ansyr Technologies Web site at `www.ansyr.com`. (The Primer Reader costs $49.95.) If you're not sure whether to purchase the product, you can download an evaluation version that runs for a 30-day trial basis. After the 30-day period, you can purchase and register the product at the Ansyr Web site.

The Microsoft Reader

Developed by Microsoft Research, the Microsoft Reader improves the look of font resolution on LCD screens (the screens used with Pocket PCs, laptops, and flat-screen monitors). The Microsoft Reader uses a patented technology called ClearType, which gives an experience similar to that of reading crisp text on paper, even when you're reading on a computer screen. Figure 1-2 shows you the difference that ClearType makes to a book that appears on a computer screen.

In addition, the reader software tries to simulate the experience of reading a professionally-published document, including quality typography, ample margins, full justification of text, proper spacing, leading and kerning, and powerful tools for book-marking, highlighting, and annotating.

A free copy of the Microsoft Reader is available for desktop PCs and laptops; you can download a copy at `www.microsoft.com/reader`.

If you install a copy of the *Encarta Pocket Dictionary*, you can look up the definition of a word while you read, just by clicking the word on the screen. A small window pops up, showing the definition of the word, as shown in Figure 1-3. To continue reading, just click the page behind the window and the window disappears.

Figure 1-2:
This
demonstra-
tion screen
on the
Microsoft
Reader Web
site shows
you the
difference
between
text with the
ClearType
technology
and text
without it.
The
ClearType
text is much
sharper and
easier to
read.

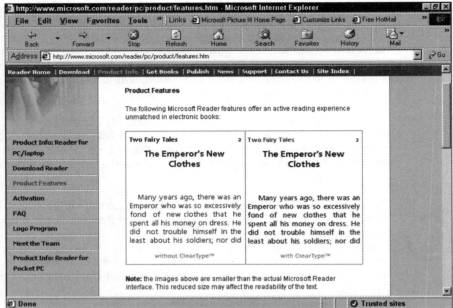

Figure 1-3:
After you
install the
*Encarta
Pocket
Dictionary,*
you can look
up a word
while you
read, just by
clicking the
word.

 An early version of the Microsoft Reader was also pre-installed on PocketPC. Unfortunately, because the PocketPC Reader was not the final version of the reader software, PocketPC users may not be able to open all the encrypted eBooks sold through publishers and online bookstores, like BN.com. Microsoft is working on a patch for the PocketPC to correct the problem.

Figure 1-4 shows a copy of the Microsoft Reader as it looks on a Pocket PC device, and Figure 1-5 shows what the beta version of the Microsoft Reader looks like for PCs and laptops.

Figure 1-4:
A copy of Bram Stoker's *Dracula,* as viewed with the Microsoft Reader on a Pocket PC device.

Figure 1-5:
The copy of Bram Stoker's *Dracula,* displayed on the Microsoft Reader for Windows PCs looks just like the Pocket PC version (but more text can be displayed on the screen).

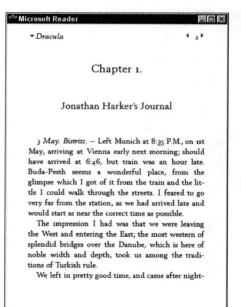

Downloading and using the Night Kitchen TK3 Reader

Night Kitchen is a New York-based company that produces TK3 — a reader and authoring tool used to create eBooks that include multimedia content (such as text, audio, and video files). The reader can be downloaded from www.nightkitchen.com/downloadreader/. Chapter 6 gives detailed instructions on how to download and install the TK3 Reader.

Downloading and using the Glassbook Reader

Glassbook, Inc., is a software company that designs eBook reading software for consumers and applications that automate the sales and distribution of eBooks for publishers, booksellers, distributors, and libraries. Adobe, which distributes the Acrobat authoring software and Acrobat Reader, has announced plans to acquire Glassbook. The Glassbook reader can be downloaded for free and installed on your computer. This reader allows you to open and read PDF files. After you install the reader, it organizes all PDF-formatted eBooks into a library, as shown in Figure 1-6.

Figure 1-6: The Glassbook Reader helps you organize your PDF files into a library of eBooks.

The Glassbook Reader requires you to have Internet Explorer 4.0 or a later version installed.

In addition to the free version of the reader, Glassbook offers the Glassbook Plus Reader. It can be purchased for $39 from their Web site. The Plus version includes an eBook version of Houghton Mifflin Company's *The American*

Heritage Dictionary of the English Language, Third Edition. Additionally, the Plus version lets you beam your eBooks to other users of the Glassbook Plus Reader, and you can also create sticky and inline notes, and highlight text. To download either version of the reader, go to `bookstore.glassbook.com/store/getreader.asp`.

Getting eBook Content

Okay, you researched all the options and decided on an eBook reader. Now all you need are eBooks to read. Thanks to the Internet, getting eBooks is easy. Most major publishing houses (including Time Warner, Random House, St. Martin's Press, IDG Books, and others) are committed to producing their new books in eBook format, in addition to the printed versions. Some publishers are going through the process of converting their *backlist* (titles which are no longer new, but continue to sell year after year) to eBooks.

eBooks are sold from distributors through online bookstores and also by direct order from the eBook publisher. The price of eBooks range from free to as much as the publisher feels the market will pay. (eBook publishers are no different than any other company selling any other products.)

Many people are participating in an ongoing debate about whether eBooks should cost as much as the pBook versions of manuscripts. pBooks are significantly more expensive for a publisher to manufacture, and in light of this fact, some eBook advocates want to see the eBook savings passed on to the consumer. On the other hand, some publishers claim that consumers are paying for content, and the price should be the same, regardless of the delivery mechanism. In time, eBooks will probably follow a pricing scheme similar to the paperback book model; the price may be less than the hardcover version of a book, but the eBook may not come out as early as the hardcover version. If they are released at the same time, the eBook will probably be closer in price to the pBook version. (Then again, I could be completely wrong about my pricing theories. That's part of what makes eBooks so interesting . . . it's a completely new distribution model and everyone's waiting to see how it all turns out.)

Some eBooks that can be downloaded from the Web come with *DRM (Digital Rights Management)* software. This software encrypts the content of the eBook so that only the person who purchased the eBook is able to open and read it. Different versions of DRM software exist; SoftLock is one example. SoftLock works with PDF files. eBooks incorporating SoftLock encryption are sold through the eBook publisher Web sites, online bookseller sites, and directly from the SoftLock.com Web site.

Buying eBooks in the correct format

You need to make sure that the bestseller you're about to buy is in the correct eBook format for your reader device or reader software. Although many publishers are now offering eBooks, most are not publishing in a wide variety of eBook formats. In fact, most publishers only offer one or two formats — usually Adobe Acrobat, the Microsoft Reader, or the Rocket eBook. So before you buy any eBook, make sure to check which formats are available so you won't be disappointed when you try to open the file.

If you have an eBook reader with a built-in modem like the SoftBook Reader, you can download files directly to the device. Other devices require that you purchase the eBook by connecting to the distributor's Web site with your PC, downloading the eBook file, and then transferring the file to your reading device through a serial or USB connection. (If your PC is your reading device, you don't need to worry about file transfers. Just double-click the file and start reading.)

eBookNet.com (`www.ebooknet.com`) is a Web site devoted to eBooks. It offers a very useful page that lets you find eBooks to read, and it is categorized according to reader type (downloadable audio, HTML, Microsoft Reader, Open eBook, PDF, Palm, Rocket Edition, SoftBook Edition, and Windows CE). Check out this page by going to `www.ebooknet.com/topic.jsp?topic=Home%3AThings+to+Read%3ABy+File+Type`.

Getting eBooks from BN.com

The Barnes & Noble online bookstore has an entire section dedicated to eBooks. You can check it out by going to `www.bn.com`, and clicking the eBooks link at the top of the page, as shown in Figure 1-7.

Connected versus unplugged

Most current eBook content is self-contained, which means that the entire eBook is contained within a single file that can be read from start to finish in a linear fashion. In the future, eBooks will contain links to supplemental content that requires a connection to the Web. If you read eBooks on a PC with an "always on" Web connection, you won't need to worry about accessing linked content. If you read an eBook on a portable device and you don't have a wireless connection, then you may be frustrated by not being able to access the supplemental content. To date, no standard exists for how to handle linking; different readers and documents handle it in various ways. Some handle broken links gracefully but others may just show ugly `File not found` error messages.

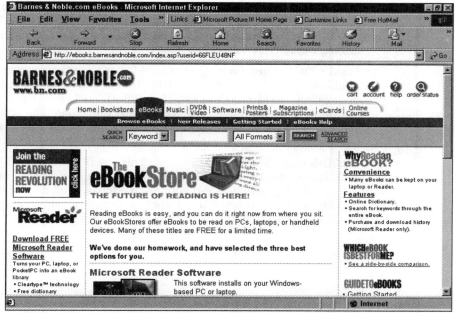

Figure 1-7:
The eBook
store at the
Barnes &
Noble Web
site is a
great place
to find one
of the
largest
selections
of eBooks
for sale.

You can purchase eBooks formatted for the Microsoft Reader, the Rocket eBook, or the Glassbook Reader (which opens PDF files). In addition to a huge selection of eBooks from major publishers (with more titles being added daily), BN.com offers a neat chart to help you decide which eBook reader best meets your needs. You can see a copy at `http://ebooks.barnesandnoble.com/education/compare_readers.asp?userid=59H9H56Q3N&srefer=`.

Getting content directly from eBook publishers

In addition to getting content from BN.com, you can also buy eBooks directly from publishers and eBook publishers. The Online Directory listed in this book gives you more information about where to go, but some of the Web sites that you don't want to miss include the following:

- **AtRandom.com:** (`www.atrandom.com`) The online Web site for Random House. Contains both fiction and nonfiction eBook titles.

- **Books OnScreen:** (`www.booksonscreen.com`) This Web site has over 100 titles in all genres, available in PDF, HTML, RTF, LIT, RB, and DOC formats. Books are available in multi-media PDF on CD or as downloads attached to e-mail.

✔ **Bookmice.com:** (www.bookmice.com) An ePublisher of new and already published eBooks. Its list includes titles available in PDF and HTML formats, Rocket eBook formats, and Palm Pilot formats. After you order an eBook, it's delivered by e-mail attachment or on CD-ROM.

✔ **DiskUs Publishing:** (www.diskuspublishing.com) A pinoneer in ePublishing, DiskUs publishes quality fiction and nonfiction titles that are available in PDF, HTML, PRC (PalmPilot), RocketEdition, and SoftBook Reader formats on diskette or by download. The company published the #1 bestselling eBook of 1999 — the first year that such rankings were kept. Audio books are also available for some titles.

✔ **iPublish.com:** (www.ipublish.com) This site is Time Warner Trade Publishing's new Web-based publishing venture to develop and distribute quality digital fiction and nonfiction eBooks. (Full disclosure time: At this point, I have to admit that I work for iPublish.com, so I'm biased, but it's a great site and I encourage you to check it out.)

Chapter 2

Finding a Great Topic

In This Chapter

▶ Picking a great topic

▶ Writing what you know best

▶ Finding your audience

So you wanna write an eBook? It helps to start with a great idea. That's what this chapter is about — finding a great idea that interests you and your audience. For a great writer, almost any idea can be great. This chapter is for the rest of us. I'm not a *great* writer, so I need to hunt for topics that make people want to read my material.

Sometimes, you know exactly what to write about because you plan to write about a specific topic for years. At other times, a topic presents itself when a newsworthy event happens or there's a breakthrough in your field of interest. When you know just what to write about, it's a great feeling; it makes writing the words much easier.

At other times, you know in general what to write about, but you haven't been able to narrow your focus on a specific topic. If you don't know exactly what to write about, it helps to learn what topics people want to read about. Focusing on an interesting topic isn't difficult. In this chapter, I show you how find a suitable topic and identify whether the idea you have is marketable. You may love the idea of writing about needlepoint techniques of the 18th century, but before you commit hundreds of hours to the project, find out whether you can sell enough copies of your eBook to make the project worth your effort.

Picking a Great Topic

Have you ever noticed how many sources seem to latch on to the same idea within the space of a few weeks? One month, everyone is writing about genetics. Another month, venture capitalism is the hot topic. After you notice which ideas are popular, it's easier to guess which ideas may become popular. You can spend hours browsing from news site to news site, trying to spot the hot topics, or you can go to the Web sites that summarize the news and have that site do the legwork for you.

The easy way to stay current

Two great sources to know about are *Slate* and the *Media Grok* newsletter. Slate.com (www.slate.com) has a daily column called *Today's Papers*. It shows which top news stories have been printed in the major U.S. papers (like the *L.A. Times, New York Times,* and the *Wall Street Journal*). Reading the column every day is a great way to see what editors deem newsworthy. Go to the Web site and click the Today's Papers link. Slate.com also has other columns devoted to timely topics, so it's worth your time to browse the site.

If you don't want to get online every day to read the news, TheStandard.com has a newsletter that can be e-mailed to you. The *Media Grok* newsletter shows what stories were featured in the top newspapers and the spin that each paper gave the story. I find the *Media Grok* newsletter to be a highly entertaining way to stay abreast of current events. To sign up, go to www.thestandard.com/newsletters/ and select *Media Grok* from the All Newsletters drop-down list.

Timing your topic

If you stay up to date with the news, you can see which topics attract the most attention. You may be tempted to write about one of these topics, but you need to figure out a way to make your information valuable to the reader. Ask yourself why a reader would want to pay for the information in your eBook when he or she can get much of the same information for free on the Web? If you want to write about a current topic, keep these pointers in mind:

- **An eBook should contain more information than an article:** This is true even for eMatter articles (which are longer than standard articles, but not as long as full-length eBooks).

- **Write and publish an eBook about the topic before it becomes yesterday's news:** An eBook about the Y2K bug may have sold well in 1999, but you waste your effort if you publish it after the year 2000.

- **Present the information in a different way:** If you're overwhelmed by all the available information, you can write a *CliffsNotes* type eBook about the subject. Presenting a lot of complex information in a compact cheat-sheet type of document can provide value to your audience, which translates into sales for you.

- **Put a comical spin on the topic:** If coverage on a specific topic reaches absurb heights (for example, Monica Lewinsky's face is plastered on every newspaper and magazine), you can write a parody eBook. By writing a parody eBook, you can give your audience information and provide some well-needed comic relief.

✔ **What goes up, must come down (this includes public interest on a topic):** If you write about something current, expect sales to cool off after the public's saturated with the topic. This is inevitable to some degree, so you don't want to spend a lot of time researching and writing about a hot topic. Cover it in a shorter format (such as an eMatter article), and get ready for the next hot topic.

Standing out from the crowd

Maybe your topic isn't sizzling hot and featured in *Wired* magazine, but you want to write about a perennial favorite. Because the books on your topic continue to sell well year after year, tons of books are already available. Does that mean you should keep hunting for a topic? No — but you should try to figure out a way to personalize the topic and make it your own. The following tips help you think about ways to make your eBook different than the competition:

✔ **Put a unique spin on the topic:** This makes your eBook stand out from the crowd. For example, if everyone writes articles about the breakthroughs in genetic research, you can write an eBook about the ethical implications of the research. You could also write a fictional work that's told from the viewpoint of Dolly, the first cloned sheep.

✔ **Put a humorous or lighthearted spin on a serious subject:** I'm not recommending that you write a title called *Laughing at Leprosy,* but try not to take yourself or your topic so seriously. Lighten up and have fun. You may make a scary or tough subject easier for your readers to deal with.

✔ **Follow the money:** If you're not sure how to make a common topic unique, try to focus on people's pocketbooks. Many people are fascinated by money (even if they don't admit it). If you can tie money into your topic somehow (for example, by showing how to make money or save money), your title becomes more interesting to people.

After you put your unique spin on a topic, make sure your eBook's title reflects your fresh point of view. You may write an eBook on how to nurture and breed exotic Koi, but if the title is *Caring for Your Goldfish,* how will a potential reader know that your eBook is different?

Writing about what interests you

You may find a topic fascinating long before the rest of the world is interested. (When the rest of the world does become interested, they'll call you a visionary.) If you think a topic is really cool, and you just can't get it off your mind, start researching the topic and see whether it's worth writing about.

Looking out for the next great topic

The more you read on a broad range of subjects, the more likely you are to find the next great topic. Anything can spark your curiosity. Even when you face a deadline, spend a few extra minutes to explore something new that intrigues you.

You'll probably specialize in a few key areas to allow you to develop expertise and become an acknowledged source. Although a focus is natural, make sure that the area is broad enough for you to branch out into new topics. This is especially important if you work in a field that is constantly evolving, like the Internet industry. Someone who specialized in writing about the Web's "push technology" a few years ago may have a hard time getting an audience now that "push technology" has been shoved aside for other content-delivery models.

This book resulted from a missed opportunity. When I was at Microsoft, I worked on small business e-commerce–enabled Web sites, but I just couldn't get the topic of eBooks out of my mind. I started researching to find out about where eBooks were heading. I collected articles and signed up for newsletters. Suddenly, every time I picked up a publishing-industry magazine, I was reading about eBooks. Finally, I gave in to temptation and put together a proposal for a book about eBooks. The rest is history.

If something has grabbed a hold of your mind and won't let go, chances are good that other people will find the topic interesting. And if you're lucky, a lot of readers will find the subject interesting, and you'll be on your way to becoming a best-selling author.

You may have a great idea for a marketable eBook, but if you're not excited about the topic, don't write about it. If you don't have passion for what you write about, you may find the process of writing an eBook to be miserable, even if you manage to finish the text.

Writing What You Know

Everyone is an expert at something. Even if what you know doesn't strike you as interesting or unique, there are probably people out there who wish they knew what you do. If you can package your expertise in an easy-to-digest format, you have the basis for an eBook. If you wonder what expertise you have, take a look at what you do every day. You can write about what you do professionally, about your hobbies, about the things you do at home, or about how you view the world.

Writing about what you do professionally

If you have a full-time job, you probably spend more than 40 hours a week doing what it is you do. Your boss pays for your expertise. If you package your knowledge in an eBook, other people may pay you for your expertise, too.

If you don't think you can write about what you do at work, take a piece of paper and write the answers to these questions:

- **What do you get paid for?** This is not a trick question and I won't pass the answers on to your boss (I promise). Anyone who gets paid to perform a task has certain skills. The skills you perform provide value; if they didn't, you wouldn't get paid. If you know what value you provide, you can learn to package that information and sell it to others in the form of an eBook.

  Even if your job is flipping hamburgers at the local fast-food franchise, you still know something about rapid food preparation and serving dinner up hot and quick. Figure out who this information is valuable to (like working parents) and you have a topic for an eBook.

- **Without using the verbage in your job description, what are the real tasks you perform?** These tasks are actually the real value you provide. Your title may be Senior Administrative Assistant to the Executive Chairman, but if you organize a digital rolodex, that's your actual job value. Write an eBook about how to organize a contact list. The eBook doesn't have to be long — it just has to provide solid information that people can use.

- **Ever wish you could tell your boss everything that's wrong with his or her organization?** You can, but tell a group of readers instead of your boss. Analyze business practices that are inefficient and propose better ways to do things in your eBook.

- **What do you do best at work?** If everyone in the office asks for your help solving a certain set of problems, write down the process you follow when you help them. You can give this guide to your coworkers and save yourself the time of talking another office mate through the solution. You can also sell the guide as an eBook.

- **Do your coworkers come to you to discuss their personal problems?** You can write *The Sensitive Person's Guide to Coworkers*. You could also write *How I Lost My Job (But Became a Shrink Instead)*.

- **Have you mastered the art of doing nothing at work but looking good in front of the boss?** You can write *The Slacker's Guide to Getting Promoted*.

Writing about your hobbies

A lot of people have hobbies that they enjoy outside of their professional lives. You work because you have to. You *hobby* because you choose to. Anything that you like well enough to devote your spare time to is worth writing about.

This is true even if you're not an expert at your hobby. Maybe you enjoy golf, but no one has ever confused you with Tiger Woods. That's okay; you can write about the best golf courses to go to in your state. You can write about Zen and the art of golf. You can write about living with Tiger-Woods envy. The possibilities are only limited by your imagination.

Have fun when you pick a topic that's focused on your hobby. If your hobby is popular, a lot of books are probably already written on the topic. In that case, you need to focus your topic on the needs of a niche audience. Here are some good ways to limit the scope of your topic to a specific market:

- Limiting the topic to the needs of a regional group, such as your neighborhood, town, county, city, or state

- Limiting the topic to the needs of a specific demographic group, such as teens, baby boomers, GenXers, or retirees

- Limiting the needs to a single gender or ethnic group, such as *The Woman's Guide to . . .*, or *The Essential Guy's Handbook to . . .*

- Limiting the topic to an economic group, such as *The Poor Guy's Guide to Spending Big*

Writing about what you do at home

A great way to come up with a topic for an eBook is to combine two different things that you do well. You can use these ideas to spark your thinking:

- **What skills have you developed in your professional life that carry over into your personal life?** My husband is the most organized person I've ever met — sometimes his perfection in this area scares me. When our daughter comes home from school, he organizes her school papers into color-coded folders. There's a green one for artwork, a red one for homework that needs to be done, an orange one for papers we need to review and respond to, and so on. He could easily write an eBook called *Whip Your Disorganized Life into Shape — Fast!* (You should see what he has done for our bill-paying.)

- **What comes naturally to you?** I have a couple of friends who are wonderful hosts and hostesses. Everytime we go over to their house, people are coming and going. They have friends in for brunch; their children have school buddies come over, and the parents stay to socialize. More friends drop by and stay for coffee and cookies. It's like a 24-hour party (and great fun everytime we go). My friends could write an eBook on *Easy Entertaining*.

✔ **How have you saved time doing the chores you hate?** If you figured out a quick way to get the laundry done, let me know so I can buy your eBook.

Writing about your environment

Sometimes, the answer is right in front of your nose. You can always write about the small things you notice and give your observations a unique twist. This technique worked brilliantly for the writers of the TV sitcom *Seinfeld;* each week, they wrote "a show about nothing." It also worked for Erma Bombeck, who wrote about being a homemaker and mother in a way that millions of readers could identify with.

If you feel like you don't have anything important to say, remember that it's not always what you say, but how you say it that counts. If people constantly laugh whenever you describe life's little troubles, maybe you should consider writing an eBook about nothing.

Ghostwriting: Write what someone else knows

What if you can't come up with a great idea? You can always hire yourself out to act as a *ghostwriter* for another person's ideas. Working as a ghostwriter, you build an initial outline from the concept, flesh it out, and write the words for someone else. Depending on how you structure your agreement, the idea orginator can be listed as the sole author or you can become coauthors of the work (another person's ideas coupled with your words). To find someone you can ghostwrite for, put an ad in the classified section of your local newspaper. Tell everyone you know that you're interested in a ghostwriting project. Many people claim that they'd write a book if they only had the time. Offer to do the task for people with no time to spare. If you don't have a resume of clips, offer to write and publish the eBook in exchange for a coauthor credit and percentage of the profits.

Even if you can't find someone to ghostwrite for, you can publish a classic if you reissue a work that's in the *public domain* (texts where the original copyright has expired). Many publishing companies are publishing these texts in eBook format because no licensing fees need to be paid after the copyright on a work expires. Authors whose works are now in the public domain include Shakespeare, Mark Twain, and Lewis Carroll. You can write an introductory essay, rewrite a plot for a modern audience, or combine classic stories into an anthology. For the most complete list of works available in the public domain, see the Project Gutenberg at www.gutenberg.net/index.html.

Finding the Audience for Your eBook

If you have a general idea about what to write, but you're having trouble refining your topic, **think about the audience you're writing for.** Define the primary group of people you plan to market your eBook to. It may help to visualize people who fall into the ideal market for your work. Are these people young? Old? In between? Single, married, parents, or grandparents? Working professionals, blue collar, in school, unemployed?

After you identify your target audience, write a short *scenario* about the needs these people have, as those needs relate to your topic. A scenario is a short scene you write about the needs and problems of one person who represents your target market. Here's how it works:

1. **Pick the general topic you know you want to write about.**

   For example, say I want to write about losing weight, but a lot of books on that topic are already on the market. I need a way to make my eBook stand out.

2. **Pick the target audience for your eBook.**

   For a book about weight loss, my target audience could be anyone who wanted to lose some weight, but that's too broad. I need to refine the market a little, so I decide to target professional women who are slightly overweight (5-25 pounds), but not obese. (Obesity is a serious medical condition. Because I'm not a doctor, I'm not qualified to address the topic from a medical standpoint.)

3. **Visualize people you know who fall into the target audience you select.**

   I picture some of the women I know. Some are women I work with and some are friends.

4. **Write the scenario.**

   In the scenario, you need to describe the problems faced by a fictional person and the reasons these problems exist. Don't try to suggest possible solutions — you're not trying to write the book just yet. Here's the scenario I came up with: Karen isn't really heavy, just a little too plump (in her opininon). Her clothes have gotten too tight for comfort and she can't afford to pay for new clothes. Plus, Karen doesn't want to think of herself as a size 12. She liked being a size 10 and wants to get back to that size. Because Karen is so busy at work, she doesn't have time to go to the gym.

   Karen gained the weight because she ate too much during the holiday season. Because Karen's job is stressful, she finds herself grabbing candy during the day to give her a quick lift. The candy has become a pleasurable habit that she doesn't want to give up.

In short, Karen has gotten bigger because of her poor eating habits, she doesn't have time to go to the gym, and, because she has a stressful career, sugar has become a daily reward.

Most books on losing weight would recommend a low-fat diet (maybe cut out refined carbohydrates) and a moderate exercise program. Karen's a bright woman; she knows what she needs to do, but she doesn't feel she has the time to shop and prepare healthier meals, and she doesn't have time for an exercise program.

5. **Review your scenario and see if it offers some topics for you to write about.**

   If I were trying to write a book to help Karen, I may decide to write about diet and exercise tips for extremely busy people.

If the scenario doesn't give you an idea of what market to write for, try changing the target market and writing a different scenario.

Realizing the size of your audience

Before you fill your head with dreams of the financial independence that *Real Men Use Real Mowers* will bring, try to find out how many people are actually interested in the topic. If magazines are devoted to your topic, write to the advertising department of the magazine (you can usually find this information on the magazine's masthead) and ask for a rate card. This card gives information about the size of the magazine's readership and the cost of buying advertising in that periodical. (I'm not suggesting you take out an ad, but the size of the magazine's audience can tell you something about a subject's popularity.) The more general the topic, the larger the size of the market (the market will also be more competitive and you may have to spend more money and effort to market your eBook in order to make it stand out from the other titles). The more defined the topic, the smaller the size of the potential audience, but you'll sell fewer eBooks because the eBook's content is interesting to only a smaller universe of people. But fewer ePublishers will be targeting the market, so your eBook has the opportunity to become a big fish in a small pond.

This is just a long-winded way of saying that *Sports Illustrated* has a larger potential market than *Fly Fishing Quarterly*. If you write about a general subject, you'll have a larger audience, but more competition from other books. If you write about a specialized subject, the size of your market may be small in comparison, but you may be able to charge more for your content.

Writing for your audience

You may be the greatest writer the world has ever known, but you can't write credibly about advances in medicine if you failed biology twice. This is especially true if you hope to write for an audience of physicians. Before you set an ambitious task for yourself, be honest about whether you're the right (write?) person for the job.

Here's an exercise that keeps you honest: Before you commit to write an eBook, write the author blurb that would go into the eBook's marketing materials. For example, an author blurb may read something like this:

John Doe, a recognized expert in die cutting, explores new procedures in medicine made possible through advances in laser technology. Designed for doctors, nurses, and others in the medical profession, this eBook discovers the benefits and side effects of laser surgery.

After you write your blurb, review it. If you were a potential customer, would you buy this eBook? If not, it's time to rethink your topic and your target audience. You can always twist the topic to be more appropriate (for example, *How Patients Feel about Laser Surgery: A Guide for Doctors*).

Thinking about what readers want

The title of your eBook and your topic need to clearly communicate the eBook's value to the buyer. Ask yourself what your eBook does for the reader, and why the reader should care enough to pay for the privilege of reading it. The eBooks that best give value to their audience either help the reader profit, save money, save time, or have fun. Mass-market books, even if they're just for pleasure reading, are bought because they fulfill one of these basic needs.

Does your topic help readers profit?

Does your topic help readers profit? Profit isn't just about making money (although it can be). A good topic may be one that profits the reader by providing guidance, advice, instruction, and so on. When you evaluate topics, ask yourself these questions:

- How will readers' lives be improved as a result of reading this eBook?
- Will this eBook teach readers a specific set of skills?
- Will this eBook provide information that's difficult for readers to get from other sources?
- Will readers be able to make direct profits as a result of reading this eBook?

Does your topic help readers save money?

Helping readers save money is just as good as helping them make money. Examples of topics that help people save money include the following:

- How to get out of debt
- How to manage and live with a budget
- How to find free deals offered on the Web
- How to look like you spend a lot when you don't

These titles generally do better during hard times, when more people are looking to economize.

Does your topic help readers save time?

As a working mother, time is the most precious commodity I know. True story: I once signed up for a time-management seminar, but I didn't have the time to go. Topics that would appeal to the chronically busy include the following:

- How to do less without feeling guilty
- How to manage your time better
- The One Minute . . . *Anything*. The clever idea behind the *One Minute Manager* and similar titles is that they're *CliffsNotes* for life issues. Readers can quickly read and absorb basic principles that may take hundreds of pages in longer books. If you can package your expertise in a concise, informative, and entertaining way, you're able to sell a lot of eBooks.
- How to *blank* while you *blank* (for example, *How to Learn French While You Commute*). These titles appeal to people who want to *multi-task* — do two things at the same time. If you can show people how to successfully accomplish twice as much, you have the basis for a good line of eBooks.

Chapter 3

Researching Your Topic

● ●

In This Chapter

▶ Researching published books on the topic that you want to write about

▶ Getting the results that you need from search engines quickly

▶ Finding and subscribing to eZines and clipping services

▶ Benefiting from forums and newsgroups

● ●

*A*fter you find the perfect topic for your eBook — what then? Unless you're already an expert on the topic you chose, you probably need to conduct some research. Luckily, if you own a computer with Internet access, gathering research material is easy.

In fact, if you're like most people who're just starting to research online, the amount of information available is likely to overwhelm you. This chapter guides you and teaches you how to zero in on the right information in the least amount of time.

Doing the Research

Before you start writing, find out who else has already written on the topic you chose. You don't need to be the first to cover a specific topic, but you do need to cover the topic in a unique way. If 100 authors write about how to design insanely great Web widgets, becoming Author #101 is pointless. Anyone who cares about the topic has already read about designing Web widgets. You're better off taking a different slant. A book with the title *Why Not to Use Web Widgets,* for example, takes a different view of the subject, and you have a ready audience for such a title (all those people who bought into the Web widgets craze in the first place).

Studying the competition by using Amazon.com and BN.com

Before Amazon.com (www.amazon.com) and Barnes & Noble.com (www.BN.com), you could spend an entire day or more researching the competition at your local library. But because these two companies offer comprehensive online databases, researching available books in print becomes a quick and easy process.

In purchasing Exchange.com in 1999, Amazon.com acquired the Bibliofind database of over 9 million, hard-to-find, antiquated, and used books. If you conduct a search on Amazon.com, you can locate both out-of-print books and books currently in print. Remember to check the publication dates of the books to see which ones are the most recent.

To see who else has covered your topic, do a quick Amazon.com and BN.com search. Even if a book is out of print, you can see how many authors wrote about your subject (and when they wrote about it). You can see whether the market is saturated with books on your topic and whether you need to put a different spin on your topic to make your book stand out.

You decide to write a book about e-commerce because you find an e-commerce article every time that you open a newspaper. You think readers may want a reference book about setting up an e-commerce division within an established company, but you need to see how much competition exists for the idea.

Researching online, step by step

You can start researching your topic by following these steps:

1. **Type your topic into the search text box on the home page of www.amazon.com, leaving the All Products option showing, and then click the Go! button.**

   If I use *e-commerce* as my topic, Amazon shows three items for the term *e-commerce* under each of the applicable product categories. In this case, the categories are books, electronics and software, zShops, and auctions. (You didn't expect to find something about e-commerce in the toys section, did you?)

   On Amazon.com, don't limit your initial search to just the books section. Many times, Amazon.com's zShops and auctions can give you information about self-published products that you can't find otherwise.

2. **Click the <u>See all results in Books</u> link, which appears under the top three books.**

   Amazon.com offers to search the auctions section and the rest of Amazon.com for e-commerce. Amazon.com also suggests related searches for e-commerce: b2b e-commerce, e-commerce development, and mastering e-commerce. Under the suggestions for these related searches, the full results of the search appear. For the *e-commerce* topic, the search finds only five books.

3. **Open a new Web browser window and type in** `www.bn.com`.

   I use Internet Explorer, so I launch a second browser window from the Windows Start menu, go to Programs⇨Internet Explorer.

   Leave the Amazon.com Web site open in the other browser.

4. **At the BN.com Web site, type your search topic in the Quick Search text box, which you find at the top of the BN.com home page, and click the Search button.**

   For the *e-commerce* topic, BN.com lists a few books (at the time of this writing), although it does showcase a book on related topics and provides a link to enable you to search the *e-commerce* topic in its rare, secondhand, and out-of-print store. (*E-commerce* is a relatively new topic, so you're probably not going to find too many out-of-print books available on the subject.)

BN.com lists its titles in best-selling order. This setup enables you to compare how well specific titles are selling. Don't read too much into the rankings — how well a book sells depends on many factors — but sometimes, you can discover which buzzwords help a book sell. If certain buzzwords keep appearing in the top-15 book titles, you may want to think some before incorporating the same buzzwords into your work. They may help people notice your title, but on the other hand, your book may get lost in the field. (In Chapter 4, I discuss how to find a killer title for your work.)

Narrowing your research to specific books

After you review the number of books available on your topic, research some titles in depth. How many books you decide to research this way depends on the number of titles your initial search produces. The most obvious way to research is to buy and read the books, but you don't want to spend the time or money on more than a couple. If your search produces many books, choose the most recent books to research first.

You can look at the publication dates to get an idea of how current your topic is and whether it demonstrates staying power. If your topic is very current, publishing an article instead of a book may prove the better course, as a book can take months to write and publish. If your topic is less current but exhibits a longer shelf life (excuse the pun), you normally face more competitors who've also written about your topic. A less-than-current topic, for example, is how to design Web pages; you can find books that are still selling four or five years after their publication dates, but the market's pretty saturated. If you write about this topic, you need to find a new angle to make your material fresh and interesting to readers.

To research books without buying them, follow these steps:

1. **Return to BN.com (at** www.bn.com**), conduct a search on the topic** *e-commerce,* **and click the link for one of the book titles that your search topic returns.**

   As a part of my search on the topic of e-commerce (which I describe in detail in the steps in the preceding section), I click the link for the book *Surviving The Digital Jungle: What Every Executive Needs to Know About eCommerce and eBusiness.* In addition to the information you expect (such as a picture of the book jacket, a synopsis of the book contents, nice quotes from executives who reviewed advance copies, and a brief author bio), you can find out how well the book sells at BN.com.

2. **Look at how readers rate the book on BN.com.**

   Surviving The Digital Jungle: What Every Executive Needs to Know About eCommerce and eBusiness displays only one customer review (at the time of this writing), which gives the book a five-star rating. I never give too much weight to just a single review, whether positive or negative. If it's glowing, the author's mom may have written it. If it's negative, the guy in the cubicle down the hall, who's jealous that he has never published a book, may have written it. You never know.

    Looking at reviews can prove helpful if you need to narrow the scope of a topic, or you're looking for a new twist on material that other authors cover. Comments such as, "I loved this book, but wish the author had covered *xyz* in more detail," tells you that a market exists for writing about the *xyz* topic. On the other hand, negative comments can prove even more informative than positive ones. A comment such as, "This book was terrible. I was hoping for informative text, but all I got was an infomercial for the author's other products," may suggest ways that you can do things differently in writing a book on the same topic.

3. **Log off of BN.com and go to Amazon.com (**www.amazon.com**) to check reader reviews there.**

4. **Conduct a search for the e-commerce topic at Amazon.com and then click the link for the book you just looked at on the BN.com site.**

   Surviving The Digital Jungle: What Every Executive Needs to Know About eCommerce and eBusiness is only 109 pages in paperback. This page count tells you that the book doesn't delve deeply into such a broad topic. Perhaps you can see here an opportunity to write an *Executive eCommerce Bible* that covers the topic in depth? After all, you're researching this book to look for a new opportunity.

In researching a book, you find that Amazon.com offers more information than does the BN.com Web site. Amazon.com makes a clear distinction between *editorial reviews* (where the reviewer receives an advance copy of the book from the publisher, who hopes to use a nice quote from the reviewer on the book jacket) and *reader reviews* (where the book inspires someone enough to comment on it).

Amazon.com also lists other products that people who bought this book purchased, other authors that the people who bought this book read, links to books on similar subjects, and the book's Table of Contents (if available).

5. **Click the <u>Customer Reviews</u> link.**

   Although BN.com features only one review for the book, Amazon.com features several more. In addition to being able to read each review, users at Amazon.com can also rate how helpful they find the reviewer's comments.

   Customer reviews can tell you what the reader feels passionate about — which is valuable information if you're trying to decide how to focus on a topic for your work.

6. **Scroll back up to the top of the page and click the <u>Check Purchase Circles</u> link.**

   One of Amazon.com's more controversial features is *Purchase Circles*. Because Amazon.com collects tons of information about each person who purchases from the site, it can aggregate the information in interesting ways. Although some people criticize Amazon.com for what they perceive as a privacy violation, this data can prove insightful as you conduct your research into specific target groups that you may want to write for.

7. **Check on how popular the book you're researching is by clicking the <u>Browse other Purchase Circles</u> link in the middle of this page to view the Purchase Circles that the site lists.**

   Surviving The Digital Jungle proves popular with employees at GE. You can also see which books are selling best in different geographical areas, in different companies, and at different universities — fascinating stuff. For anyone working on regionally oriented content, Purchase Circles are a gold mine.

You can find a lot of good material at the BN.com and Amazon.com sites to help you focus on a topic. After you decide how to present your topic in a new way, you're ready to start conducting additional research to help you in the writing process.

Make sure that you read Amazon.com's tips for searching successfully throughout the site. On the Amazon.com home page, click the <u>Help</u> link. The Help page lists links to additional Help topics. Click the <u>Books & Audiobooks</u> link under the Search Tips section of Help topics. Amazon.com's search Help shows you how to perform the following tasks:

- ✔ Efficiently conduct a keyword search.
- ✔ Search for an author if you're unsure of how to spell the name.
- ✔ Search for a book title if you know only some of the words in the title.
- ✔ Search by publisher or publication date.
- ✔ Search for children's books by narrowing the field to an appropriate reading level (for example, ages 0–3).
- ✔ Perform *Boolean searches* (by using the words *and, or,* and *not* to link different parts of the book description together).

Researching what your competition's likely to publish

Although seeing what books on your topic are already in publication is useful, you also need to research bestsellers and the books that people are likely to publish in the coming year. You want to study both eBooks and print-based books that are debuting in the near future.

Sometimes, what's going to appear in print in a given period is obvious. After Princess Diana died, for example, seeing every major publisher rush a book about her to market was hardly surprising. Publishers often copycat one another on what they perceive as a "hot" topic. After the success of Arthur Golden's *Memoirs of a Geisha,* which Knopf published in 1997, many larger publishing houses began releasing books with an Oriental theme. You can look at this year's bestsellers to get an idea of what topic to write about in the near future — that is, as long as you can give the topic a unique twist.

The New York Times offers expanded bestsellers lists on its Web site at `www.nytimes.com/books/yr/mo/day/bsp/index.html`. You can find the bestsellers for fiction and nonfiction, and advice for hardcover and paperback sales. The Web site also provides information on how well books are selling through the independent book stores verses sales through the chain stores, such as Barnes & Noble or Borders. As you check out *The New York Times'* bestseller lists, pay attention to how many weeks each title stays on the list. If you want your eBook to sell for more than a couple months, you want to determine which topics exhibit longevity.

To find out more about coming trends in books, subscribe to *Publishers Weekly,* often known simply as *PW.* Most people in the know consider *PW,* a trade magazine, the bible of the publishing industry. Each week, it covers publishing-industry news, bestseller lists, top author interviews, and early reviews of adult and children's books. The reviews also give you information about books to be published in the coming months.

In reading *PW,* remember that print titles can take months to reach the market. If you spot a trend, often you can write and publish an eBook before some of the print versions become available. The shorter publishing schedule of eBooks can prove a big advantage to you in getting your book to market first, but unfortunately, you can expect this advantage to last only until publishers start releasing their own eBook versions earlier than their print versions.

A good place to find out what eBook titles are becoming bestsellers is on the eBook Connections Web site (at `www.ebookconnections.com`). This useful site breaks down eBook bestsellers by sales per quarter, sales per year, and sales over the book's lifetime. The site also gives interesting summary information — for example, that in February 2000, the romance category accounted for 57 percent of all eBook titles sold. (Happy Valentine's Day!)

Working with Search Engines

After you decide on a topic and research competitive books, are you ready to start writing? No . . . not yet. (But hang in there, you start writing in the next chapter.) Now you need to conduct some additional research to broaden your knowledge about your topic and to check your facts.

How much research and the type of research you do depends on your topic, but you're likely to start your search by using an online search engine. A *search engine* is a Web page that lets you search for a word or term and displays a list of Web pages that relate to the term that you searched. (For example, if I type the word **brownies** into a search engine, I get a list of pages that focus on chocolate desserts, but I also find Web pages that relate to the Girl Scouts.)

Although search engines can help you quickly find Web sites that relate to your subject matter, they can't vouch for the credibility of the editorial content. In browsing a Web site, you need to decide how much confidence you can put in the source of the material. Relying on content from established editorial sources, such as the Web-published versions of print newspapers and periodicals, is safer than believing what you read on *Billy Bob's Gossip Web Page,* although you may miss out on some breaking news.

As you start to work with search engines, you need to know only a handful of Web sites to achieve the results you want. If you start your search with several of the larger search engines (such as Yahoo! or Altavista.com), you generally find just what you need, unless you are searching for highly specialized content.

Searching effectively

Like any skill, searching effectively on the Web takes a little know-how and a little practice. If you follow the tips given in this section, you discover how to find what you're looking for quickly and with less frustration.

Most of the larger search engines enable you to perform Boolean searches. In a Boolean search, you join terms together by using the words *AND*, *OR*, *NOT*, and *NEAR*. (*Note:* Not all search engines support the use of *NEAR*.) You can type these words, known as *operators,* in uppercase letters to distinguish them from the words you're searching for.

If you want to do research on a competitor search engine, you should do a search on a highly popular Web site, such as AOL.com, to find the information. More than 22 million people use AOL for Internet access. If the majority of these users go to AOL's search engine, you want to search there as well to see how highly AOL users rank a competitor's Web site. To use AOL's search engine to find info on your topic, follow these steps:

1. **Go to AOL's search engine at** `http://search.aol.com/` **and type the primary word you want to search for.**

   In this example, I want to find out what eBook and ePublishing companies exist. I start by typing **eBook** in the search text box on the AOL site and clicking the Search button.

2. **Take a look at how many matching categories and matching sites the AOL search engine returns and determine whether you want to reduce the number of hits by performing a Boolean search.**

   For the term *eBooks,* AOL returns several matching categories and hundreds of matching Web sites. Because I don't want to browse until 6 a.m. the next morning, I decide to try a Boolean expression to narrow the field.

   In a rush and don't want to bother with Boolean searching? You can scan the first group of hits that AOL's search engine returns to see whether any are close to what you want. If you find one that you like, click the Show me more like this link to see similar Web sites.

3. **Review the search results that the engine returns and see whether any of those Web sites clearly don't meet your expectations.**

   The first query returns several Web sites, including How to Create an eBook and eBook Secrets, so I ignore these.

4. **Click the Search Options link under the search text box.**

   You go to AOL's advanced search page.

5. **On the Advanced Search page, type your search phrase (eBooks in my example) into the text box and select Exact Phrase from the three questions shown below the text box.**

6. **Refine your search further by selecting where you want to search and selecting other specific words to add to or eliminate from the search.**

   Next, you can choose whether to search on AOL.com and the Web or the Web only. In this example, I choose On AOL.com and the Web by clicking on the radio button for this option.

   Finally, you can choose words or phrases that further refine your search. Now you're getting somewhere! For my example, I select Must not Contain from the first drop-down list and then type the word **secrets** in the text box next to the drop-down list.

7. **After you refine the search, click the Search button and review the results.**

   For the refined search, AOL returns a smaller amount of matching categories and matching Web sites. Better, but I probably need to refine my search even further, until the search engine returns a manageable number of hits.

Discovering how to search effectively is the key to saving extra effort. You soon figure out how to weed out the undesirable sites just by looking at the results that the search engine returns.

In addition to AOL's search engine, some good search engines to try include the following:

✓ **Yahoo.com:** www.yahoo.com

✓ **Altavista.com:** www.altavista.com

✓ **AskJeeves.com:** www.askjeeves.com

✓ **Google.com:** www.google.com

Always be on the lookout for great new search engines. Ask your friends and family what engines they use, and give each engine at least one try. To evaluate a newfound search engine, try performing the same search on that site and on other different search sites to compare the results that you receive from each site. (I like to use the search term *antique maps.*) Notice how many results each engine returns and which sites make the top-ten list. Which search engine returns the results most relevant to your topic? A Web site that ranks high in one search engine may not even show up in the list of another. Some search engines rank sites according to how many other sites link to that particular Web site, while others rank them on keywords. Each time that you come across a new search engine, try your stock search term and compare the results against those of the search engine that you usually use.

A (key)word about RealNames

RealNames is a company that's trying to promote the use of keywords instead of URLs to help people find Web sites. Instead of typing a Web address, such as www.microsoft.com, into your browser, you can type the word **Microsoft** and go directly to the Microsoft Web site. This approach is similar to AOL's popular Keyword system. RealNames is gaining popularity; Microsoft's Internet Explorer Web browser now incorporates it, and MSN.com uses it as well.

The main drawback to RealNames' service? Companies must pay to appear on its listings. If the service catches on and many Web sites sign up, RealNames is likely to become an easy way to search for Web sites. If you try RealNames today, you see only the Web sites that currently pay for a listing.

So many search engines exist on the Web. Some are highly specialized and others are very general. Because no search engine can cover every Web site (and, in fact, most Web sites don't appear on the lists of any search engine), you need to experiment with each new search engine that you hear about to see which ones work best for your needs.

Remember, too, that each search engine works a little differently, so you want to refer to the Help section whenever you try a new search engine. Sometimes, you can find this information after you click the engine's Advanced Search link.

Some search engines, such as AltaVista.com, are case sensitive. Typing **dog** into the search form produces different results than if you type **Dog**. Make sure that you try your search term both ways.

After refining your search in your selected search engine, I suggest that you take the time to browse while doing your research. Start reviewing the sites that the search engine returns, and follow some of the links shown on each site. Give yourself permission to get lost and lose track of the time. You generally discover valuable new sources of information, although the information that you find may not be exactly what you were looking for.

You want to keep your word processor open while you research various sites so that you can jot down notes or copy URLs from the browser to visit again later.

If you're too lazy to copy and paste URLs into your word processor, you can use the Bookmark feature under the Favorites menu in your Web browser to "save" an important Web page. The next time you connect to the Internet, you'll be able to quickly go to the Web page you bookmarked by simply clicking the Favorites menu and selecting the Web page you want.

Using automated searches

Shareware programs can automate your Web searches. A shareware program is software that you can download and use for a limited period of time. After the evaluation period, if you want to keep using the software, you will be asked to pay a nominal fee to purchase a software license. You download and install the file from a Web site, type the words you're searching for, select which search engines to submit the search to, and you're off. After submitting the query to each search engine, the software returns all the results.

Some people swear by these tools, but I'm not a big fan of them. They're generally slow because they must submit the query multiple times, and they return so many results that sorting through them is hard. If you're conducting a very targeted search on a specific subject, however, one of these shareware programs may prove helpful to you. To find one, follow these steps:

1. **Go to the ZDNet Downloads Web page**
   (www.zdnet.com/downloads/specials/free.html).

2. **Select your operating system (PC, Mac, and so on) from the drop-down list, type** All in one Searches **in the search form, and click the Go button.**

   ZDNet returns a list of shareware programs that you can download. These programs carry ratings (from one to five stars), and you can see the number of times that people have downloaded a program.

New York Public Library's Express Information Service

If you need help with your research, contact the New York Public Library. The NYPL Express service helps you research and responds to any questions you send to them. While researching for you, the staff searches through hundreds of databases; they also can access print and non-print reference sources, professional and trade associations, and government agencies.

The service is sometimes expensive, but it's well worth the cost if you can't find what you need anywhere else. Standard research is billed at $75 per hour of research time and the search is completed within two weeks. If you're in a rush, the fee increases to $90 per hour, but the research is completed within three to five business days. If you're frantic, you can get the research completed within two business days, but the fee increases to $125 per hour. The findings can be faxed to you (50 cents per page within New York City, $1 per page for long distance, or $3 per page for international) or you can have the information sent by FedEx (at a cost of $11 for up to one pound of material). For more information, see the New York Public Library Web site at www.nypl.org/research/docdelivery/ResearchServ.html.

Knowing when enough is enough

As you research, you often find that so much information is available that knowing just when to stop can prove difficult. How much research is enough? If you start to form an outline in your head, you've probably done enough research to begin writing. You may need to research some more for specific sections of your document, but at this point, you can generally feel pretty confident about your knowledge of the topic.

To avoid plagiarism, you want to put your words on paper without referring to your notes. After absorbing the material sufficiently, you start to merge this knowledge with your own thoughts and viewpoints. You may need to refer back to your sources for highly detailed information, but as you write, you want the words and concepts to come from you — not from your research.

If you never get to the point of spontaneous writing, you may want to question whether this topic is the right one for you. If necessary, consider going back through your research to look for a related topic that makes better use of your area of expertise.

Using eZines for Your Research

The easiest way to get information? Have it come to you. That's why you should subscribe to as many eZines as possible in your area of interest. *eZines* are newsletter-style publications that you receive by e-mail on a regular basis. Because eZines are cheaper to deliver than printed publications, publishers can send out weekly, or even daily, issues. Many publishers issue free eZines because they're a great way to promote products without spamming potential customers.

Finding eZines

Most of the large consumer Web sites publish associated eZines, which you can subscribe to for free. Many of the smaller topical Web sites publish eZines as well.

There's no such thing as a free lunch, as the old saying goes — or a free eZine subscription. Generally, either advertising funds all those "free" eZines, or the publisher designs the eZine especially to entice you to buy a certain product. Most eZine publishers list their privacy policies on the home page. Before you subscribe, look over the privacy policy and decide whether you're comfortable with how the publisher may use your personal data. If you can't find a privacy policy, that's a bad sign. Unless you know that the publisher has a solid reputation, be wary of signing up.

A number of Web sites enable you to subscribe to multiple eZines from a single page. If you want to get your feet wet with eZines, take a look at InfoBeat, Inc., Tip World, or The Standard.com. You can find information about these Web sites (their addresses, for example) and other places to find eZines in the Internet Directory section of this book.

Subscribing to eZines

You can subscribe to an eZine quite easily. Most Web sites offer a subscription form on their home page. This form enables you to enter your e-mail address, and then all you need to do is click a Subscribe or Go button to submit your request to subscribe.

If you get an eZine someone forwards to you, and you want to subscribe, look for a list of URLs somewhere in the text of the newsletter. Most of the time, you find subscription information at the bottom of the eZine, but occasionally you may find it at the top. These links usually appear as <u>To Subscribe</u> and <u>To Unsubscribe</u>. If you don't see a <u>To Subscribe</u> link, click the link to the Web site's home page. (You can usually find the Web address in the body of the newsletter.) From there, although you may need to do a little hunting, you can usually find either the sign-up form or a link to a page that enables you to sign up.

The following list offers some reasons for you to consider subscribing to an eZine:

- ✔ **Staying in touch with what's new in your field:** Daily eZines offer information that's more current than printed periodicals.

- ✔ **Interesting links:** Good eZines include links to Web sites with additional information.

- ✔ **Finding new forums and newsgroups:** eZines can often steer you to interesting forums and newsgroups where you can participate in lively "discussions" about your topic.

- ✔ **New topics:** eZines often get you thinking about new topics for your writing.

- ✔ **Building a list of editors:** You can start building a list of editors to submit a press release to when you're ready to publish your eBook.

Advertisers sponsor many eZines. You can usually determine what's editorial content and what's an ad, but if most of the links turn out to be ads, you probably want to unsubscribe from that eZine.

Overcoming e-mail overload

The only disadvantage to subscribing to many eZines is that overwhelmed feeling you get as you look at the number of messages in your inbox every morning. Because of the nature of my work at Microsoft, I got as many as a hundred e-mail messages each day. If you add eZines to the total, it's a lot to process before I even begin to do "real" work.

The following tips may help you survive the overwhelming number of e-mails in your inbox if you start subscribing to eZines:

✔ Create an e-mail account specifically for your eZine subscriptions. Many Web sites, such as Hotmail.com (`www.hotmail.com`) offer free Web-based e-mail.

  After you create your free e-mail account, use it whenever you subscribe to an eZine; this strategy helps keep your e-mail account at work free of excess e-mail.

✔ After you start receiving eZines, get in the habit of scanning each one as quickly as possible to determine what you want to read. Don't waste time reading each article.

✔ Be ruthless about unsubscribing. Your time is precious; if you find that you consistently don't read an eZine, take a few minutes to unsubscribe. Doing so cleans up your inbox, leaving you with less e-mail to process.

✔ Don't get compulsive about getting through all the eZines. At times, your day is just so busy that you can't read all your e-mail. If you subscribe to a number of eZines on the same topic, you soon notice that they all cover the same information. Scanning through one or two to find out whether anything major's happening is usually sufficient.

✔ If you find too much similarity between your eZines, pick out the two that you like the best and unsubscribe from the rest.

HTML versus text e-mail

Many eZines give you the choice of subscribing to HTML-formatted e-mail, instead of ASCII (plain) text e-mail or other mail formats.

The HTML version can make scanning the page easier, because HTML gives the author more page-layout options. After you become familiar with the layout of a particular eZine, you can quickly scan its headlines and jump to the sections that you usually read.

You also find advantages to subscribing to the text version of a newsletter. If your Internet connection is slow, downloading the text version is usually faster than downloading the HTML-formatted e-mail. If animated GIFs or banner ads easily distract you, go with the text version. If your e-mail program doesn't support HTML formatting, however, you're pretty much stuck with the text version.

Don't bother sending e-mail to the sender if you want to unsubscribe from an eZine. An automated program known as a *ListBot* manages most eZine e-mail subscriber lists. Nobody's actually there to read or respond to your e-mail.

If you look through the text of the e-mail, you usually find an e-mail address where you can send mail to unsubscribe. (Many times, the e-mail asks you to enter the word ***Unsubscribe*** as the subject of the e-mail.) If you can't find an e-mail address, look for a link to a Web page that enables you to stop receiving the e-mail.

If you can't find an e-mail address or link, go to the home page of the Web site publishing the eZine and send an e-mail to the customer-support contact, who can usually help you.

If you know how to get through your eZine e-mail efficiently, you wind up with more time to write.

Signing up for clipping services

Another way to get news to come to you via e-mail is to sign up for a *news-clipping* service. (These companies got their names back when all news was print-based.) For a fee, such a company clips and sends you articles about a specific subject or company.

With the advent of the Internet, the companies that provide these services became very sophisticated. They can now search through thousands of databases to deliver very targeted information. Most clipping services charge hefty fees for the information that they provide, but other ways exist to obtain this research with less expense.

Excite (www.excite.com) offers a free *NewsTracker* service to users who register at its site. This service enables you to define a search term; NewsTracker searches through more than 300 online newspapers and magazines available on the Web. (***Note:*** Retrieving articles from some of these sites requires registration, although you need not pay to register.) The results from NewsTracker don't come to you via e-mail, but you can view them from the Excite Web site.

One of the most popular fee-based clipping services is *DowJones.com,* where you can perform a business search from the front page. By typing a word, phrase, or symbol, you can elect to search through the Newswires and the DowJones.com index of 2,000 top business Web sites; or you can search for a specific term through 250 news and business publications, including *The Wall Street Journal.* Any headlines that you retrieve are free, but purchasing the full text of the article costs $2.95. Go to http://dowjones.work.com/ to perform a business search or just browse through the large amount of free data available.

Before paying Dow Jones to retrieve an article, first go to the Web site of the periodical originally publishing the article. Sometimes, you can read the article for free just by going to the source.

Mining Forums and Newsgroups

Many eZines can steer you to related forumsand newsgroups that can prove moderately useful for research. These forums and newsgroups are often useful for publicizing your material, a topic that I cover in Chapter 15.

Talk to me . . .

A *forum* (or *chat*) enables you to communicate with other people by typing comments in a public chat room. Your comments appear to other participants as soon as you type them, which adds a certain amount of tension to the process if you're not a fast typist. Other people are adding their comments as well. A chat moderator manages the entire process, redirecting comments if people get off the subject and kicking people out of the chat room if they don't adhere to the rules of conduct. With a great moderator, chats are lively and interesting. With a mediocre moderator, chats can become chaotic.

You can't rely on information that you get from a chat because you don't know the identity of your source. The exception is if you attend a well-publicized chat with a public figure. In this case, the chat takes on more of an interview tone, and you can often gain some relevant information. Most of this information is very general, but sometimes you find out something new.

Newsgroupies

A *newsgroup* is a Web site that posts threaded "discussions" from people who leave messages for others to read. Person 1 leaves a comment or question on the newsgroup bulletin board. This message becomes the start of a thread. Person 2 responds to Person 1, either by answering the question or by making a comment in response to the first message. Person 2's comment causes Person 3 and Person 4 to leave responses. Person 5 responds to Person 3, but no one may respond to Person 4.

Each response usually appears indented under the message that spawns it. This layout makes seeing which response goes with each originating message easier. On a good thread, you can obtain a lot of useful information, especially from newsgroups that provide technical support.

That's the theory. In practice, it often works as follows:

✔ You want to know which Web browser is better. You enter your question into a form on the Web site's newsgroup page and after clicking the Submit button, your question is shown on the Web site for the entire world to see.

- Bob, who works for Microsoft, has some strong opinions about the subject. He leaves a lengthy message extolling the virtues of Internet Explorer. His message appears underneath your original message.

  - Karen, a retired Netscape employee, is equally passionate on the subject of browsers. She leaves a scathing message for Bob, ripping into his arguments and finishing with a summation of why Netscape always has — and always will — rule. Her message appears under Bob's.

  - A nasty flame war breaks out between Bob and Karen, who hurl comments at each other that have nothing to do with browsers. Your question is completely lost in the crossfire.

- Sam, who doesn't work at all, goes off the subject completely and starts discussing what screen savers he has downloaded using his browser and how cool they are.

Relying on "tips" you get from newsgroup threads can prove very dangerous. In the preceding example, Karen may claim she worked for Netscape — but how can you really know? I don't want to turn you into a cynic, but don't believe something you read in a thread until you confirm the information with an outside source.

Some newsgroup threads are very informative; some are a waste of time. The owner of the newsgroup helps create a great thread by weeding out the foolish postings on a regular basis.

Forums and newsgroups can prove useful if you want to take the pulse of a group in reaction to a major news event. After the Clinton-Lewinsky scandal broke out, the chat rooms and newsgroups were flooded with postings by people offering their opinion about whether President Clinton should be impeached. This reaction can become a newsworthy event in its own right. If reporters don't have enough data on a breaking story, they sometimes report how people are reacting to the story. MSNBC often uses this technique; the TV cable service reports on activity on the MSNBC.com newsgroups. If you're searching for a topic to write about, this technique may prove of interest to you.

How to find forums and newsgroups

To find forums on your area of interest, go to Yahoo! (www.yahoo.com) and click the <u>Chat</u> link at the top of the page.

To find newsgroups of interest, follow these steps:

1. **Go to** www.yahoo.com **and click the <u>Computers and Internet </u>link.**

   Note: You can select any of the Yahoo! areas that interest you; I just used <u>Computers and Internet</u> in this example.

2. **Under the Inside Yahoo! section, click the <u>Post a Message</u> link.**

3. **Click any of the Yahoo! message boards links that you find interesting.**

   From here, you can read messages and post your own responses.

Most of the portal and other large Web sites (such as MSN.com, AOL.com, and Go.com) feature their own message boards and chats in which you can participate. Go to the home pages of these sites and look for links to their <u>Community</u> or <u>People and Chat</u> areas.

Part II
Starting to Write

In this part . . .

So, you're ready to write. Now what? If you find the idea of a blank screen scary, Part II contains tools to jumpstart your writing.

Chapter 4 explains how to structure your document. I provide tips to help you break through writer's block, and I give you online resources that you can use.

In Chapter 5, I give you advice on how to write effectively. This chapter explains how to use outlines to organize your content and how to write a first draft.

Chapter 6 shows you how to move beyond the concept of a text-only book through the addition of images, sound, animation, and video. This chapter shows you how to get media clips and how to incorporate them into your eBook.

In Chapter 7, I explain that ePublishing is more than just printing to a Web page. This chapter shows you how to add interactivity to your document. This chapter also discusses what kind of media works best for fiction, children's literature, nonfiction, and technological eBooks.

Chapter 4

Jumpstarting Your Creative Process

In This Chapter

▶ Thinking about what type of eBook you want to write

▶ Creating a template for your eBook

▶ Curing writer's block

▶ Finding a great title

*Y*ou picked your topic and did the necessary research, but now you're overwhelmed about where to go from here. The thought of writing dozens, if not hundreds, of pages seems like too large of a task to tackle. Take a deep breath and relax — you're just suffering from information overload. You may be too close to the topic to see how it needs to be structured and organized into an eBook.

In this chapter, I show you how to structure your eBook. I also discuss templates that are available on the CD-ROM to help you create articles, booklets, manuals, and eBooks. I also give you helpful tips to break through your writer's block, if that should happen. I end this chapter by helping you find the right title for your eBook.

The tools in this chapter are designed to help organize content for nonfiction. Fiction, by its very nature, doesn't fall easily into organizational categories. If you have an idea for a novel, jump ahead to Chapter 5, which gives you some tips on how to organize fictional material.

Getting Organized

This section contains tools you can use to help organize your material. If you do the exercises in this section, you may have a better understanding of the following points:

✔ The type of eBook you're writing

✔ The needs of the audience

✔ The main points your eBook needs to discuss

✔ The main sections that go into your Table of Contents

✔ Additional sections that may be added to your eBook

Deciding what type of eBook you're going to write

Before you structure your content, you need to think about the type of eBook that you want to write. To help you decide, write down the answers to the following questions:

✔ **What type of nonfiction are you creating?** For example, are you going to write a how-to eBook, a technical eBook, or a biography?

✔ **What type of group are you writing for?** I use *group* as a deliberately generic term. For example, are you writing for parents, job seekers, new investors, or teachers?

✔ **How long will your eBook be?** Give a rough idea of the page count. For example, do you plan to write a ten-page article, a 50-page manual, a 200-page eBook?

By thinking about the length of the manuscript in advance, you help define how detailed you want your eBook to be, and how much subject matter you want to cover. Don't feel like you have to cram everything into a single eBook — unless you're writing the ultimate reference on a specific topic. You can save some material for follow-up articles or for the sequel.

Figuring out what your readers want

To help you identify what people want to read about, you can write a short *scenario* about your topic. To create a scenario, write a short scene in which you identify the needs of one character that represents a typical reader from your target audience. When you write the eBook, try to provide solutions for your character's situation, which is, in fact, your audience's situation. To write a successful scenario, follow these steps:

1. **Describe the situation the character faces.**

2. **Describe the specific problems that the character hopes the eBook will solve (don't try to provide solutions just yet, however).**

3. **Keep writing down your character's unique problems until you can't think of any more.**

4. **Analyze the problems you list in your scenario and describe them in a more generic way.**

   This list represents what your target audience wants you to solve when they read your eBook.

5. **As you organize the material for your eBook, create chapters that provide the answers to the questions you created.**

Deciding what readers should know after reading your eBook

When you organize the material for your eBook (check out Chapter 5 to see how to create an outline based on your material), you're writing to help readers understand the topic you've selected to write about. In addition to meeting your readers' needs, think about what they should know or understand after they read your eBook.

For example, let me list the main things I hope the audience understands after reading this book:

- What an eBook is and the different types of eBook readers that are on the market

- How to choose a topic for an eBook and conduct necessary research

- How to organize research material to create an outline for the eBook

- The basics of writing well and knowing where to go for help in improving his or her writing

- The advantages eBooks offer and an appreciation for how alternative media can be integrated into eBooks

- How to structure an interactive document and organize the content contained within the eBook so it's optimized for onscreen reading

- The differences between articles, booklets, manuals, and eBooks and how to reuse the same content in various packages

- How to build a simple eBook either by coding the eBook or using an authoring tool

- The fundamentals of ePublishing: distributing content by working with an ePublisher or becoming an ePublisher. The readers should also be able to make an informed choice about which option to choose.

Create your own list for what the audience should know after reading your eBook; organize the list in a way that makes sense to you. Depending on the items in the list, the items can be ordered chronologically, in order of importance, and so on. Use the list you create as the basis for the chapters in your eBook.

Including the necessary sections in your eBook

No matter what type of nonfiction eBook you write, certain sections are necessary for you to include:

- ✔ **Cover:** Although this cover won't be like a physical cover on a bound book, you probably want to include a cover page that's the first page the audience sees. It should contain the cover image for your eBook.

- ✔ **Title page:** The title page should show the title of the eBook, the name of the author, the name of the ePublisher, and the copyright notice. The title page should also contain a link back to the Web site where you sell your eBooks to allow readers to buy other titles that you publish.

- ✔ **Table of Contents:** You may want to include a Table of Contents or a List of Links if you plan on linking to the page that begins each chapter or section.

- ✔ **Index:** A detailed list of items mentioned in the eBook. Each item should be linked to the section of text that mentions it. If an item is mentioned in multiple places within the text, provide a link for every instance where the item's mentioned. The index item should look something like the following example:

```
Index Item (e.g. Table of Contents)
    1st mention in text (this should be a link)
    2nd mention in text (this should be a link)
    3rd mention in text (this should be a link)
    Etc.
```

Including extraneous sections in your eBook

The following sections are useful to add to your document, especially if you worry that you don't have enough content to write a full-length eBook:

✔ **Expert tips and tricks:** A list of shortcuts and tricks can be listed at the end of each chapter, or listed at the end of the last chapter.

✔ **FAQs:** This stands for Frequently Asked Questions, which are often found on Web sites. FAQs are a list of commonly asked questions that contain the answers underneath each question. FAQs are a great way to help the audience understand difficult issues or to review material. FAQs can be included at the end of each chapter.

✔ **References and Resources:** These should contain links to online references; but, you should know if the eBook reader's hardware can access the Web while the audience reads the text.

✔ **Glossary:** A list of words found in the eBook that some of the audience may not know because the terms or acronyms are specific to your topic. List the words in alphabetical order and provide the definition after each word.

✔ **Appendixes:** Sections of content that are added to the end of a book because they contain *supplemental material* (content that may be useful to have, but isn't critical to understanding the main points of the book). Very detailed or technical information is appropriate for an appendix.

Building Your Own Template

Sometimes, the easiest way to start organizing your own content is to see how someone else structures his or her content. If you want to jumpstart the structure of your manuscript, look at the sample templates I created and added to the CD-ROM to help get you started.

The CD-ROM that accompanies this book contains sample templates that you can use to create articles, booklets, manuals, and full-length eBooks. Go to Chapter 9 to find out more about ePublishing in these different packages and how to reuse content created for one format in another format.

To build your documents, you can use the sample templates on the CD-ROM or you can create your own template. After you find out how to build a template, you can reuse it to author new eBooks.

To create your own template, do the following:

1. **Open Word 2000.**

   Word 2000 opens with a new blank document.

2. **Create a series of custom styles to use with the document. (See Chapter 10 if you need help on how to use custom Word styles.)**

   At a minimum, you should select the formatting to be used for normal text, Heading 1, Heading 2, and Heading 3. You can also create formatting for captions, hyperlinks, and other elements you think will be used extensively throughout the text.

3. **Create a document that has no content, but contains the structure of the eBook you plan to write.**

   For example, for Chapter 1, write Chapter 1. Create another line and write some sample text using the normal style. Then create a subheading; format it using one of the heading styles you create, and write some sample text. Under the subheading, write some sample text using the normal style again.

   You may continue to create subheads and sample text entries until you have a document that uses each of the major styles you want featured in your eBook. The document will look similar to the document in Figure 4-1.

4. **Save the document by choosing File⇨Save As.**

   The Save As dialog box appears, as shown in Figure 4-2.

5. **Select a name for the file and the folder where you want it saved; click the Save button.**

   With the document you just saved, you can now create a template.

6. **Select File⇨Save As.**

   The Save As dialog box appears.

7. **Select Document Template (*.dot) from the Save as Type drop-down list.**

   After you make this change, the folder automatically changes to the default directory where Word stores templates.

   Don't try to change the folder from the default template directory. If you do, you won't automatically see your new folder as a choice when you select from the available templates.

8. **Give your template file a name and click the Save button.**

9. **Close the Word document you created the template from by choosing File⇨Close.**

10. **Create a new document in Word by choosing File⇨New.**

    The New dialog box appears.

11. **Click the General tab.**

    Your template shows in the icons displayed in the dialog box. Make sure that Document is selected under the Create New section of the dialog box.

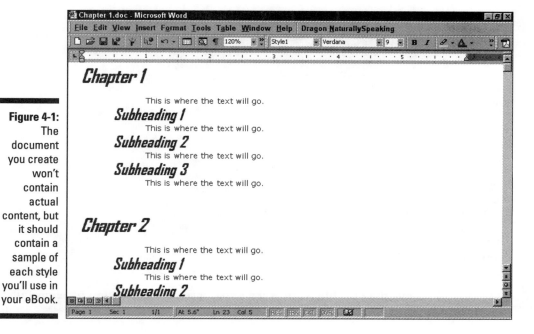

Figure 4-1:
The document you create won't contain actual content, but it should contain a sample of each style you'll use in your eBook.

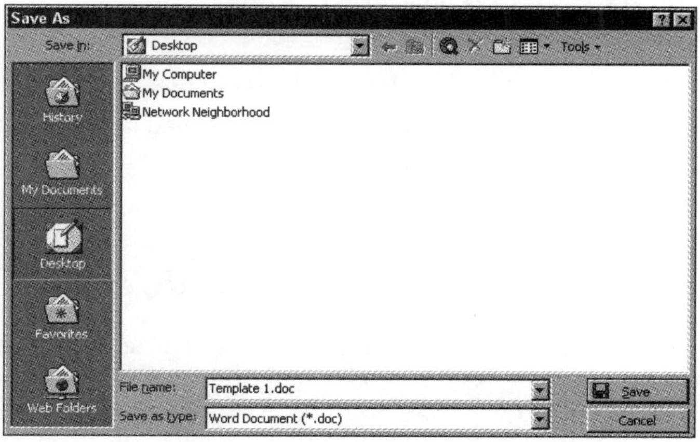

Figure 4-2:
You can save your document in the Save As dialog box.

12. **Click your template icon and click the OK button to create a new document based on your template, as shown in Figure 4-3.**

13. **Overwrite the sample text that you used when you created the template and enter the content you want to have in your eBook.**

Figure 4-3:
As long as
you select
the
Document
option under
the Create
New section
of the dialog
box, a new
document
opens in
Word that's
based on
your
template.

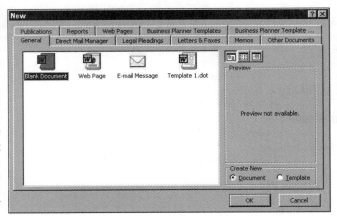

14. **Save the new file (with Word's standard .doc extension) by choosing File⇨Save.**

    The Save dialog box appears.

    The Word Document (*.doc) option should be showing in the Save as Type drop-down list.

15. **Select the name and folder for the file and click the Save button.**

    Your document, based on your template, is saved in the directory you choose.

Breaking through Writer's Block

Sometimes, you may feel stuck when you try to organize your thoughts. The same thing may happen when you try to write and can't think of a single thing to say. If this happens to you, you have *writer's block,* an ailment that seems to hit all writers at some point in their careers. The most important thing to do when you have writer's block is to take a break from writing — it could be that you're working too hard and need a little time off.

If taking a break doesn't help your writer's block, try the following tip to help you get writing again. Sometimes, writing something that's completely different from your work can get your thoughts flowing again. Try sending an e-mail to a neglected friend. Try writing a letter to your mother. Write a short children's story (and read it to your children). After you take a mental break and try your hand at a different type of prose, you may find that you're able to work again.

Playing the expert

REREAD
DON'T KNOW
if it
works.

If you're racing to make a deadline and are hit by writer's block, you may want to try this technique to get your creative juices flowing again. I call this technique *playing the expert*:

There are a number of Web sites where people post questions (in multiple categories) and other people "bid" to provide the answer. Other Web sites don't involve a transaction, but participants are invited to post their opinions about products and events. A similar forum is bulletin boards and chats, which give you a chance to voice your opinion about a specific topic or subject.

1. **Find a site that allows you to participate in your area of expertise.**

2. **Look for questions that you can answer and provide answers for any questions that cover the material you want to cover in your eBook.**

3. **Save the questions and your responses in a file on your desktop.**

4. **After you answer the first question, rewrite the text so you can use your response in your manuscript.**

   Sometimes, just the act of answering one question relieves your writer's block. If it doesn't, keep answering questions until you feel like writing again.

Interested in trying this technique? Here are some Web sites to check out:

- ✔ www.epinions.com/
- ✔ consumerreview.com/
- ✔ www.deja.com
- ✔ www.about.com

If your writer's block never goes away, at some point, you'll have enough responses to publish an eBook that's formatted in FAQ (Frequently Asked Questions) style.

Getting help from other writers

If you can't break through your writer's block, but still want to ePublish, don't worry. You can acquire content in other ways and compile it into an eBook. You can work with other authors to package their work and create an anthology. (Visit Chapter 6 to find out how to use an author's work in the eBook you're creating.) If you use a substantial amount of another's writer's text, you need to license the content instead of just getting permission to use a small excerpt. (See Chapter 14 for more information on how to license content.)

You can also hire a *ghostwriter* to write your ideas for you. This person can take your initial outline, expand it and write the document for you. You may decide to become an eBook *packager*. (An eBook packager comes up with the initial concept for an eBook, finds the authors to develop the title, collects the additional media, hires a graphic artist to create the cover design, and compiles and formats the finished document. The ePackager can either ePublish the title or work with an ePublisher for distribution.) If you're not ready to write the title yourself, you can find a ghostwriter by putting an ad in the classified section of your favorite writers Web site. (A list of Web sites devoted to authors and eBooks is listed in the Online Directory.)

Finding a Killer Title

First impressions are important. Your eBook's title is the first thing people notice. If your title is dynamic and gets people's attention (in a positive way), people may take the time to find out more about your eBook, and maybe even buy it. If the title makes the book sound dull, even the most exciting eBook will have a hard time getting the sales it deserves.

Creating knock-'em-dead titles

Titles must be short, clever, and suggestive of the content in the eBook. The title should jump out at customers. Here are some tips to help you find a great title:

- ✔ **Shorter is better:** Try to describe your eBook in four words or less.

- ✔ **It's good to be clever, but don't be corny:** If you have a hard time coming up with a really catchy title, stick with something simple. A title called *Guide to ePublishing* is preferable to the irritating *ePublish/ShePublish*.

- ✔ **Use verbs in your title:** Verbs energize the title.

- ✔ **Do a search on book-selling Web sites:** Search on Amazon.com and BN.com for competitive books. Make a list of the top-three titles (in your opinion). Try to analyze what makes these titles so good and keep these thoughts in mind as you play with words for your title.

- ✔ **Certain words grab people's attention better than others:** Words like *Secrets, Success, Profit, How To,* and similar terms suggest that readers will benefit from your eBook. Try to include these words if they're appropriate for your title.

- ✔ **Make someone smile (or, even better, laugh out loud):** If you can make someone feel good just by reading the title, he or she is more inclined to find out about the eBook.

Creating a brand

Why did you buy this book? The chances are that you looked at it because the words ...*For Dummies* were in the title. ...*For Dummies* represents a powerful brand that IDG Books, the publisher, has put time and resources into building. Readers associate the words ...*For Dummies* with technical or difficult subject matter that's presented in an easy-to-understand, friendly, tongue-in-cheek fashion.

If you're thinking about creating a line of eBooks (especially if you plan on working with other writers to create the titles), you need to think about the brand you want to build. Try to come up with a single term or phrase that describes the line and include this in the title of every eBook. If the line becomes successful, customers may seek out your titles because of the brand you established (instead of seeking an eBook because of the credibility of a single author).

After you establish it, your brand becomes the symbol for your credibility. Make sure that people continue to associate your brand with a high-quality product. Never publish a manuscript before you think it's ready (or if you're not sure that it fits your brand of eBooks). One poor-quality title can hurt your brand's reputation.

Chapter 5

The ABCs of Effective Writing

In This Chapter

▶ Organizing your thoughts

▶ Writing the first draft

▶ Editing essentials

▶ Structuring copyrighted material

▶ Working with an editor

*I*f you haven't written much since high school, don't worry. Writing comes as naturally as speaking — just don't worry about how a manuscript reads after the first draft. No one sits down and composes publication-ready text in the first sitting. Writing is a process. First, you must organize your thoughts, then get something (anything!) down on paper, and then refine, refine, refine. When you can't improve the text any more, ask someone to review the document. Edit the document again based on the feedback you receive. Now you're ready to have an editor review the manuscript before it's published.

Sound like a lot of work? That's because it is — but it can also be a lot of fun. As you get more experienced, you won't have to spend as much time editing your documents. Some stages of the process are more enjoyable than others. For example, I love writing the first draft, but I hate editing. My sister, who wrote many papers for her master's degree, enjoys doing the research but breaks into a cold sweat at the thought of writing the first draft. So no matter which part of the process you enjoy the most, spend enough time on each step so that your final document provides value and enjoyment to your audience.

Outlining Your Thoughts

Different writers have different writing styles, but most start with a structured way of tackling a project. Most people need to put a few notes into an outline before they sit down to write a beautifully organized document. If you have a general idea about what you want to write, but you're not sure where to begin, your best bet is to start with an outline.

Avoid the urge to over-outline, especially if you're doing it to avoid writing.

Different people have different outlining tools that they like to use. I always use Microsoft Word's Outline feature, so here's how to create an outline with Word:

1. **Open Microsoft Word and create a new document by choosing File⇨New.**

   The New dialog box appears.

2. **Select the Blank Document option and click the OK button.**

3. **Choose View⇨Outline, as shown in Figure 5-1.**

   When you change to Outline View in Word, the Outlining toolbar appears; it replaces Word's ruler (if you had the ruler showing).

4. **Start your outline by typing the first top-level heading at the cursor and press the Enter key.**

   The type of document that you're writing determines your top-level headings. If you're writing an article, you may only have two or three top-level headings. If you're writing a full-length eBook, then each chapter title should correspond to a top-level heading. Later, as you begin to flesh out your outline in the writing process, you may want to turn each chapter into a separate outline.

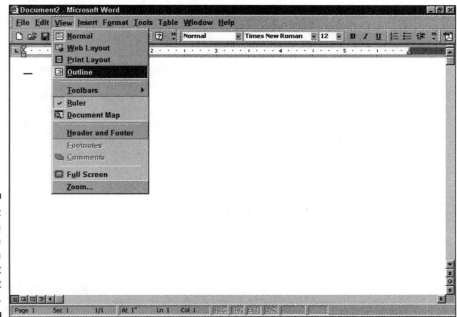

Figure 5-1:
You can use the Outline feature in Microsoft Word to get started.

For example, suppose I want to create an outline for this chapter. For my first top-level heading, I enter "Outlining Your Thoughts" and press the Enter key. Word formats your first top-level heading using the Heading 1 style. (For an explanation of how to format text using Word's styles, see Chapter 10.)

5. **Continue to enter the top-level headings for your document, pressing the Enter key after each entry, as shown in Figure 5-2.**

   Now you're ready to enter the second-level headings.

6. **Move the cursor to the end of the first top-level heading and press the Enter key. Under this top-level heading, type your first second-level heading.**

   After typing the second-level heading, you must convert it from a top-level heading to a second-level heading.

7. **Move the mouse over the dash-like symbol that's located to the left of each heading.**

   The symbol changes from a dash to a plus sign with an arrow at each point. When you see this symbol, drag it to the right until you see a gray vertical line appear on the screen. After you stop dragging, the heading is demoted to a second-level heading.

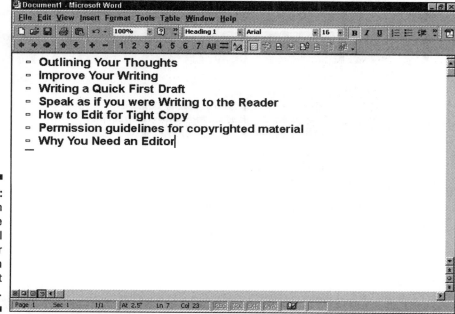

Figure 5-2:
You can enter all the top-level headings for each chapter that you write.

An alternate way to demote a heading: Click somewhere in the heading and click the Demote button (it looks like an arrow pointing to the right) in the Outlining toolbar. The heading is demoted one level every time you click this button.

8. **After you convert the paragraph to a second-level heading, press the Enter key.**

9. **Enter the remainder of your second-level headings under the first top-level heading — press the Enter key after you type each heading.**

   Your document should look something like Figure 5-3.

10. **Now you can enter all the second-level headings for the rest of the top-level headings.**

    If you want to detail your outline further, you can create third-level headings under the second-level headings.

After you enter many headings at different levels, it may be hard to see the overall structure. To simplify the document, you can *collapse* some headings. To quickly collapse the entire outline to show just the top-level headings, click the 1 button in the Outlining toolbar. All the sub-headings in the document collapse, and only the top-level headings appear. To expand a collapsed heading, place the cursor on the heading that you want to expand, and click the Expand button (it looks like a plus sign) in the Outlining toolbar. The collapsed subheads appear.

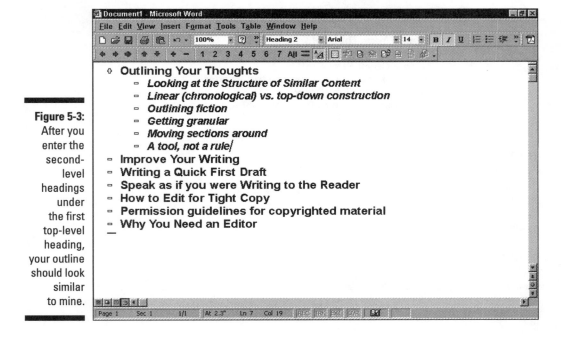

Figure 5-3: After you enter the second-level headings under the first top-level heading, your outline should look similar to mine.

REALLY?

After you're happy with your outline and are ready to write, you can easily convert your outline into a document.

11. Choose View⇨Normal.

All the outline headings are converted to document-style headings. Now you can start typing the text into your document.

As you work on an outline, you may discover that a subheading originally placed in one section of the document should actually go into a different section. You can move a heading to a different location by dragging the symbol up or down — all the subordinate subheadings and body text under the heading moves with it.

Organizing your content

Sometimes, after you spend a lot of time researching a topic, you know exactly what you want to write about. You can bang out a pretty decent outline in about an hour because you know the material so well. Other times, you can feel completely lost about where to begin your outline.

Whenever I find myself in this situation, I use two different methods to get me moving. The methods in this section help you break through the panic that can set in when you have no idea how to get started.

Start anywhere

When I have no idea how to structure a document, I write a quick outline of all the random thoughts I have in my head. I don't even structure them. I make everything a top-level heading. And when I run out of ideas, I stop and do more research on the topic. As I research, new thoughts come into my mind and I add them to the outline. Using this method, I can quickly come up with an outline that is 20 to 30 pages long (and makes absolutely no sense to anyone else).

hmmm.

If you try this method, as you add to the outline, you begin to see that some headings actually belong under some others. You should now begin to demote headings and move them as necessary. As you do this, remove duplicate ideas from the document. (Much of those 30 pages of mine are actually redundant, so I trim it down by weeding out the repeats.) You should keep working at the outline until a structure emerges. The process can be slow and tedious, but it helps you to get organized when nothing else works.

Expect some structural changes as you as begin to write. You may have included a section when you were building the outline, but if you find that it no longer works in the same context when you're writing the first draft, take it out. This is especially true in works of fiction — an author may expect the story to end a certain way and is surprised when he or she writes a completely different ending. After you start writing, an eBook takes on a life of its own . . . just go with it.

Outlining fiction

Outlines work best for nonfiction, but outlining can help you even when you work on a novel. Before you tackle the first page, you can put together an outline that can help you think through the plot and characterizations. If you already started a draft, but you got a case of writer's block, step away from the keyboard and try writing the following:

- **Detailed character descriptions:** For each major character, write a detailed character description. Describe what the character looks like, his or her family background, the schools that the character attended, where he or she grew up, what motivates this character, the character's likes and dislikes, and anything else you think is relevant information.

- **Descriptions of minor characters:** For each minor character, write a paragraph or two that describes that person.

- **Plot outline:** Write a short sentence or two that describes each major scene. You should do the same for each subplot. Regardless of how the novel is written, the plot outline should be written in chronological order so you can refer back to it when needed. The plot outline doesn't need to be written in a document; you can use note cards, put the outline in a spreadsheet, or draw it on paper.

See how others do it

I would never recommend plagiarizing another writer's material, but you can sometimes find it helpful to see how someone else organizes material, especially with structured documents.

If you're trying to organize an eBook, take a look at the Table of Contents for books and eBooks with similar content. Many times, you can find the contents listed on Amazon.com or BN.com. Viewing the Table of Contents allows you to see the structure of a book without having to pay for it. Also, looking at outlines without actually reading the text protects you from accidentally using another writer's material.

Structuring your outline in different ways

You can structure a work of nonfiction in a few different ways. Before you organize your outline, think about which organizational style works best for your target audience. The type of structure that you should use depends on what you're writing (for example, an article or a manual) and the sophistication of your audience. Here are a few ways to structure your work:

- **Chronological:** This is the easiest organizational structure to understand. Start at the beginning, and when you reach the end, stop.

✔ **Simple to advanced:** This is similar to a tutorial structure. You start the document with simple concepts and then move to increasingly sophisticated concepts (based on the assumption that the audience understands the early concepts). Most math books are written in simple to advanced format. If you don't understand simple algebra, you'll be completely lost when you get to calculus.

✔ **Inverted pyramid:** Newspaper articles and Web sites use an inverted pyramid structure, in which the most important content is presented in the first paragraph, and the supporting concepts or materials are mentioned in later paragraphs. The concluding paragraph contains supplemental material that isn't critical to the story or presentation. Newspaper and Web site articles are written this way because people tend to scan through the content instead of reading every word. By reading only the first paragraph or two, the reader determines whether the topic is of enough interest to continue reading.

✔ **Focus around the topic's structure:** Suppose I'm writing an eBook about house maintenance — I could organize the structure of the outline around the structural elements of a house. I could include a section about maintaining the plumbing, the electrical wiring, the roof, the exterior, and so on. When a reader scans through the Table of Contents, he or she can easily find the required section. When the topic that you're writing about has a well-defined structure, you can use that structure as the basis of your outline.

✔ **Reference:** People don't read reference books from cover to cover — they just look up the material that they need. If you're designing a reference book, then you need to organize the content in any way that makes sense (alphabetically, chronologically, or topically structured), but remember that the Table of Contents and the Index are the pages that get read the most often. Make sure that any article in the reference book can be quickly found by using these sections. If you write the most complete reference eBook of all time, but the user can't find what he or she is looking for, then your eBook is useless.

An outline should be a helpful starting point, but that's all it should be. Many times, as you write, you think of things that should be added to or removed from the outline. That's okay. The outline is a tool for you — no one else ever needs to see it. You can start the writing process by creating an outline but still end up with a very different document than the outline dictates.

Writing a Quick First Draft

You developed a great outline, you did lots of research on the topic, and now you sit down at the computer with a cup of coffee. You start Word and . . .

nothing happens. You freeze up and can't think of how to structure the first sentence. You drink a little coffee, check your e-mail, browse a few Web sites, and glance at the newspaper. Two hours later — you haven't written anything.

Getting started is hard, especially if you tend to procrastinate. I'm a genius at not starting unless a deadline looms over me. Because my husband is tired of listening to me panic, he now pops his head into my office to ask me how many pages I've written since the last time he checked up on me. Annoying? Yes, but it works. If you procrastinate, ask someone to be your "page police officer." At least once a day, have this person call and ask how many pages you wrote. Knowing that someone is checking up on you can keep you working when you'd rather be surfing the Web.

The most important thing is to get the words down on the paper. You don't need to worry about their readability, or whether they're spelled correctly, or anything else at this point. Just get the words outta your head. Writing quickly helps your writing sound more natural than if you take the time to craft each sentence. The craft part comes later. When you write your first draft, type as much as you can as quickly as you can.

Filling in the outline

When you start writing, your goal is to fill in the outline that you created. If you are writing nonfiction, just focus on getting out the facts, details, and information that you want your audience to know. If you are writing a work of fiction, you can be less structured — but try to keep the story (plot) moving along, especially if you're writing a fast-paced thriller.

Books to help improve your writing

It would be grossly arrogant of me to tell you how to improve your writing. I'm not an English teacher, an editor, or a journalist. So, instead of teaching you how to write like me, let me introduce you to two books that can teach you how to write really well.

The Elements of Style by E.B. White, author of *Charlotte's Web,* is a classic on how to improve your writing. One of the best things about the book is how much information is compressed into a short volume. The book covers the elementary rules of usage, elementary principles of composition, a few matters of form, words and expressions commonly misused, and 21 pointers for improving the way you write.

Although *The Elements of Style* is like a dictionary (you'll want to keep a copy on your desk), *On Writing Well,* by William Zinsser, is more inspirational. Instead of getting just the rules, you get the background information that you need to improve your writing. This book also does a good job of discussing the different forms of writing: interviews, memoirs, business writing, humor, and so on.

When I write, I pretend that I'm explaining something to my younger sister or my husband. I try to explain things in a way they can understand, and I pretend that they ask me questions as I write. I make sure to answer all the questions about a specific topic before I go on to the next section of the outline.

When you fill in your outline with text, don't start at the beginning and work straight through until you're finished. That may be the hardest way to write a document. You can get stuck at the beginning and never finish the first draft. The easiest way to write a document is to start at the section that you understand the best. Jump around the outline and fill in sections as quickly as you can without referring to your research (which slows down the process of writing). Write what you can, straight out of your head, and then jump to another section where you know just exactly what you want to say. Avoid introductory and summary sections until the rest of the content has been written. (After you know what you say in the chapter, it's easier to introduce and summarize the text.)

Taking notes along the way

It never fails. You're working really well on one section of your document when you get a brilliant idea about something that you should mention in another section. The idea is so great that you know you won't forget it, so you keep writing in the current section. The phone rings and — Poof! — you can pick up the thread of what you were working on, but you can't remember that brilliant idea.

Avoid this aggravation and keep a notepad close to your desk while you write. Whenever you get an idea, jot down a couple of notes so you won't forget the idea altogether, and then return to the section that you're writing. I used to scroll through the document to the place where the great idea belonged, but by the time I found it, jotted the notes and then scrolled back, I had lost my momentum on the section I was originally working on.

Editing Your Work for Tighter Copy

The quality of your writing is the result of how well you edit, rather than how well you write the first draft. For many writers, editing takes more time than writing the initial set of pages.

Editing is more than just making sure that your punctuation is correct and that all the words are spelled properly. Editing lets you listen to the sound of the text when you read it aloud and enables you to fill in the textual holes, so that you can turn your document into a manuscript that you're proud to show other people.

Tell your story

One mistake that novice writers usually make is to write too formally. Unconsciously, they write phrases like, "Conceptually, we can postulate that . . ." and, "In conclusion, let me add the following . . ." Maybe pompous people talk that way in real life, but I bet you don't! If it sounds stuffy when you write it, it sounds stuffy to someone reading it.

One of the tricks to writing well is to sound natural. You should talk to your readers through the text. Like most things that seem easy when done well, this can be surprisingly difficult to do. If your words sound stilted to you or if an editor tells you that your text doesn't flow, then I have a suggestion: Stop writing and start speaking.

Voice recognition software (sometimes called *dictation software*) has improved in quality in the last few years. Now, after you install the software and train it to recognize your voice, you can speak into a microphone and have the words that you dictate show up onscreen. It's a wonderful way to get a first draft down on paper, especially if you're a slow typist.

One reason to use this software is to help make your text sound more natural. If this is your goal, don't look at the screen when you dictate your text. If you watch the words appear on the screen, you may get self-conscious and then pompous phrases may start to creep into your speech patterns. Look away from the screen and pretend that you're talking to your best friend.

One of the most popular dictation packages is Dragon NaturallySpeaking, by Dragon Systems. The NaturallySpeaking software provides continuous speech recognition, which means that you can blab on and on, and the software keeps up with you. The text is entered into your word processor. For more information about Dragon NaturallySpeaking, check out this Web site: www.dragonsys.com.

Remove the words that you don't need

When I write a first draft, I'm wordy. I include unnecessary words and bulky phrases. The words sound clunky when I read them. To improve my work, I remove as many words as possible without changing the meaning of the text.

Here's an example sentence that shows you how to remove extraneous words from your document. My first draft of the sentence reads like this:

> I include a lot of words that aren't needed and phrases that add bulk.

After I edit the sentence, it looks like this:

> I include unnecessary words and bulky phrases.

It can be hard to sharpen your pencil when editing, especially when you need to produce a certain number of pages. Lousy writing fills up more pages than tightly edited (good) text. But it's better to delight your readers with a well-crafted document than to bore them with every page.

Remove redundancy, remove redundancy, remove redundancy

I repeat myself. I say the same thing several different ways to make sure I get my point across. When I edit a chapter, I find the same idea expressed in slightly different terms. I often . . . well, you get the idea.

Don't repeat yourself throughout the document. This is easy to do, especially when you write different sections at different times. The tendency to be repetitive happens most often at the start of a new section of text. You try to make the text flow by recapping the ideas of the previous section. When you edit, reduce the repetition and keep the text flowing by using different text as a bridge between sections.

Although you may be writing different sections at different times, your reader may read every word in a single sitting. You don't want to waste his or her time by repeating text, so edit carefully. You may need to delete entire sections, but the sacrifice is worthwhile when the end result is a manuscript in which every sentence is valuable.

Read your material aloud

After you finish editing, take the time to read your manuscript aloud. You may feel silly and self-conscious, but find a spot where you have some privacy and do it anyway. This is a quick and easy way to notice the clunky phrases that need to be edited.

You may think that you can spot sentences that need editing by reading the text silently to yourself. Reading to yourself works better than not reading the text at all, but it still doesn't compare to the benefits of saying the words aloud.

Have someone else read your manuscript

Unless you plan to stay unpublished, someone else will read your work at some point. You can ePublish a document as soon as you're finished with it, but you should ask a second person to review it before you do. This person should be someone that you respect and can listen to when he or she gives constructive feedback. If this person loves everything that you do and never has a negative word to say, however, ask someone other than Mom.

When you ask this person to read your manuscript, let him or her know that you really want feedback to improve the document (and you have to mean it). The feedback that you solicit may vary depending on the type of eBook that you're working on. If you're authoring fiction, you may want an opinion on the following:

- ✔ Are the characters believable?
- ✔ Does the dialog sound like people talking?
- ✔ Is the plot credible?
- ✔ Is the plot easy to follow?
- ✔ Does the writing elicit emotions from the reader?
- ✔ Does the first page grab the reader's attention?
- ✔ Does the reader enjoy reading straight-through until the end of the story?
- ✔ What changes can improve the reader's experience?

 Someone who likes you can have a hard time giving you honest negative feedback. Type up the questions and ask the reader to write the responses down instead of saying the criticisms directly to you. This method is easier on the reviewer, and you'll probably get more honest feedback that way.

If your work is nonfiction, you may want to ask the reviewer the following questions:

- ✔ Are the instructions clear and easy to understand?
- ✔ Are there any holes in the text where the audience wants or needs more information? Every document has some holes early on in the editing process. Just make sure that your holes aren't gaping.
- ✔ Does the document follow a logical structure?
- ✔ Can the audience find specific information using the Table of Contents or the Index?
- ✔ Can the audience define the manuscript's benefit after reading it?
- ✔ What changes can improve the audience's experience?

Check your spelling

Finally, don't forget to proofread your document for basic mistakes in spelling and grammar. Your word-processing program can help you with 90% of the job, but you still need to do an editing pass yourself.

Printing out the document to do your editing pass can be very helpful (as long as it's not too many pages). For some reason, you're more likely to spot typos on a printed page.

Using Copyrighted Material

Even if you're a prolific writer, occasions may arise when you want to reference or quote another author's material. When you want to use a quote, you should keep two important things in mind:

- ✔ **Ask permission to use the material:** This falls into the category of better-safe-than-sorry advice.

- ✔ **If you're unsure about using a quote, consult with a copyright lawyer:** This falls into the category of much-better-safe-than-sued advice.

On the CD-ROM that is bundled with this book, I provide a letter that you can use as a template when you want permission to use a media clip in an eBook. With a little modification, this letter can be used to request permission to use a quote within your manuscript. In the section of the letter that describes the work to be used, provide an exact quote of the full text you want to use. You should also include the page number and edition number that features the quote, to help the publisher identify the exact section to be used. Here's a quick cheat sheet for including quotes in your work:

- ✔ Enclose the quote with quotation marks.

- ✔ If you mention the source of the quote before the quotation, you should add a comma before the quote. *Example:* E.B. White and William Strunk say, "A basic structural design underlies every kind of writing."

- ✔ When the attributive phrase follows the quotation, the comma should be enclosed within the quotations marks. *Example:* "Please stop writing now," my daughter begged.

- ✔ When you include a quote that's more than a single line, distinguish it from the rest of the text by using a different font, by beginning the quote on a new line of text, and by indenting it. In this case, do not use quotation marks (unless quotation marks were used in the original quote).

Working with an Editor

You polish your writing until it's perfect. Each word is a jewel — each sentence can stand proudly alone as a work of art. So it's obvious that you don't need an editor, right? Wrong. Nothing beats a great editor for taking your draft and turning it into a marketable manuscript.

By the time you read this book, the editorial team at IDG Books will have reworked this text so that you'll never know how this text improved with editing. But trust me, I wouldn't want to publish something without an editorial review (and neither should you). You may be a good author, but you're too close to your manuscript to see some of the flaws that a professional can catch and work with you to correct. Only after you see the editorial comments do you realize how much your work can be improved.

When you work with a publisher or an ePublisher, they provide you with editorial support. If you are ePublishing your own content or publishing through an online distributor (like MightyWords.com), you need to find and pay for your own editor. Nobody likes to spend extra money, but paying for a professional editor isn't where you should try to save a buck.

As an author, your ability to sell future eBooks depends heavily on the reputation that you earn with your first few titles. If your early work is professional, well-crafted, and presented in an easy-to-read fashion, your readers will buy your work again (especially if you publish a sequel). If your eBook is poorly organized and filled with incoherent sentences and typos, not only will your readers never buy your work again — they will also tell other people that your work stinks. (Sorry to be so blunt, but I want to make sure that this doesn't happen to you.)

Finding editorial help

Many companies specialize in providing editorial-consulting services to authors. You can type **Editorial Services** into a Web search engine and find plenty of companies willing to help you. However, this is a hit-or-miss method — you can get lucky and find some great companies, or you can waste time contacting people who may not be able to give you what you need to produce a great manuscript.

Getting a recommendation is a better way to find a good editor. You can post a notice on some of the top writer-support Web sites stating that you're looking for a good editor. *Note:* You can find a list of these Web sites in the Online Directory within this book.

If you read an eBook that you think is especially well done, contact the author and ask if he or she worked with an editor. If the author didn't work with an editor, ask if the author wants to serve as an editor for your manuscript.

Affording an editor

A good editor is a valuable commodity. The really good ones can charge top dollar. If you're trying to publish a book on a shoestring budget, here are some suggestions for ways to save when getting editorial help:

✔ **Get your manuscripts as error-free as possible:** If your editor charges by the hour, try to get your manuscript as perfect as possible before you send it in. You should use the spell-checking and grammar-checking features of your word processor, and you should ask a friend or two to read the document before your editor sees it. With luck, you can catch most of the errors, so your editor won't spend time fixing obvious problems.

✔ **Ask your editor to reduce the hourly rate in exchange for a percentage of the eBook's profits:** Most editors won't do this, but it doesn't hurt to ask. This option may get you more support than you can otherwise afford.

✔ **Ask your editor to work for a flat fee instead of an hourly rate:** You may not save money, but this way helps you budget the cost of your eBook.

✔ **Visit the local college:** If you can't afford a professional editor, contact your local community college and find out who teaches writing classes. This person may be interested in a freelance-editing project, or they may suggest another qualified editor.

What to expect from an editor

I worked with a group of editors at IDG Books to create this book. My acquisitions editor made the decision to publish this book based on my proposal. My project editor, Sheri Replin (a sweet and patient person), is responsible for the overall book project. She works to make sure all the deadlines are met and all the project resources are pulled together to publish the book on time. Sheri also makes sure that the book reads well and is structured in a logical way, and she makes gentle suggestions when I go off track.

My copy editor, Rebekah Mancilla, reviews all my text to make sure I don't embarrass myself. (It would be humiliating to create a chapter about writing well that's filled with grammatical errors.) The technical editor reads through every chapter to make sure that my facts are technically accurate. A media development team works to collect the materials that are available on the CD-ROM.

Let's face it: I'm spoiled. Compared to what an eBook author has to do, my job is simple. All I have to do is get the words down on paper — a big task, but nothing compared to doing everything yourself. That's the point of having an editor: *You shouldn't try to do everything yourself.* The editor that you work with should take on the role of copy editor, but if you're lucky, he or she will also take on some of the tasks of a project editor.

When you negotiate the contract with your editor, you need to specifically define what you require. Some of the support that you can expect from your editor includes:

- ✔ Review the structure of the document and make suggestions for improvement

- ✔ Determine whether the document has some conceptual holes that need to be addressed before the document is published

- ✔ Copy edit the document to make sure no misspellings or grammatical errors exist

Many editors charge by the hour. If you're worried about the budget, you can go without a review of the document structure and an analysis of content, but make sure that you get your manuscript copy-edited.

Checking your ego at the door

Getting your work reviewed with a critical eye is not exactly fun, and getting comments back from your editor can be a humbling experience. You may find yourself feeling misunderstood and you may wonder if your editor is really any good. You can handle this situation in only one good way . . . get over it! You're paying this person to help you improve your eBook. As long as you're confident about your editor's professional qualifications, it would be foolish to ignore his or her advice. Unlike you, your editor is not emotionally invested in your manuscript. An editor can approach the text from a professional viewpoint. Remember that you're paying for this detachment, so don't fight the feedback.

Most good editors are sensitive to the pain that they can inflict on the author. They tend to couch their suggestions in gentle terms. If you still find yourself feeling raw despite the gentle approach, however, the following suggestions may help you:

- ✔ **Remember the words of Michael Corleone in *The Godfather*, "It's not personal; it's just business."** If you want to publish and get paid for your work, you must approach it like a business and act professionally about the editorial feedback that you receive.

- ✔ **It's far better to hear criticism from an editor than from a reviewer.** If you get negative feedback from your editor, you can revise and correct the problem. If you get negative feedback from a book reviewer, it can impact the sales of your eBook (and embarrass you).

- ✔ **If you feel strongly about not wanting to change something, discuss it with your editor.** Explain why you like the original version (and listen to your editor's feedback about why the change was requested). You can probably brainstorm a compromise that pleases you both.

- ✔ **In the end, it's your name on the eBook.** If you really don't want to make a change, you don't have to. The role of the editor is to help you make improvements. In the end, what goes into the manuscript is up to you.

Chapter 6

Going Beyond Text

*A*dding media to your eBook makes your book more exciting and meaningful for the reader. Think of media like makeup for a book: A little, applied well, can make a good product even more beautiful. Too much can make the overall effect appear garish and cheap.

Figuring out when and where to add media is not easy when you first start working on eBooks. Some types of eBooks, such as children's books, benefit from images, which can hold the interest of young readers. Interactive examples and animated illustrations can help clarify complex content in technical books. However, media in other types of eBooks can distract or annoy the reader. So before adding images or sound, ask yourself whether the addition of a clip could interrupt the reader's concentration. If the clip complements the text without distracting the reader, you can plan for its inclusion.

Planning to Add Media

When you work on the outline for your eBook, make notes of where additional media should go, and what type of media you plan to use. As you review the outline, be careful to avoid including too many images or clips.

Don't let the fear of using too much media keep you from using any images at all. You should include some pictures — they may save you the trouble of writing thousands of words. But, should you include sound? Animation? Video? I help you figure out what kind of media you should use in the following sections.

Figuring out how much media to add

When you add media to your eBook, you add to the overall file size of the package that readers download. Because most people still use modems for dial-up access to the Web, try to keep your eBook as small as possible. If someone has to wait a long time to download your product, any clips that you've added need to be worth the wait.

To avoid gratuitous media, don't add an image or a clip unless it really contributes to the overall value of your document. An image should enhance or explain the accompanying text. Many Web pages contain graphics that have little purpose other than to make the page look nice.

eBook authors can't afford to add such "eye candy." Unlike a Web page, where the user downloads one page at a time, your eBook may contain hundreds of pages that are downloaded at a single time. Resist the urge to design for the sake of a nice look. You can make your eBook look pleasing through the effective use of fonts, rules, and other typographic devices.

You should limit your images to no more than one per chapter, if possible. (Obviously, you need to use more images if you're writing for small children.) If you need more than one image per chapter, minimize the size and resolution of each image. Although the final images won't look as good as the originals, you're still doing your readers a favor.

Sound, animation, and video files are even larger than images. Add them only if they provide a value that you can't give the reader in any other way. If you need sound, animation, or video in your eBook, limit the number to only a handful of clips. If this isn't possible, serialize your eBook. This enables your readers to download it one chapter at a time.

Acquiring media for an eBook

When planning what type of media to include in your work, you need to think about where to acquire this media and how the acquisition fits into the general timeline that you scheduled for completing your book. If you plan to include other people's work (in exchange for credit in your book), then you need to get their permission for inclusion. Beware: This can be a time-consuming process.

I include a sample permission letter, formatted as a Word 97/Word 2000 document, on this book's CD-ROM. This letter can be sent to the people whose media you want to incorporate into your eBook. Feel free to modify this letter to meet your needs.

Maybe it doesn't seem sensible to request permission to use the work in "all media" (images aren't required in an audio book and a sound clip isn't necessary if your eBook is re-issued in print format). However, you're better off getting all permissions now, so you can avoid making a second request at a later date.

Although the sample permission letter on the CD can meet most of your needs, it's always imperative to run a copy past your lawyer. He or she can change the text to meet any specialized requirements your business may have. Your lawyer can also ensure that the letter meets any specialized requirements in your state or country.

Adding Images to Your eBook

You should try to reduce the number of images in your eBook, but don't explain a concept by writing page after page of text when an image can do the same job in just half a page. When a picture can explain a concept more easily, substitute it for the text that you planned to write.

A picture can be detrimental to the experience when you are writing a work of fiction. Ideally, you want your readers to be swept up by your story — you want them to form their own mental pictures without being interrupted by an image on the page. An exception to this rule is children's books. Children's books need pictures to keep young readers interested in the plot of the story, as shown in Figure 6-1.

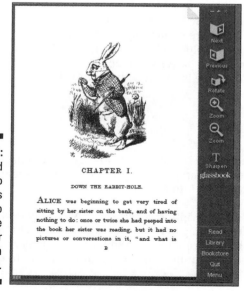

Figure 6-1:
You can add an image to a children's book to help keep the reader focused on the story.

What about animated GIFs?

Animated GIFs are images that seem to be moving because they cycle through a number of small images in a rapid sequence. Documents formatted in accordance with the basic Open eBook specification can't incorporate GIF image files. In light of this, you shouldn't use animated GIFs in your eBook because many OEB-compliant readers won't know how to display them.

If you create an eBook in a format that does support animated GIFs, however, go ahead and add them. But make sure not to overdo it. Using too many animated GIFs on a Web page (or an eBook) is one of the marks of an amateur designer.

Animated GIFs can be very effective on the cover of your eBook. If you know that the cover image will be listed on a Web page, then you can use an animated GIF to draw the eye of a potential buyer to your eBook. Just promise me that you'll use something subtle . . . .

Formatting your images for eBooks

If you want to create an OEB-compliant eBook (see Chapter 10 for more information on the Open eBook standard), then PNG and JPEG are the two image-file formats to use. Most eBook readers are capable of displaying embedded PNG or JPEG files, although not all readers can display color images.

PNG stands for Portable Network Graphics and was developed as a patent-free replacement for GIF files — the image format used on most Web sites. But because Unisys owns the patent for the GIF image-file format, the OEB Forum decided to support the PNG format instead.

JPEG stands for Joint Photographic Experts Group format. These files are recognized by a .jpg extension and are commonly used on Web sites. JPEGs do a good job of displaying high-resolution images with lots of colors, like photographs. Although the images look better when compressed, the image size tends to be larger than when a file is saved with the PNG format.

Using clip art

Non-graphic artists out there may be thinking, "How can I add images to my document? I have no skills as a graphic artist." You're in luck — many images can be licensed for incorporation into an eBook.

You can easily sign up for a subscription service, like ArtToday (www.arttoday.com). For $99.95 a year, you have access to the searchable database of clip art, Web graphics, photographs, and fonts. The license agreement allows you to use the content in commercial projects, and to modify the content as needed. However, the license agreement does include some restrictions. For example, you can't redistribute the content as stock photography and clip art. You also need to get explicit permission if you plan to distribute in excess of 100,000 printed copies of a commercial work. Be sure to read the license agreement, but the content is probably permissible for use in most eBooks.

To sign up and find a clip, follow these steps:

1. **Go to** `www.arttoday.com` **and click the <u>Join ArtToday</u> link in the middle of the home page.**

2. **Select the level of membership you wish to have. (Prices vary according to the type of membership you choose.)**

   In this case, I want the Professional level membership for $99.95 a year.

3. **Enter the e-mail address that you want to use with the account, and whether you want to receive updates about ArtToday and special promotional offers.**

4. **Select a username and password for the account. You must enter the password twice.**

5. **Enter your company and address information.**

6. **If you are selecting anything other than the basic level of membership, enter your credit-card information.**

7. **Click the <u>Usage Guidelines</u> link to read the license agreement.**

   Don't skip this step — you must make sure that the ArtToday license agreement won't prevent you from using the media that you need for your eBook. One of the restrictions prevents you from using their media to "create obscene or scandalous works." If you plan on publishing an erotic eBook novel, you may not be able to use their material, so read the agreement before you commit.

8. **Click the Submit button to sign up.**

Now comes the fun part . . . searching for images and other media:

1. **Go back to the ArtToday home page and click the Member tab.**

   At the top of the page is a search form that lets you search through the database of images.

2. **You choose whether to search for Clip Art, Photos, Web Art, or Fonts by selecting one of the radio buttons associated with each choice.**

   For this search, I decide to search only through the photographs by clicking the radio button next to the word *Photos*.

3. **Enter the term that you are searching for in the search form under the radio buttons.**

   Because I am working on a document about books, I enter **Books** as the term to search.

4. **ArtToday lets you search for specific image formats by checking the appropriate check boxes, which are to the right of the search form.**

   For the eBook that I'm creating, I can only use JPG or PNG image file formats, so I unselect the GIF, WMF, and EPS formats by clicking in these boxes. (ArtToday selects all options by default.) I want to search only for color images, so I also unselect the Black and White option by clicking in that check box.

5. **After you make your selections, click the Search button (located to the right of the search form).**

   If you're not logged in, ArtToday shows you a dialog box and prompts you to enter your username and password. Enter the username and password that you used when you signed up for membership and then click the OK button.

   ArtToday shows you thumbnails for each image that matches your search criteria. In my case, four images are returned.

6. **Click any of the thumbnails to get download information for that image.**

   The image that I select is called "Tobak: Miscellaneous 2" (1996).

   You are given information about the format of the file, the download size of the file (it's important to use small files if you plan on using a few images in the book), the dimensions of the image, and the resolution (in this case, 300 pixels per inch). The title of the image, the artist, and the publisher are also available, as shown in Figure 6-2.

   By clicking the <u>Title</u> link, I can see related images (usually images offered by the same artist). Remember to click the link if you like the style of a particular artist and want to see what else is available.

7. **Click the <u>Add to Cart</u> link if you want to collect a variety of images to be downloaded all at the same time. Click the <u>Download Separately</u> link to get the chosen image immediately.**

   I only plan on downloading a single image right now, so I click the <u>Download Separately</u> link.

   ArtToday retrieves the chosen image and displays it in the browser.

8. **You can copy this image to your clipboard, or select the <u>Click Here to Download the Image</u> link to save the image to a folder.**

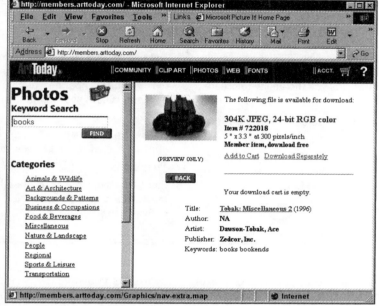

Figure 6-2:
ArtToday
shows you a
thumbnail
image and
information
about the
file to be
downloaded
for use in
your eBook.

I right-click the <u>Click Here to Download the Image</u> link and select Save Target As from the menu. In the dialog box, I choose to save the file to my desktop by clicking the Save button. After the file saves, I can incorporate it into my eBook.

Another source of clip art to try is PhotoDisc (`www.photodisc.com/am/default.asp`). PhotoDisc offers professional quality images in a variety of resolutions. You can license a 600K-72dpi image for $24.95. Don't worry about purchasing the higher resolution images — they're too large to include in your eBook.

Creating your own images

You can also create your own images to add impact to a document. Even if you're not a talented artist, you can still create some visual interest by using an image-editing program to create graphical-looking text. This text can be used instead of chapter headings within the body of the text. (I've been warning you against the gratuitous use of images, and now I'm suggesting using images as chapter headings? Sometimes, you need to break the rules. But, the most important thing to remember: Don't overdo it!)

Creating text effects with WordArt

If you have Microsoft Word 2000, you can try using WordArt, a free utility that comes with Word. WordArt gives you the ability to create impressive text effects very quickly:

1. **Choose Insert⇨Picture⇨WordArt from the toolbar.**

2. **Select the WordArt style that you want. (You can modify these styles later if you want to customize the look.)**

3. **Enter the text that you want to use in the Edit WordArt Text dialog box.**

4. **You can change the formatting by playing with the different options, accessible from the WordArt floating toolbar (which appears when you click the WordArt object).**

5. **To capture the image, select the image by clicking it. Click the right mouse button and select Copy.**

6. **Paste the image into an image-editing program. You can then save the image for inclusion in your eBook.**

Make sure that your image-editing software lets you save the resulting image in PNG or JPG format, unless you know that your eBook reader supports other types of images.

Capturing images

You can also acquire images by using a digital camera. Many good models are available for a moderate price — between $250 and $500. Each year, the quality of the cameras keeps improving, and prices keep dropping. When researching different brands, focus on which one provides the best picture quality at low resolutions. Three brands to look at — if you plan to spend under $500 — are the Kodak DC280 Zoom Digital Camera, the Nikon Coolpix 800 Digital Camera, and the Olympus D460 Zoom Digital Camera.

You need to reduce the size of any images that you shoot with your camera, so it doesn't make sense to spend extra money to get top-quality resolution. You're better off spending the cash to purchase lighting equipment, to help make your resulting images look more professional.

As with any kind of equipment, you should spend time learning how your digital camera works by reading the instruction manual completely. Prepare to spend a couple of weeks playing, before you are ready to shoot images that can be included in your eBook. Use this playtime as a great excuse to get new photos of your family and friends!

After you download the images from your camera into your PC, use a good image-editing program to crop and resize the images. You may need to experiment with saving the images at different resolutions and learning to make trade-offs between small file sizes and better-looking pictures. No general rule exists about how large image files should be, but try to remember the following points:

- ✔ The more images you use in an eBook, the smaller you should keep your files. Large files can cause a long download time for your reader, which is always irritating.

- ✔ Don't use the file size of images on Web pages as a guideline for how large your eBook images should be. A user only downloads a single Web page at a time, but readers download all 400 pages of your novel simultaneously.

- ✔ If you need an image on every page (as is the case with children's books), you should reduce the number of pages in the book.

- ✔ The largest file size should be reserved for the cover image. This image is seen in marketing materials and may have an impact on whether a user decides to purchase your eBook.

- ✔ If you produce an eBook that's really media-rich (with lots of images, sound, animation, interactive applets, and so on), consider distributing it on CD-ROM, rather than letting readers download it from the Web. Although this increases your material and distribution costs, it's better to have a more expensive product than risk making users unhappy.

You can capture images by using a scanner and cropping or resizing the image to meet your needs. Just be sure to own the rights to the material that you scan to avoid copyright infringement. It may seem easy to grab an image, and manipulate it with an image-editing program so that it's no longer easy to recognize, but it's not worth the risk. Any eBook profits that you make will only get eaten up in the resulting lawsuit . . .

Creating and Including Sound

Before adding sound to your eBook, you need to determine when it will really be effective, and when it will just be annoying. Sound can be great for setting a mood, but it can also interrupt your train of thought. (How many times have you been irritated by the phone ringing at the wrong time?)

Most readers don't currently support sound, although some, such as Microsoft Reader and Adobe Acrobat, are designed to work on PCs where sound is available because the PC includes a sound card, speakers, and a media or sound player application.

Sounds good . . .

Some types of eBooks are natural candidates for the addition of sound:

- ✔ **Children's books:** Sound can be added for fun effects.
- ✔ **Encyclopedia and reference books:** Sound can be used for pronunciations or in an explanatory fashion.
- ✔ **Textbooks:** Quiz questions can be added to the end of every chapter.
- ✔ **Biographies:** Sound clips can be added to make the subject seem more real to the reader.
- ✔ **How-tos, gardening, and cookbooks:** Listening to instructions enables the reader to take the necessary actions without having to look back at the book every few minutes.

Sounds not so good . . .

The most difficult type of eBook to add sound to is fiction. How can you add to the reader's overall experience, instead of just interrupting the story? Sound in fiction is made more difficult because of the issue of synchronization. When do you play the sound? When the user gets to a new page? When the reader is leaving a page? Or do you force the user to click something to hear the sound?

Unless you think of a plan for great integration of sound into a fictional experience, you should probably leave it out.

Sounds downright terrible . . .

If you plan to include sound, your first inclination may be to get a good-quality microphone, and record it yourself. First, you need to ask yourself a few hard questions (and be honest about the answers!):

- ✔ Do you cringe at the recorded sound of your own voice?
- ✔ Do strangers ask you to repeat yourself when you say something on the phone?
- ✔ Did anyone wince and leave the room the last time you sang karaoke at a bar?
- ✔ Do dogs in the neighborhood howl when you sing in the shower?

Your eBook needs to come across as a professional, high-quality product. Nothing ruins good writing faster than a bad sound clip.

If you don't have a great voice (ask friends and family to be honest with you about this, if you're not sure), you should get help recording clips for your eBook. Your local community college may offer voice instruction to drama students. See if you can hire the voice coach to read your clips.

After you record your sound clips, they need to be digitized and edited using sound-editing software. Although many software packages are available, you need to research whether the editing software can save clips in a format that can be imported by your eBook-authoring software.

Licensing sound clips

You can license sound clips to include with your eBook, but this can be an expensive proposition. To find sites that sell royalty-free clips, do a search on the term *royalty-free sound clips* in your favorite search engine. As you research the relevant Web sites, remember to look for sites that allow use of the sound clips in digital or multimedia products, or that provide the clips in a digital format, such as WAV files, MIDI files, and MOV files.

Instead of using a text link to play the sound clip, it's a better idea to use an image as a sound icon. Then, if the eBook reader doesn't support sound files, an error message displays on the screen, stating, "Sorry, this sound file cannot be played by your reader." Using an icon instead of a text link helps the reader to understand that a sound file can't be played (instead of the reader wondering why the link is "broken").

When you purchase a sound clip to include in your eBook, don't bother paying for higher resolutions — the file sizes are simply too large to include in your package. Although the sound quality won't be as good, the most compressed sound byte works better for your eBook (and it's cheaper, too).

Adding sound or video to an eBook

Adobe Acrobat 4 makes it easy to add a QuickTime sound or video clip to an eBook formatted as a PDF file. Just follow these steps:

Note: If you need a copy of the QuickTime player, you can download one for free from www.apple.com/quicktime/.

1. **Open Adobe Acrobat 4 by double-clicking the Acrobat icon on your desktop.**

   To create a PDF file and add a sound clip, you need the full version of Acrobat — not just the Acrobat Reader that can be downloaded from Adobe's Web site.

2. **Choose File➪Open to launch the Open dialog box.**

   Make sure the Files of Type drop-down list shows Acrobat (*.pdf), and select a file to open.

3. **Click the Movie Tool button that's located in the vertical toolbar on the left side of the screen.**

   The Movie Tool button looks like a little film clip with the words *Movie Tool (M)* in a tooltip that appears when you hold your mouse pointer over the button.

4. **When you click the button, your mouse pointer changes into a plus sign.**

   You can determine where to place the sound or movie clip by clicking your document at the location where you want to place the clip and by dragging your mouse to create a rectangle. The place that you specify is where the clip is placed.

5. **Acrobat launches the Open dialog box to let you select the clip that you want to add to your document.**

   Only QuickTime clips (MOV) can be added to an Acrobat document. Select the clip that you want to use and then click the Open button.

   If you are looking for a MOV file to play with, QuickTime provides a file called Sample.mov, which was copied to your hard drive when you installed QuickTime player. Look for it in the folder where QuickTime was installed (normally, this is C:\Program Files\Quick Time). This sample file is a video, not an audio clip, but you can use it with your PDF file as a test.

6. **In the Movie Properties dialog box, under Player Option, click the Show Controller checkbox and select the Play Once, Stay Open option from the drop-down list. Click the OK button.**

   After clicking somewhere else in the document, you no longer see the box that you drew for placement of the clip. Don't worry — the clip is still there.

7. **Choose File➪Save to save your PDF file. Close Acrobat after the file has been saved.**

8. **Open the PDF file that you just created by double-clicking the file. Move your mouse pointer over the location where you inserted the clip. The mouse pointer changes into a movie clip when you're over the right place. Click when you see the movie clip appear.**

   The sound clip starts playing. You can start and stop the clip by using the controller, as shown in Figure 6-3.

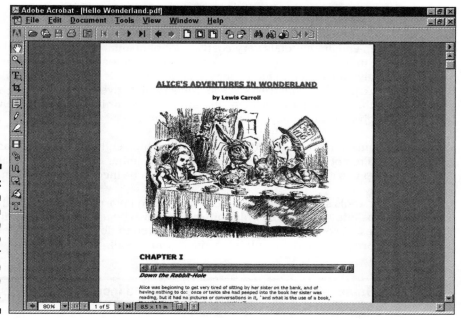

Figure 6-3:
You can easily add a QuickTime sound clip to your eBook with Adobe Acrobat.

If you include a movie or sound clip in this fashion, you should make sure that the clip is in the same directory as the PDF file that you create. When you send the eBook PDF file to a user, you will also need to send the clip and instruct the customer to keep the two files located in the same directory. An easier way to include a sound clip is to insert a WAV file via a link or page attribute. If you do this, the sound file will be packaged as part of the PDF file and no additional file is required when you distribute the eBook.

Animation and Video

Some writing software tools don't support the inclusion of animation and video files in the eBooks that they create, because these files greatly increase the size of the overall package and the complexity of the software required to play back the media clips.

If the addition of moving images will truly increase the value of your eBook, you should include animation or video — but make sure that the type of eBook reader used for your eBook can support these files.

Acquiring animation and video

High-end animation is very costly. A lot of manual effort is involved to create the individual *cells* (the images shown frame after frame in rapid succession to give the illusion of movement). 3D animation is also expensive. First, a software program constructs a *wire frame* (which gives the underlying structure to the final image). Then, images are *rendered,* or laid on top of the wire frame to give the final image a lifelike appearance.

Teams of people are required to produce high-end animation. But as long as you're not trying to create *Toy Story III*, a number of tools are available to help you create simple animations that can be incorporated into an eBook.

The tools shown in Table 6-1 can be used to incorporate sound and video clips into your eBook. This software can also be used to create simple animations. In some cases, your reader is required to download and install a viewer in order to see the resulting media in your eBook.

Table 6-1	Tools for Creating and Incorporating Clips
Tool	*Web Site*
Macromedia Flash	www.macromedia.com/software/flash/
Macromedia Director	www.macromedia.com/software/director/
Adobe LiveMotion	www.adobe.com/products/livemotion/main.html

Most video must be digitized before the clip can be incorporated into a multimedia product, which makes using video costly. If you produce your own video using a video camera, you need to install a *video capture board* into your computer. You connect your video camera or VCR to the video capture board and start playing the tape. Then the board copies the images, and converts them to a digital format, which is saved in a file on your hard drive. Generally, a very fast computer and a lot of room on the hard drive are required to be able to digitize video. After the video has been digitized, edited, and compressed, it's ready to be incorporated into your eBook.

Exploring a media-rich eBook

For a great example of how media (including video) can be effectively used in an eBook, download a copy of the Night Kitchen TK3 eBook Reader and view one of the sample files available from its Web site.

1. Go to the Night Kitchen Web site and download a copy of its TK3 eBook Reader (www.nightkitchen.com/downloadreader/).

2. Enter your name and e-mail address into the form on the Web page and indicate whether you want to be notified about TK3 Reader upgrades and other Night Kitchen software offers, or other special offers, by clicking the appropriate checkboxes. After you fill in the form, submit it by clicking the Download button.

3. On the next page, click the appropriate link for either the Windows or Mac version of the reader.

4. In the File Download box, select the Save This Program To Disk option and click the OK button.

5. In the Save As dialog box, select the folder that you want to copy the file to, and then click the Save button to start downloading the file.

6. On the same Web page, click the link to go to the TK3 Samples page.

7. From the Samples page, click the link to download and install the Introduction to the TK3 Reader sample.

   To uncompress the files and see the video, you need a copy of WinZip (if you're downloading the reader and the sample for use on the Windows platform) and a copy of the Apple QuickTime viewer.

   A copy of WinZip can be obtained from www.winzip.com/. A copy of the Apple QuickTime viewer is available from www.apple.com/quicktime/.

8. After downloading both files, double-click the TK3_Reader_B61_ Setup.exe file and follow the instructions to install the TK3 Reader on your computer.

9. After the reader installs, make sure that WinZip has been installed on your computer and double-click the Intro_to_TK3_Reader.zip file to unzip the file.

10. Start the TK3 reader. From the Windows Start button, go to the Program menu and then go to the menu for TK3 Reader. From this menu, select the TK3 Reader item to launch the eBook reader.

11. After the eBook reader begins running, choose File⇨Open Book.

12. In the Open Book dialog box, go to the folder where you saved the Introduction to the TK3 Reader sample, after unzipping the file.

    Note: This file has a .tk3 extension.

    The entire sample is worth taking the time to explore; it provides a terrific glimpse of where eBooks will be evolving in the future. As you explore, notice how sound and video have been incorporated without detracting from the text.

On the NightKitchen Web site, you can also sign up to participate in the beta test of TK3's authoring software. See www.nightkitchen.com/ for more information about how to participate.

Providing Down-Level Versions of Media

A general rule of thumb: Readers that work on PCs and high-end PDAs, like the PocketPC or the Handspring Visor Deluxe, will have support for more media because the platforms like these have applications that can play the media clip. This is only useful to you if your eBook has the ability to open the player application when a user clicks a link. Check your authoring software to see if it allows your eBook to launch an external application in response to a clicked link.

The *OEB (Open eBook) specification*, which attempts to define the standard for eBooks, permits the incorporation of additional media files (like QuickTime movies), but requires a *down-level* version in one of the standard file formats. This means that if you add a video file to your eBook, you should also supply an image (in JPG or PNG format) for those readers that can't display the movie. This ensures that your eBook can be displayed on all OEB-compliant reading systems.

Converting color images for a black and white display

Some eBook readers (usually those that work on a PC) display images in color. Most eBook readers (such as the Rocket eBook or the SoftBook Reader) are only capable of displaying black and white images, because the cost of color screens would make the reader too expensive for most people to afford.

If you create images for viewing on a black and white reader, these images need to be converted to grayscale before you add them to your document. This process is usually simple if you have an image-editing program. To convert a color image to black and white in Microsoft's Photo Editor, follow these steps:

1. **Open Photo Editor and choose File⇨Open.**

   The Open dialog box appears.

2. **Select the folder and name for the file that you want to edit and click the Open button.**

3. **When the image appears, choose File⇨Properties.**

4. **In the Properties dialog box, select Gray Scale (8 bit) from the Type drop-down list. Click OK.**

5. **Choose File⇨Save As to save the file.**

   You can give the image any name you like, but make sure that you pick JPEG File Interchange Format (*.jpg, *.jpeg) from the Save As Type drop-down list.

   Your image converts from color to black and white and can be incorporated into your eBook.

Note: If you plan to use images in eBooks created for the Rocket eBook, the screen is only capable of showing black and white images (no gray scale). Any images you incorporate will look grainy, so test all the images by viewing them on the eBook reader before you create the final version of your eBook.

Although adding media to your eBook can make the product more interesting for your audience, media's only a benefit when a person is able to view it or hear it. If you're not sure whether all the people reading your eBook can enjoy your media, don't add it. No matter how great the media, your text should be the most important component of your eBook.

Chapter 7

Authoring Content for eBooks

. . . .

In This Chapter

▶ Arranging your content to work in an eBook

▶ Making your eBook interactive

▶ Creating different genres of eBooks

. . . .

*e*Publishing's more than just "printing" a document to a digital file. In this chapter, I show you how to make your eBook interactive by adding links, multiple storylines, or add-on software applications. This chapter also tells you about certain techniques that work best for fiction, children's literature, nonfiction, and technology eBooks.

Structuring Your Content to Work in an eBook

Most eBooks available today are *linear* in format, which means that the content of the book has a beginning, middle, and an end. The reader is expected to start at the first page and read straight through until the end. The only difference between eBooks and printed books (pBooks) is that they're formatted for electronic distribution.

However, eBooks will evolve from a linear format into text that the audience interacts with as writers experiment with the development of non-linear story forms and add interactivity and other media. Because people are used to Web pages with these elements, it won't take long for eBooks to follow this direction.

TIP

One reason more authors haven't started experimenting with non-linear eBooks is because so much work is needed to create a non-linear title. You need to plan for interactivity when you begin working on your book's outline. If you write all your text first and then try to retrofit the interactive techniques described in this chapter, you wind up wasting time because you have to write and rewrite the text. In the end, your work appears disjointed and incoherent.

Reading online versus reading the printed page

When you're absorbed in a good book, you're not conscious of reading each word at a time. Your eyes skim over the page and the words seem to fade away as your mind follows the flow of the text. This experience is called *immersive* reading. You become so involved in getting the content that you no longer notice the act of reading.

Reading text onscreen is a different experience because of the poor resolution of most computer screens (compared to the crisp look of text on paper). Reading a Web page is even less immersive because of the way the pages are laid out. When people read Web pages, their eyes tend to jump around, looking for headings and links, or people tend to skim over the content quickly to get the gist of the words, and then move on. The act of clicking or scrolling to get from screen to screen also interrupts your reading when moving from page to page.

Although companies like Microsoft and Adobe are working to improve the resolution of text on the computer screen, reading text on a screen is not yet an immersive experience. Because of this fact, you should anticipate that readers of your eBook won't experience your content in the same way as if they were reading a pBook.

You can structure your content to make the most of the way someone reads on a screen. This tactic ensures that your eBook takes advantage of the medium instead of fighting against it.

Readers won't read everything

Because reading on a screen can be tedious and can strain the eyes, readers skim for the content that matters to them and skip what they don't find useful. If you're working on a nonfiction title, anticipate this and write in a way that lets the user focus on what he or she needs. A reader should be able to read and understand a section of the text without having to read the preceding sections. You should include the following elements in a nonfiction eBook:

- Extensive use of headings and subheadings.
- Detailed Table of Contents.
- Comprehensive Index.
- A glossary of terms that may be new to the user. The first time you include a new word or term, link it to the definition in the glossary.
- Lots of cross-references between related sections of the document (these should also be links).

When creating an eBook, end each chapter or section with a list of links that lets the reader decide where to go next. The list is not meant to be a substitute for the Table of Contents, but it should contain related material for the reader to review. Although the reader is in control of where to go next, your links provide a road map through the content.

Adding Interactivity to Your eBook

At the simplest level, you can add interactivity to an eBook by using links. Links are a great way to start adding interactivity to eBooks, but in the next few years, eBooks will evolve beyond just providing text with links. eBooks will become a new medium that gives the audience a rich interactive experience by enhancing the text with video and sound clips.

Experimenting with non-linear content

The reader, not the author, directs his or her own path when reading non-linear content. This can be tricky because your job as an author is to guide the reader through the content. So how can you be a guide if the reader makes his or her own choices about where to go and what to experience? You can present non-linear content effectively in numerous ways, depending on the type of book that you publish.

When you plan to write non-linear content, keep in mind that you have to write much more text than you would write for a linear book. You should add time for this into your schedule, and you may decide to increase the price of the eBook when you sell it.

Planning a non-linear eBook

You can create a non-linear eBook in five primary ways. These include the following:

- ✔ **Adding links:** You can add interactivity simply by including links to additional content within the body of text. These links can lead to related parts of the same eBook, or to external sources of information.

- ✔ **Creating multiple storylines:** If you're working on a fictional title, you can create multiple storylines or points of view. The reader is presented with one or more endings, and he or she can choose which ending to follow by clicking the appropriate link. Multiple storylines also work in situations where the story doesn't change, but the reader can choose which point of view to experience by selecting the story as told by different characters. (This last approach doesn't need to be restricted to fiction, but can be used in nonfiction as well. Think of this as the "he said, she said" approach.)

✔ **Letting the reader navigate:** You can let the reader determine where to go and in what order by creating a rich index and Table of Contents, and by featuring links to the content that the reader wants. Reference and how-to books work best with this approach.

✔ **Creating an experience that the user navigates through:** You guide the reader by providing compelling links at key times, but ultimately, the reader is in charge of making choices that lead through the content. Although you can create the road map, the reader still decides when and where to turn the car. Fiction works well with the road map approach, but other types of eBooks can work as well.

✔ **Adding Java or similar applets:** For eBooks that are read on devices connected to the Internet, applets can be used to let people interact with other readers. For example, textbooks may incorporate small applications that test how well a student understands a section of material.

When you plan a non-linear eBook, you need to create a schedule that is at least three times as long as the schedule for a linear title. (You need an even longer schedule if you're creating more than two storylines in an eNovel.) You need to write twice as much material, plan for the integration of the links, and test your eBook to make sure that there are no *dead-ends* (places in which you drop the reader but don't give a way back out).

In addition to planning more time to create your eBook, you need to be highly organized about writing all the material. The following steps show you how to create a *content map* that keeps you on track:

1. **Draw a rectangle on a piece of paper.**

   This rectangle represents the first screen the reader sees after opening your eBook. The screen may actually contain several pages of text, but don't worry about that just yet.

2. **Draw a second rectangle just below the first rectangle and give it a name.**

   The second screen is the first point at which the reader can make a choice about where to go.

3. **Draw an arrow from your first rectangle to your second rectangle.**

   This arrow represents the link from the first screen to the second screen.

   If you want the reader to be able to go back to the first screen from the second screen, draw an arrow going back to your first screen.

4. **Keep drawing rectangles for each possible storyline in the eBook.**

5. **Look carefully at the flow chart you have created.**

   Are there any screens where the reader is stuck with no place to go? Unless it's the end of the eBook, this is a problem. Make sure that you resolve all navigational problems before you begin writing your text. You don't want to leave a reader lost in your story without a way to get out.

   Your paper should look something like Figure 7-1.

Figure 7-1:
You should map out the different screens that the reader can choose from.

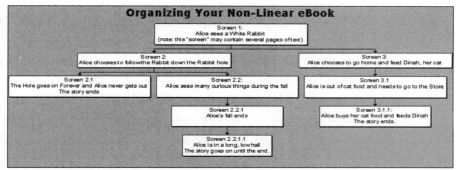

Mapping (charting out) your eBook helps you organize the content and the structure of your eBook. It shows you how much text needs to be written to ensure that your reader has a good reading experience from every vantage point.

When you look at the size of the map, plan for an extra 30 to 50 percent more time than you think it'll take you to write the text. This extra time will be used to correct navigational problems and to resolve other issues that occur when you create a non-linear title.

Linking within your document

How you add links to an eBook depends on what type of authoring tool you use and the eBook reader that the document is displayed on. In the following two exercises, I show you how to add links to an eBook by authoring the content and adding links in Microsoft Word. After you add the links, you can convert the document to an eBook with the SoftBook Personal Publisher. Although your authoring tool may be different, the principles of adding links are the same.

To add links to your eBook, follow these steps:

1. **Open a document in Microsoft Word 2000 that contains headings formatted using Word's styles. (See Chapter 10 if you're not sure how to use styles.)**

   I open the document that I created for Chapter 18, which contains ten second-level headings. A copy of this Word document is available for you to play with on the CD-ROM that comes with this book.

2. **Select the section of the text that you want to make a link.**

   For this eBook, I want to turn each of the bulleted items listed under the "In This Chapter" section into a link. Each link, when clicked, takes the reader to that section of the chapter.

   I highlight the text that reads, "Forgetting to test whether you have a marketable idea."

3. **Press Ctrl+K to open the Insert Hyperlink dialog box.**

4. **Click the Place in This Document icon, as shown in Figure 7-2.**

   The list in the dialog box shows each of the headings that have been added to the document. To create a link, I click the "Forgetting to test whether you have a marketable idea" heading from the list in the dialog box, and then I click the OK button.

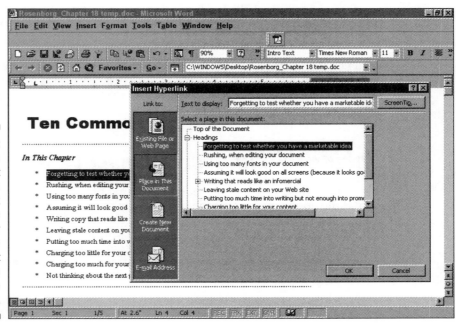

Figure 7-2:
You can turn text into a hyperlink that takes the reader to a different section of the document.

The selected text turns into a link. (You can tell it's a link because the text is now displayed in blue and it is underlined.)

5. **Test the link by clicking it.**

The mouse pointer changes into a hand when you move it over the link. Clicking the link takes you to the "Forgetting to test whether you have a marketable idea" section of the chapter.

After you add links, make sure that you test every link to see if it works properly. Nothing looks more unprofessional than a broken link!

Now it's time to turn the document into an eBook:

1. **Install the SoftBook Personal Publisher by going to** `www.softbook.com/corporate/contactus/download.asp`.

Follow the instructions shown on the page to download the Personal Publisher software.

2. **Double-click the software file and follow the instructions to install the software on your computer.**

After the software installs, Word's File menu displays a new Export as SoftBook Edition menu item.

3. **After adding hyperlinks to your Word document, save the file. Choose File⇨Export as SoftBook Edition.**

The SoftBook Personal Publisher Settings dialog box appears. From this dialog box, you can set the properties for the SoftBook eBook that you're creating.

For this document, I make sure the Save SoftBook Edition and Preview Converted Document options are checked, and I click the OK button. The Personal Publisher converts the document and displays the new eBook.

The links that you created in Word show as underlined text in the SoftBook Reader, as shown in Figure 7-3.

4. **Click one of the links while the eBook is displayed in the SoftBook Reader.**

I click the <u>Forgetting to test whether you have a marketable idea</u> link and the document jumps to that section of the chapter.

If you add links to external content, like other eBooks or Web sites, make sure that the person reading your eBook has access to these external sources (generally, this means access to the Web). Stand-alone eBook readers, such as the SoftBook Reader, have an internal modem, but many times, the audience won't be plugged in while they read an eBook.

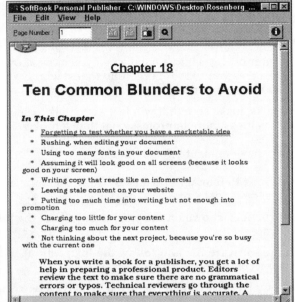

Figure 7-3:
The link is
displayed as
underlined
text.

Including other software

You can add more interactivity to your eBook by including other software. Some authoring software, such as Adobe Acrobat, supports the inclusion of other software, but most don't. Although software can add a new level of excitement to your eBook, you should keep a number of things in mind:

✔ Make sure that the type of reader for which your eBook is formatted is capable of playing back the added software. This isn't as simple as firing up the reader and seeing if it works. If your reader runs on a computer, does the software work on both Windows and Mac? On other platforms? On which versions of these platforms?

✔ Does the software require installation before the eBook can be played?

✔ Will antivirus software or security settings on the user's PC prevent the software from installing properly?

✔ Unless you coded the software yourself, do you have a license to distribute the software with your eBook?

✔ If you coded the software yourself, are you prepared to provide customer support for the software in the event that a customer has a problem? How will you provide support (through e-mail or by phone)?

✔ How will you bundle the software with your eBook? Will you compress the two files together or distribute them separately?

✔ Is there any chance that your software could cause problems on the user's PC? Problems can include freezing up the user's PC, catastrophic data loss, or the dreaded Windows Blue Screen of Death.

✔ In case your software causes data loss on the user's PC, total PC meltdown, or other issues that make users unhappy, do you have liability insurance or a good lawyer in the family?

If I haven't scared you off and you're still determined to add interactive applets, JavaScript (and other features commonly found on Web pages) plans out how the software will work within the context of your eBook. You should figure out whether to add interactivity to the end of each document section or to disperse it throughout the text to get the user's attention.

If you know that your eBook reader can handle it, consider adding Gizmoz to your eBook. Gizmoz are Java applets that can be customized and added to an e-mail or a Web page, but they can also be effective within an eBook. See www.gizmoz.com for more information.

Creating Digital Fiction

Because of the unique nature of the medium, eBooks can do more than just tell a linear story. In the next few years, eBooks will bring about a new type of digital fiction, featuring multiple story lines, unique user interfaces, communities that revolve around story characters and settings, media clips (including sound, animation, and video), and serial stories. If you're interested in learning more about digital storytelling, you can check out an excellent resource on this topic — The Center for Digital Storytelling at www.storycenter.org/.

Building multiple story lines

A technique that can be used most effectively in eBooks is the use of multiple storylines. Because it's easy to link one part of a story to another, and because book length is no longer determined by what is practical to print, authors will begin experimenting with the following:

✔ Different endings to the same story.

✔ The same story told from different points of view.

✔ Background information (more flashbacks, explanations, asides, and so on).

- Stories that are like interactive games where the reader must follow a specific path of links to access the entire story and find the solution to a mystery.

- Author notes, edits, and comments (similar to a director's cut version of a movie, where the audience can see what never made it into the final version of the eBook). For example, DVD movies include outtakes, extra film clips, and interviews: Your eBook can contain equivalent material.

Creating a user interface to lead the audience through the content

A user navigates through a linear book easily: He or she starts at the beginning and reads straight through, turning pages when necessary. When the last page is read, he or she stops reading. Simple.

M.J. Rose's thoughts on interactivity

M.J. Rose, author of *Lip Service* and coauthor of *How to Publish and Promote Online,* was one of the first eBook success stories. M.J. packaged *Lip Service* as an eBook and sold the novel on her Web site (www.mjrose.com) for $12.95. After selling hundreds of copies online, Doubleday Book Club and the Literary Guild picked up the book.

I asked M.J. for her thoughts on what type of best-selling author would be most likely to create the first interactive blockbuster novel. According to M.J., "The author who breaks this form open will be visually oriented, will have adapted one of his or her books into screenplay form, will know how the Net works, will have a good musical sense, and will be someone who is not bound by the traditional. Someone who thinks out of the box.

"My guess is that it will be a collaborative effort between a bestselling author and a creative group that includes a filmmaker, a composer, and a graphic artist.

"The biggest negative to an interactive novel is how long it will take to create it. As a writer, I can see getting lost in addendums that the reader might enjoy . . . substories, background imagery, diary entries, etc.

"Horror, historical fiction, and sci-fi are great bets for the genre. All offer rich back stories and texture. For instance, a character travels on a train between Paris and Venice in 1889 — the reader will hear the appropriate music.

"The writer will write about the view out the window and the reader will be able to click on some of those words and see that view. The character will wonder about a day she spent with an old lover who died in the last war and the reader will be able to click the lover's name and see a photo, read some old love letters, read a brief history of that war and on and on — all info that is interesting but not pertinent to the plot."

The more rich and interactive an eBook is, the easier it is for the user to get lost or confused. To avoid losing your audience, you need to provide a navigational structure to your content. The authoring software that you use to build the eBook automatically generates some navigational structure for you. Most software packages create a Table of Contents and forward and backward links to let users move through the pages. Some packages also create an index, which helps the audience zero in on specific information.

Depending on how non-linear your content is, and how much you want to direct the user through the text, you can provide a *digital map* (a collection of links that gives the user a choice of where to go next). You can feature the digital map at the beginning of the eBook, at the beginning of each section, at the end of each section, or even on every page. The type of fiction that you create determines how you implement the map. A digital map isn't an actual map. (Although this can be a great device for children's eBooks, think how much fun it would be to click Milo's map in the *Phantom Tollbooth* and go to that part of the story.)

This collection of links can be textual, like the row of links found in the navigation bar on the left side of many Web pages. These links can also be hotspots that are laid on top of an image (this is how you could click on a map to go to a part of the story). Another name for these hotspots is *image maps*. Earlier in this chapter, I show you how to add a link to an eBook. Here I show you how to create a simple image map using Adobe Acrobat:

1. **Open a Word document in Adobe Acrobat 4 by choosing File⇨Open.**

   The Open dialog box appears, as shown in Figure 7-4.

Figure 7-4:
The Open dialog box in Adobe Acrobat allows you to open Microsoft Word documents, which are then converted to Adobe's PDF format.

2. **Click the Files of Type down arrow and select Microsoft Word (*.doc) from the list. Click the name of the Word document that you want to open and click the Open button to open the file.**

   The document that you open should contain an image to be converted into an image map. In this case, I open a document named ImageMap.doc, which is included on the CD-ROM that comes with this book.

   After the Word document opens in Acrobat, the Acrobat distiller starts converting the document to PDF (the Acrobat file format). This process can take several minutes.

   After the file is converted and is displayed in Acrobat, you can begin adding links.

3. **Click the Link Tool button in the vertical toolbar located on the left side of the screen.**

   Note: The Link Tool button looks like two interlocked pieces of chain.

   When the mouse pointer rests over the button, it changes to a symbol that looks like a plus (+) sign.

4. **Position the mouse pointer over your image and click at the top-left corner of the location for your first hotspot.**

5. **Drag a rectangle over the area to create your first hotspot.**

   After you finish dragging, the Create Link dialog box appears, as shown in Figure 7-5. The Create Link dialog box lets you set properties for the link area that you just created.

   Because I'm creating an image map, I don't want the boundaries of the rectangle to show over my image, so I choose Type➪Invisible Rectangle. I also don't want the look of the image to change when someone moves a mouse over the hotspot, so I choose None for the Highlight option.

   When someone clicks the hotspot, I want to display the second page of the document. To do this, I make sure that Go to View is displayed in the Type option (in the Action section of the dialog box).

   By clicking the Next Page button (located on the horizontal tool bar at the top of the screen), I go to the second page of the document. The Create Link dialog box continues to display on the screen. On the second page of my document, I click the Set Link button on the dialog box and the hotspot is created.

6. **You can create other hotspots on the same image by repeating Steps 3 through 5 until the image map is complete.**

7. **When you finish your image map, choose File➪Save to save the document as a PDF file.**

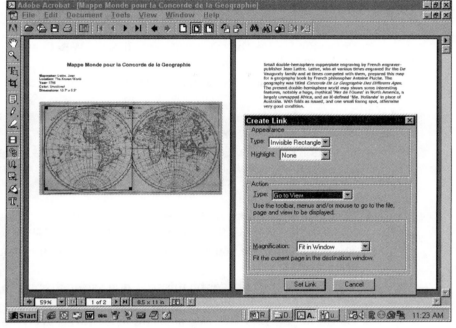

Figure 7-5:
The Create
Link dialog
box pops
up after
you drag a
rectangle
over the
area where
you want to
create a
hotspot.

Adding community around your story

A great way to build interest in your work is to create a community around the characters, settings, or plots in your novel, and ask your readers to participate. This is especially effective if you're issuing a serialized version of your work and you want to solicit feedback for sections of the novel that haven't been written yet.

MSN.com (`www.msn.com`) makes it easy to create a community that can be used to increase interest in your eBook and to promote new eBooks that you plan to release in the future.

Follow these steps to create a community for your eBook:

1. **Go to** `www.msn.com` **and click the <u>People & Chat</u> link.**

   Note: In the current version of MSN, this is located at the top of the page, but MSN has announced an upcoming redesign, so it may be located someplace else in the future. If you can't find a similar link, search for the word *communities* and MSN should take you to the correct page.

2. **Click the <u>Web Communities</u> link.**

   The Web Communities page opens.

3. **Under the Create Your Own column, click the <u>Web Communities</u> link, as shown in Figure 7-6.**

   Note: You need an MSN Passport or Hotmail account to create a community.

   If you have an account, click the <u>Click Here To Sign In</u> link to sign in and create your community.

   If you don't have a Passport or Hotmail account, click the <u>Click Here To Sign Up</u> link to sign up for a free account. Follow the instructions shown on the next series of screens. After you create your account and sign in, go on to Step 4.

4. **Click one of the links on the page to select the type of community that you want to create (such as music clubs or computer games).**

   The community that you select should be oriented to the content of your eBook.

   The types of communities on this page don't seem to apply to my eBook, so I click the generic <u>All the Fixings</u> link.

5. **On the Set Up Your Web Site page, fill in the forms to create your new community, as shown in Figure 7-7.**

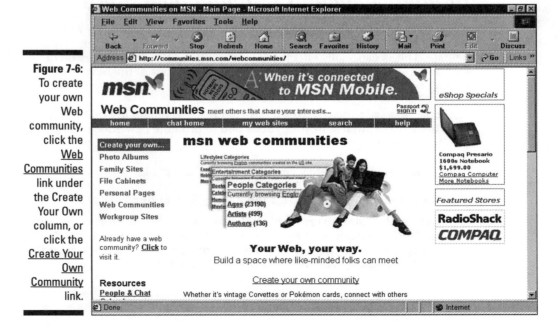

Figure 7-6:
To create your own Web community, click the <u>Web Communities</u> link under the Create Your Own column, or click the <u>Create Your Own Community</u> link.

Figure 7-7:
Using
the Web
Communities
service
available
from
MSN.com,
creating
a Web
community
is as simple
as filling in
a series of
forms and
inviting
readers to
join your
community.

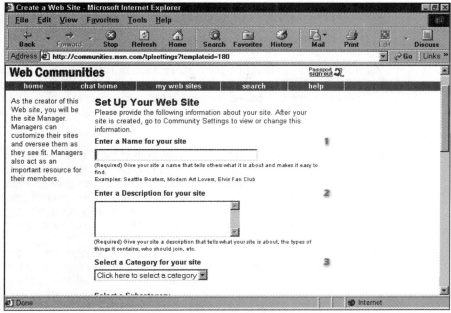

Most options are self-explanatory, but remember to set the privacy level for your site to Public if you want to create a community around your eBook that any reader can join.

6. **After you read the Code of Conduct for the MSN site, click the check box to indicate that you have read and do accept the agreement, and then click the Create My Site! button.**

MSN builds a community Web site where others can join as members, leave messages, post pictures, hold chats, and share a common calendar. The URL of the community site is `http://communities.msn.com/ <Your Site Name Here>/homepage`.

I create a site called *Vickyrtest*, so my URL is `http://communities. msn.com/Vickyrtest/homepage`.

You can include the name and the URL of your community Web site within the text of your eBook. Readers accessing your eBook from a PC — if they are connected to the Web — can access your community when clicking a link in the eBook.

Adding interactivity in a non-disruptive way

Readers like to get lost in a good story. Remember this when deciding where to add links and interactivity in a work of fiction. If you place a link in the middle of a very fast-paced section of the story, you create tension for the reader. If the tale is very absorbing, a reader may perceive a link as a rude interruption.

However, deliberately adding this tension may be effective in some situations. In a murder mystery, making the reader choose whether to keep reading one section of the story or follow the actions of a different character in another part of the story makes the eBook feel more like an interactive game — to click or not to click? In other genres, such as romantic comedy, the tension caused by having to choose whether to click may be unwelcome.

Before you add a link in the middle of a block of text, you need to determine whether you want to guide where the reader's mind goes (don't add a link) or whether the reader should choose where to go (add the link).

The return of the serial . . . novelist

Because it's possible to distribute eBooks through e-mail, many authors will be releasing serialized versions of their work, and readers may start subscribing to a particular story or author instead of paying a single price for a stand-alone novel.

Stephen King was the first mega-author to experiment with eBooks when he published *Riding the Bullet* (available only as an eBook). At the time of this writing, he is releasing *The Plant,* a serialized novel available only from his Web site.

Every month, King plans to release a 5,000 to 7,000-word segment. He's asking readers to send a dollar when they download and read the new chapter. A note to his readers on the Web site states, "My friends, we have a chance to become Big Publishing's worst nightmare." If readers don't send the money (he's relying on the honor system), King will stop publishing the story. For more information, you can check out Stephen King's Web site at www. stephenking.com.

You may not be Stephen King, but if you gather a community of people interested in your work, you can certainly experiment with releasing a novel in installments. For an interesting example of how serial novels can be distributed through e-mail, see Email Shows at www.emailshows.com/.

eBook fiction tips

When writing fiction, you should keep the following guidelines in mind as you write your eBook:

- If you provide links throughout the story, don't overwhelm the reader with choices. Give the reader a few options to click, but keep it simple.
- Don't interrupt the reader by adding a link at an inappropriate time in the story.
- Before you add links to Web sites in your eBook, test what happens to a user who doesn't have Internet access.
- Interactivity is no substitute for good writing. Make sure that you have a well-crafted story before adding interactivity.
- When planning your eBook, remember to schedule lots of time to complete your text if you're featuring multiple story lines.

Creating Nonfiction

Creating nonfiction eBooks is different from creating nonfiction pBooks because authoring an eBook is more like writing content for a Web page. The reader's eye should be able to skim over the headings to find interesting modules of content. The reader should be able to click an unfamiliar word to look up the meaning in the eBook's glossary. And finally, the reader should be able to link to relevant content, whether that content is located in a different section of the text or on a Web page.

Studying Web pages for examples of what works

If you need to get a sense of what works (and what doesn't) for digital nonfiction content, fire up your Web browser and look at some of your favorite Web sites. A well-designed Web site presents information in a logical, structured way. Good use of headlines lets your eye scan for what you need. A well-defined content hierarchy lets you select from a list of links in the Web site's navigation bar.

Although many differences exist between Web sites and eBooks, the principles of good design are the same for both. *Fortune* magazine calls Jakob Nielsen "the reigning guru of Web usability." Although he focused on user interfaces for much of his career, Nielsen became famous as Sun Microsystem's expert on Web design. See his article on how to gear your eBook for the way users read online at www.zdnet.com/devhead/alertbox/9710a.html.

When studying Web pages for ideas to incorporate into your eBook, keep in mind the following tips:

- It's better to link than repeat yourself.
- Break up long blocks of text with headings, bulleted items, and numbered lists.
- Don't use gratuitous images.
- Keep a single idea in one paragraph and make sure that the idea comes through at the beginning of the paragraph.

Using links to Web pages for updated content

If you write for a very targeted audience (such as employees of a specific company or people who want information about downloading MP3 music files), you can assume that the person reading your eBook has Internet access and the ability to view Web pages. If so, you can put links to new and updated content on your Web site. This is useful if you reference statistics, lists, and other changing content in your nonfiction work. (This can also be useful if you're a procrastinator on a deadline, and you don't have time to get everything into your eBook.)

Linking to a Web site can be a great way to sell other eBooks. If you put the latest and greatest content on your Web site, you can also put an advertisement or two for your other eBook titles.

Creating content modules

As eBooks become more prevalent, the concept of buying an entire nonfiction book about a general topic will change. Readers will purchase individual chapters containing the desired content and will be able to create customized anthologies of information. Links to content available in other books will let readers purchase additional content only when they need it. As a result, our definition of a book will change.

This is more than an idle prediction. The publisher of this book, IDG Books Worldwide, has announced an agreement with iUniverse.com to form a Web site where people can assemble and purchase custom books. Readers will be able to build the books that they need, drawing from available IDG content. Soon, you'll be able to buy a chapter or two from the *...For Dummies* line of books, combine the chapters with a map from the *Frommer's* series, and add some information from the *CliffsNotes* series. The resulting title can be downloaded as an eBook or printed, using *print-on-demand* technology (which makes it possible to print a single book at the time of purchase). If you happen to be reading this chapter as part of a customized book, now is a good time to buy more great chapters from *ePublishing For Dummies!*

As customized books become popular, you'll find that it's important to create *content modules* when writing nonfiction. A module is a stand-alone unit of content. It doesn't require the reader to review preceding chapters for comprehension of the material. Keep the following tips in mind when you create content modules:

- A module doesn't have to be an entire chapter; it's actually any section of text that can stand on its own. (For example, this block of text under the section "Creating content modules" could be a separate module.)

- Before you begin writing, you need to determine how granular (or how small in quantity) to make your modules. If you determine that your content should be divided at the chapter level, it's a lot of work to go back and create content at the subhead level. It's easier to start with small modules at the beginning of the process and then increase the module size if necessary than to try the reverse.

- If preceding modules are necessary to understand a section of content, list the required modules at the beginning of the section and provide links to the modules (if they're available). This allows the reader to acquire the necessary modules before starting the section.

- Modules don't have to be text. Items that can be packaged as modules include:
    - Images
    - Maps
    - End of chapter content (like summaries or quizzes)
    - Added media included with the eBook (like animations, sound files, or video)

- You should include a definition of terms in a comprehensive glossary instead of providing them within the body of the text. It's easier to bundle a copy of the glossary with each content module rather than provide the same definition in multiple modules.

Creating Children's Literature

Before I got my first eBook (the SoftBook Reader), I didn't really think about the possibility of writing children's eBooks. Because reading hardware is still expensive, I anticipated that most eBooks would be for the adult market. Then, my six-year-old daughter asked to see my eBook . . . I thought I'd never get it back. She *loved* it (even if she couldn't read most of the words in the biography that I was reading). I didn't show her how the SoftBook worked, but after ten minutes, she figured out the menu, how to highlight passages of text, and how to scribble on the screen.

Now for years I scolded, "Don't draw in books," so being able to draw on the screen impressed her most of all. Here was a book she could draw on, read under the covers at night without a flashlight, and play with like a computer. Watching her, I realized how big eBooks will be for a new generation of readers.

As prices come down for dedicated reading devices, and as more textbooks are published in eBook format, children will become a new (and large!) market for eBooks. Unlike some adults, these children will be comfortable with the technology and will see the devices as cool — and not as a poor substitute for printed Books.

Moving beyond linear

Because eBooks allow for interactivity, you can include the following elements in the children's titles that you create:

- **Puzzles and brainteasers:** Because children will be able to draw on the screen, you can include crossword puzzles, tic-tac-toe games, and mazes within the text of your eBook.

- **Blank spaces:** You can create spaces to let children draw their own pictures onscreen. This is easy to do if you include a *blank* picture (just white space) and, in the caption, instruct the reader to draw in the blank space.

- **Fill in the blanks:** You can let a child personalize a story, or you can encourage young writers to compose their own endings by leaving underlined blank spaces throughout the story.

- **Fun use of media:** You can add fun sound clips to your eBook (like squeaks, oinks, and crashes) that play when the child clicks a link. You can also add animation and video. Printed storybooks are available that include a chip that plays a sound when a child clicks a button.

Traditionally, these books have been expensive to produce (because a sound chip and speaker must be combined with the bound pages). eBooks provide the same experience, but with much less expense for the publisher.

Creating intuitive user interfaces

By using images, you can create user interfaces for pre-readers that don't require them to do anything other than click icons to go to different parts of the story. *Oops! At Breakfast* is a story I wrote about two mischievous children who mess up a kitchen before going to school. The story includes a clock, orange juice, eggs, waffles, and ants. Figure 7-8 shows an interface created for a pre-reader — the pre-reader can click one of the images to go to that part of the story.

In addition to images that the child can click, and depending on the capabilities of the eBook reader, you can include a soundtrack for the story so the child can hear the words being read aloud on each page.

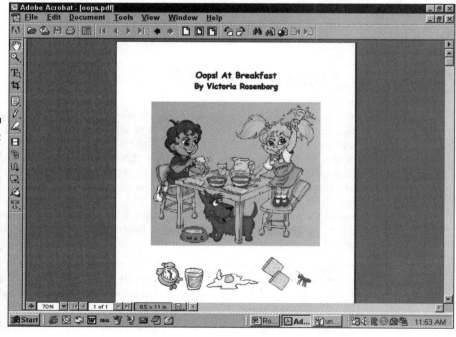

Figure 7-8: A child can click an icon, such as an alarm clock, orange juice, eggs, waffles, or ants, to jump to that section of the story.

What to avoid in children's eBooks

You should keep the following points in mind as you create a children's eBook:

- ✔ Children's books should remain simple; avoid using complicated interfaces that may confuse young readers.

- ✔ Don't use a vocabulary level that's too advanced for the age group that you're trying to reach. The child can look up unknown words in the eBook dictionary (if one is available), but if unknown words are used too often, the child becomes frustrated and the flow of the story is interrupted.

- ✔ Don't overwhelm a story with too many interactive devices and sound clips. If you have a good story, the rest should just be icing on the cake.

- ✔ Don't try to duplicate the experience of a CD-ROM. With an eBook, the emphasis should be on the text. Children's CD-ROMs usually focus on animation and interactivity.

- ✔ Young children take comfort in a story told in the same way, over and over. If you have a two-year-old in your life, you know what I mean. Using a device like multiple story endings may confuse or upset a young child. These devices should be saved for eBooks that are written for older children.

Creating How-to Books

Not only do how-to books sell well when they're published, they are often perennial favorites and sell well year after year. A how-to eBook can be fun to write and very profitable; you can update the eBook on a regular basis and sell the new version to people who bought the previous version. How-to books cover thousands of different topics, but the best of them have certain elements in common:

- ✔ **Solving a problem:** How-to books solve a problem that the reader is experiencing and shows the reader a better way to accomplish a goal (or set of goals).

- ✔ **Giving readers hope:** How-to books give the reader hope that he or she can perform the method that is described in the text. Hope usually comes in the form of inspirational stories about someone who could be the person next door.

- ✔ **Friendly tone:** How-to books don't talk down to the reader. The author speaks like an understanding and likeable friend, not an irritating know-it-all.

- ✔ **Clear instructions:** How-to books give clear, easy to understand, step-by-step instructions that the reader can follow.

Authoring a set of instructions

In school, during show-n-tell, I always liked it better when someone showed something instead of just talking about it. The same idea holds true when writing a set of instructions for a how-to book. Don't talk about the principles of how something works — instead, *show* the reader by listing step-by-step actions to be taken. Not only will your readers have a better idea of what you're talking about, they will also have a chance to learn by *doing* instead of *reading*.

Later in this chapter, I explain how to author instructions for technical material. Many of the principles that apply to writing software documentation are the same for writing any set of instructions:

- ✔ If you're describing how to use a product, make sure to detail which version of the product that you're using and any specialized features that may be required. You don't want your reader to be frustrated because his or her version of the product is different from yours and your instructions can't be followed.

- ✔ After you write your instructions, ask someone else to go through your steps and let you know what is confusing or unclear. Someone who isn't so close to the subject matter can spot problems with your text more easily than you can.

- ✔ Organize your information in a way that's easy for a reader to follow. Usually, this means starting with the basics and then taking the reader through increasingly difficult steps, until a certain level of proficiency has been reached. Don't try to take someone from novice to expert in a single eBook. This goal isn't realistic and would make for a very lengthy book. It's better to create three different eBooks targeting the beginner, the intermediate user, and the advanced user. An added benefit is that you have the chance to sell a second or third eBook to someone who was happy with your beginner-level text!

- ✔ Include definitions of specialized terms in a glossary at the end of the eBook. Don't assume that the reader understands the term after reading it in context.

Adding other media for best effect

In addition to your how-to text, don't be afraid to include other media in your eBook. Pictures should be included whenever they can help make the meaning of the text more clear. When you are detailing a complex set of steps, add an image for each step that shows the action that the reader should take.

Animation and videos can be highly informative because they can show more than a static image. (One short animation can take the place of multiple images.) If you don't have access to someone who can create clips for you, search on Web sites that cover the topic of your eBook. AltaVista (www. altavista.com/) lets you search through images, MP3, audio clips, and video clips for a specific topic. If you find an appropriate clip, ask whether the Web site owner would be willing to let you use the clip in exchange for mentioning his or her site in your eBook.

Audio can be used to narrate a series of steps. This can be helpful for someone who can't look at the eBook while working on something. By clicking a link, he or she can hear the instructions being read aloud, which frees the reader's eyes and hands for following your instructions.

What to avoid when writing a how-to book

When you work on a how-to eBook, try to avoid these issues:

- ✔ **Don't repeat yourself:** Don't repeat yourself. Don't repeat yourself. If you've already given the reader a set of instructions for building a Widget, don't repeat these basics when explaining how to build the advanced Widget. Instead, link back to the earlier chapter. Let the user know that after basic Widget Step K, he or she needs to follow Advanced Widget Step L, which is to gild all exposed surfaces before firing up the iron.

- ✔ **Don't assume that the user knows what tools are needed just from reading the instructions:** Before the instructions, provide a list of the items that the user needs to complete the steps. This lets the user gather all the required materials before starting. (You won't find anyone more frustrated than a cook who realizes that he or she doesn't have any chocolate chips in the middle of baking chocolate-chip cookies. . . .)

- ✔ **Don't try this at home:** Don't forget to warn the user before giving instructions that might be dangerous. You don't want to be responsible for someone's injury because you forgot to mention that all smoking materials should be extinguished before opening the box of fireworks.

- ✔ **Don't forget about international differences:** If you sell your eBook on the Web, it can reach a global audience. Provide conversion tables at the end of the text to help someone convert from feet to meters and vice versa.

Creating Computers and Technology Books

Computer and technology books are among the best-selling eBooks in the marketplace. Software is updated very quickly compared to products in other industries. It takes less time to write and publish a technical eBook compared to a technical pBook. This fact gives eBooks a competitive advantage when bringing a book to market quickly.

Authoring instructions for technical material

Technical eBooks should give step-by-step instructions that the user can follow while using the software. Keep the following tips in mind as you write a technical eBook:

- **Many different versions of software may be available:** I'm writing this text on Word 2000, which was preceded by Word 97, which followed Word 95, which . . . well, you get the idea. Don't assume that the reader has the latest version of the software. Make it clear which version of the software you are writing about.

- **Not everyone has the same operating system as you:** I have Windows 98 at home, but I work on Windows 2000 at the office. If your instructions only work on a specific platform, you need to mention this fact in the text.

- **Be precise about the terms you use:** If you're describing a window on the screen, specify whether it's a dialog box, or a new instance of the application running in a separate window. If a user needs to click a menu item from the toolbar, explain which toolbar and which menu item so the user is not confused about what to do.

- **Don't assume that you know what you're talking about:** Don't try to write a set of instructions straight from memory, no matter how well you think you know the subject matter. Actually perform the steps and write down what you're doing as you go through the process. You'll find that you may have forgotten many things, or that you want to mention other items in the text.

- **Structure your information logically:** You can begin with simple examples of how to use the product, and then work up to increasingly sophisticated features. Another way to structure your information is to follow the user interface of the product. If I was writing about Microsoft Word, for example, I could explain each of the items under the File menu, and then explain each of the items under the Edit menu, and so on. The first method of organization is better when you are writing for novices. The second method may work when you are writing for more advanced users of a product, or when you are writing a very comprehensive guide of every available feature.

- **Provide a glossary of definitions:** One reason that non-technical people can be intimidated by technology is because people who like technology seem to speak a different language. Your eBook gives you a chance to act as an interpreter. Make sure that you explain every term, even if you think the term is elementary. No one knows what a term means until someone else explains it to him or her for the first time.

✔ **Explain acronyms:** When I was a technical evangelist for Microsoft, we held a seminar. My husband asked me what the seminar was about and I told him that we were holding "a seminar for ISVs to explain the benefits of ASP on the IIS platform." He looked at me as if I were talking gibberish, so I explained it in a way that he could understand: "We're holding a seminar for independent software vendors to explain how to use the server-side script engine, which is available on Microsoft's Web server." I'm not sure if he understood the second time around either, but at least he knew that he didn't care to hear a more in-depth explanation.

✔ **A picture is worth a thousand words, if you'll forgive the cliché . . . :** If you give the reader a detailed set of instructions, include images showing the steps that you're explaining. Getting these pictures is simple — if you know how to capture images from the screen and include them with your document. Here's how you can capture a screen image with Windows:

1. **Find an image that you want to capture.**

2. **Press the Print Screen key on your keyboard.**

   Note: This key is often found near the Scroll Lock key.

   The image is captured to the Windows clipboard where it can be pasted into other applications.

   To capture the Window that is currently active, hold down the Alt key while you press the Print Screen key. Instead of capturing the entire screen, just an image of the active Window is copied to the clipboard.

3. **Open another Windows application, like Microsoft Paint, and choose Edit⇨Paste.**

   The screen capture image is copied.

   Figure 7-9 shows a screen capture that has been copied into Microsoft Paint.

What to avoid when writing a technology book

The following tips help you avoid problems when writing an eBook about a technical topic:

✔ **Don't ramble:** When someone buys a technical eBook, they want information that will help them quickly understand how to work a piece of hardware, or run a software application. Just present the information that they need — save your philosophical musings for a different book.

✔ **Don't show off:** You're writing for someone who needs help — you're not writing to impress power users or your buddy in the next cubicle. (If you are writing *Tips and Tricks for Power Users,* just ignore the rest of this paragraph.) A novice user wants clear, simple-to-understand instructions. You may be the greatest macro programmer that the world has ever known, but this doesn't mean much to someone who is learning to use Word for the first time. Write at the level of the person that you're writing for, and save the guru-level knowledge for a different eBook.

✔ **Don't forget to add a little of your own personality:** Software manuals can be dry and you don't want the reader to fall asleep while reading your eBook. Have some fun and lighten things up with a little humor. You'll have more fun writing, and the reader will have more fun reading.

✔ **Don't forget that software is a moving target:** No matter how quickly you write and publish an eBook, the information in the text may be dated by the time your eBook is distributed. This is especially true if you write an eBook about Web pages because these are constantly updated. Make sure that you review your eBook often after you publish it and be prepared to update it on a regular basis. You can also publish updated material on a Web site and then provide a link to the site within your eBook.

Figure 7-9:
After the screen shot is copied into Microsoft Paint, I can crop, clean up, and save the image for use in an eBook.

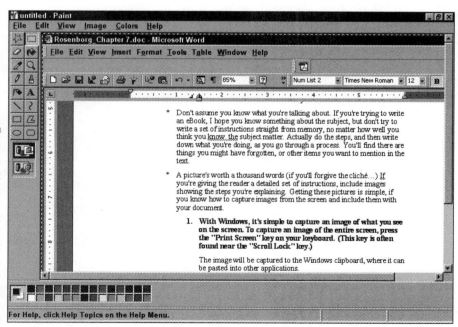

Part III
Packaging Your Content

In this part . . .

After you write your eBook, you need to package and
format it so users can download and read it. Part III
shows you how to do this.

Chapter 8 shows you how to structure your document. It
explains how to organize the content into readable chunks
and how to create the document's navigation. I explain the
fundamentals of page layout and the correct use of colors
and fonts.

Chapter 9 explains how your content can be packaged as
an article, booklet, manual, or eBook. This chapter also
shows you how to convert your eBook from one package
to another.

Chapter 10 shows you how to construct a simple OEB-
compliant eBook by hand. This chapter shows you how to
download and install the Word HTML filter. Finally, this
chapter shows you how to create the eBook package file
and open your eBook in a Web browser.

Chapter 11 is a hands-on tutorial that shows you how to
use authoring tools to create eBooks that are compatible
with different eBook readers. This chapter explains how
to install and configure each authoring tool and shows
you how to build an eBook using the tools.

Chapter 8

Creating a Professional Document

• •

• •

*Y*ou picked a great topic, did the research, prepared an outline, and wrote the text, but you're not done yet. You still have to format the document so it works well for onscreen presentation. Reading onscreen is different from reading on the printed page; you need to structure your material to work well as an eBook. In this chapter, I explain how to organize your content in a professional manner.

As you read through this chapter, adopt the techniques that work best with your material. Some of the suggestions work better for some types of eBooks. For example, using headings to chunk content is more applicable for a how-to eBook than a novel. But knowing how to structure your document helps you, no matter what type of work you author.

Structuring Your eBook

In this section, when I talk about the *structure* of your eBook, I don't mean how the text flows and how you organize the content of the eBook. Instead, I'm talking about how to provide a navigational structure for your eBook so the audience knows how to go to the next page, how to find the Table of Contents, and how to look up an item in the index. Some of this structure is created automatically by eBook-authoring tools. Sometimes, the navigational structure is an inherent part of the eBook reader. In other cases, you may need to provide all the structure when you create the document.

Figures 8-1, 8-2, 8-3, and 8-4 show the same document formatted as an eBook for the four most popular eBook readers. The figures show the different navigational aids that come with each reader.

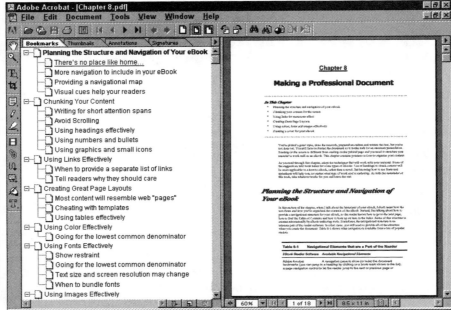

In addition to the navigation you get with your eBook reader, you may want to think through how you want to help your audience move through your eBook. You can do many things when you structure your document to make life easier for your audience. I describe some of these techniques in the following section.

There's no place like home . . .

When a user navigates through a well-designed Web site, there's always a link that takes you back to the home page. Because eBooks are based on a book-like interface, there's no home page to take the user back to, but you should include a Table of Contents, an index, or a list of links page, that serves a similar function. This is especially important if you plan to include interactive elements or multiple storylines in an eBook. Your audience needs a familiar place to go to in the event that he or she gets "lost."

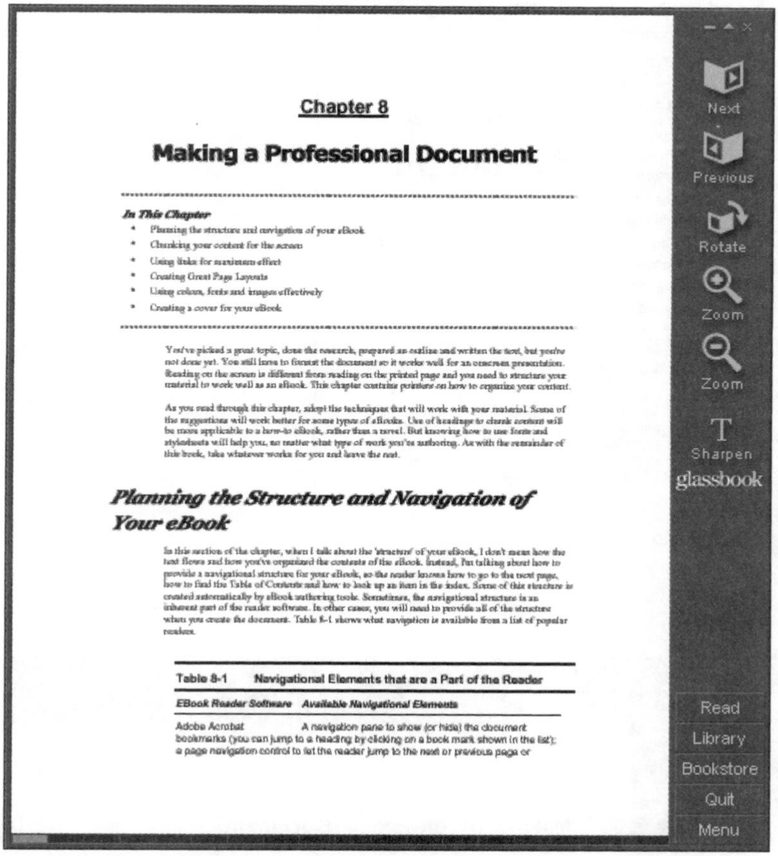

Figure 8-2:
Because the
Glassbook
Reader
opens
Acrobat-
formatted
PDF files,
documents
viewed in
this reader
retain all the
fonts and
formatting
of the
original
document.
The Rotate
button
allows you
to view the
reader
rotated at a
90 percent
angle.
Buttons let
you zoom in
or zoom out
of the text
so you can
adjust the
document to
a size that's
best for you.

Figure 8-3:
The Microsoft Reader displays a main menu when you click the down arrow shown next to the eBook's title. The reader's navigational aids include a Library, a Bookstore, a Guidebook, and a Return feature.

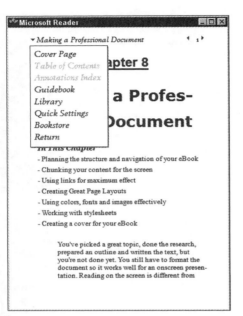

Figure 8-4:
The Rocket eBook Reader contains five sets of controls that allow you to move within the current document or to open a different document. The controls also allow you to search and annotate documents.

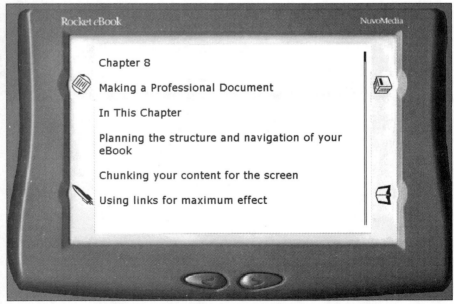

Although there's a tool in Word that automatically generates a Table of Contents based on the headings included in the document, you need to be careful before you use this tool for an eBook title. Some authoring tools won't work with the Word tags generated by the Table of Contents. If a user views your title on a Pocket PC, or another small-screen eBook reader, the eBook may be thousands (instead of hundreds) of pages. The page numbers shown in the Table of Contents won't correlate to the page numbers shown on the screen of the eBook reader.

The best way to create a Table of Contents is to use hyperlinks, which can be recognized by a majority of readers and which reduce the page-number problem for reading your eBook on different eBook readers. The following instructions show you how to create a Table of Contents in Word and convert the document to HTML so links are automatically generated between the pages:

1. **After you write the document, save the file in HTML format by choosing File⇨Save As Web Page.**

   The Save As dialog box appears.

   Make sure that the document you create includes headings and subheadings because Word uses these to generate the Table of Contents. See Chapter 10 if you're unsure how to add headings within the body of your text.

2. **Select the name and folder for your HTML file, and click Save.**

   Depending on the formatting used in your document, Word may display a warning dialog box that lets you know some formatting may be changed upon conversion to HTML format. (See Figure 8-5 for an example of the warning that may appear.) If you want more information about the changes that will happen, click the Tell Me More button. If you want to continue with the conversion, despite the formatting changes, click the Continue button. If you want to retain your document's specialized formatting, you can click the Cancel button, but you may be forced to create your Table of Contents manually instead of using Word's tool.

3. **Move the cursor to the place in the document where you want the Table of Contents to be generated and choose Insert⇨Index and Tables.**

   The Index and Tables dialog box appears.

4. **Click the Table of Contents tab.**

   In the Index and Tables dialog box, make sure the Show Page Numbers option is *not* selected. When you click the option to deselect it, the other options pertaining to page numbers are grayed out.

   You can choose how the Table of Contents text should be formatted by selecting a style from the Formats drop-down list. You can also choose how many levels of content should be displayed in the Table of Contents by changing the number in the Show Levels option (see Figure 8-6).

Figure 8-5:
Word may
show you a
warning if
the
formatting
used in your
document
cannot be
saved
properly in
HTML
format.

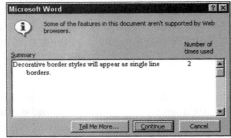

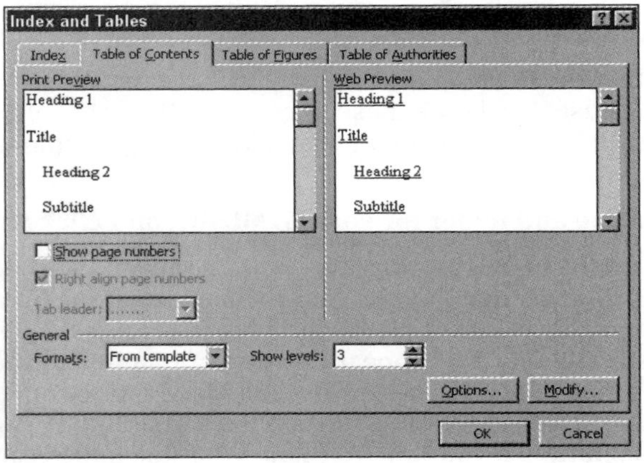

Figure 8-6:
The Index
and Tables
dialog box
lets you
customize
your Table
of Contents.

Because you're creating a Web document and you removed the Show Page Numbers option, your final Table of Contents will look like the example shown in the Web Preview pane of the Index and Tables dialog box.

If you want to fine-tune how the Table of Contents is generated, click the Options button. The Table of Contents Options dialog box appears, and you can select which heading styles will be used to build the Table of Contents.

5. **After you set the options for the Table of Contents, click the OK button.**

Word generates the Table of Contents and links to corresponding passages of text. It adds the links to your document in the place you selected. See Figure 8-7 for an example of what the Table of Contents looks like.

By clicking any link shown in the Table of Contents, you jump to that section of text.

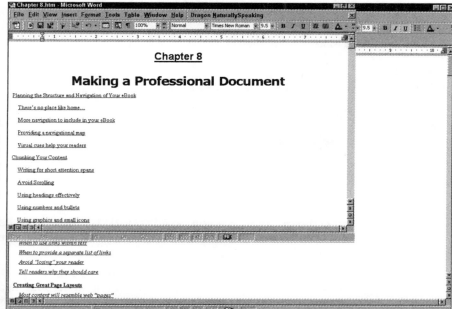

Figure 8-7:
Word generates the Table of Contents automatically and inserts the text where your cursor's placed.

A Table of Contents doesn't need to be a textual list of links. Certain types of eBooks are visual and include lots of pictures or graphical elements (for example, children's literature or comic eBooks). If you design a visual eBook, you may want to include a "map" with links that can be clicked instead of a textual Table of Contents. You won't be able to generate this type of map automatically, but the presentation may be worth the effort of creating an image map with links as hot spots.

You can now import the document into the authoring software you use to create eBooks:

1. Open Adobe Acrobat from the Windows Start Menu.

2. **Choose File⇨Open.**

   The Open dialog box appears.

3. **Select HTML (*.htm,*.html,*.shtml) from the drop-down list of file types, as shown in Figure 8-8.**

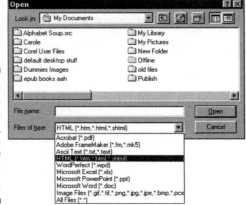

Figure 8-8:
You want to select the HTML option from the Files of Type drop-down list.

4. **Select the folder where you saved your HTML file that contains the Table of Contents you generated. Click the name of your file and click the Open button.**

   Acrobat converts your document to PDF format and retains the Table of Contents links. After the conversion is complete, Acrobat displays your document with the Table of Contents.

5. **Save the PDF file by choosing File⇨Save As and choosing a name for the PDF file and a folder to save the file to. Click the Save button.**

6. **Close Acrobat.**

Including more navigational features

The following navigational elements are useful to help your readers move around easily in your eBook:

- ✔ Forward and Back buttons.
- ✔ An index (unless the eBook is fictional).
- ✔ A list of links to Web sites that provide additional information about a specific topic.

✔ A link whenever you mention content that can be found in a different chapter.

✔ Links at the end of a scene (or at a dramatic point of the story) that let the audience choose where to go next.

✔ Small graphics that act as visual cues to let the audience know their options for where to go next. Too many textual links may clutter up the page and the audience has no way to determine which links should get priority. Using graphics allows you to create a set of icons for links that are common to specific sections of text. These links can look different from the contextual links that are specific to the information contained in the text.

Using icons to direct your audience

Most people are visually oriented, so good use of graphics can help direct your audience's attention to what to do next. To create an icon, add an image to your eBook and create a link so the audience jumps to a different section of the eBook when they click the image.

The following tips may help you incorporate icons in your eBooks:

✔ **Make sure each icon has only a single meaning:** It may confuse your audience if a down arrow means Go to the Next Page in one instance but Look at the Next Set of Information in another instance.

✔ **Don't give your readers too many ways to do the same thing:** If the audience can click a back arrow, click a <u>Previous Page</u> link, click the B button on the keyboard, or scroll up to move back to the previous page, it's too much. Ideally, there should be no more than two ways to accomplish the same task.

✔ **Be a follower rather than a leader:** If the rest of the world recognizes a forward arrow as a way of moving to the next page of text, you may confuse your audience if you decide to use a bolded *N* instead. Try to stick with those interfaces that are commonly accepted. It makes things easier on your readers.

✔ **Play around with fonts if you're worried about including too many images in your eBook:** Using a large font size for an exclamation point, for example, is a great way to draw the audience's eyes to an important passage of text. Also, it keeps the file size from getting too large for eBook readers to download in a short amount of time.

Chunking Your Content

People don't read onscreen content the same way they read content on a printed page. When people read onscreen, they scan a document, pick out the headlines, and read the first few lines under each. When people read a document that's printed, they slow down and focus on each word at a time. Although I don't know of any studies to support my theory, I think people try to get through a document as quickly as possible because reading onscreen is tiring to the eyes. When you create an eBook, take advantage of how people read onscreen by sectioning your content into easily digestible *chunks*. Chunks are sections of content that can be quickly scanned. The easiest way to separate content is by using headings to separate groups of paragraphs. A person's eye has an easier time scanning headings to see whether the related paragraphs are of interest, rather than scanning over the text of an unbroken page of content.

If you look at well-designed Web pages, you'll notice a lot of chunking. Web designers do this to support the way people read onscreen. Other techniques used on Web pages that can be adopted for use in eBooks include the following:

- ✔ Keep all your content to a single page of text that can be viewed without scrolling.
- ✔ Use bullets and numbered text when possible to break up the text on a page.
- ✔ Use graphics to explain something instead of writing paragraphs and paragraphs of solid text.
- ✔ Use small icons to help direct the audience's eyes to sections of the text that contain important or useful information.
- ✔ Use headings that describe the text that follows it.

Writing for the computer generation

I used to be the queen of run-on sentences. I wrote endless spans of text, separated only by commas, that seemed to go on forever and ever. Anyone who read one of these endless passages felt his or her eyes begin to itch and blur as he or she fought valiantly to stay awake and still keep up with my train of thought. It wasn't until I wrote using Microsoft Word that I realized how often I lapsed into stream-of-consciousness writing. As I put the period at the end of each run-on sentence, a green squiggle appeared under the sentence to let me know I had blown it — again. After a while, I got tired of seeing the green squiggle and I started to shorten my sentences.

This type of writing is bad enough on the printed page, but it can be absolutely deadly when you write eBooks. To help make your eBooks more professional, remember the following tips:

- ✓ **Keep your writing short and sweet:** Reading onscreen strains the eyes, so don't make your audience read more than absolutely necessary. When you edit, be sure to delete all the words that aren't needed to express your thoughts (the Delete key is your friend).

- ✓ **Break up run-on sentences:** Try to separate run-on sentences into two or three shorter ones.

- ✓ **Explain concepts as simply as possible:** This can be surprisingly difficult to do well. Try reading your document to a friend with no prior understanding of the material, and ask him or her to explain the concept back to you. By doing this, you're able to see whether your explanation helped your friend to understand the concept.

- ✓ **Break long passages of text into multiple paragraphs:** When the audience tries to scan through your material, long passages of text slows down the reading process. Try to break up the material and add headings, if appropriate.

Scrolling's a no-no

Some eBook readers (like Microsoft Reader, for example) automatically *reflow* (resize and repaginate) documents so the page fits within the length and width of the screen without requiring the reader to scroll down or to the right of the text. Other eBook readers try to retain the dimensions of the original document, so you may need to scroll to see an entire page when the eBook launches on a smaller screen. For example, if you take a PDF file that looks great on your desktop PC and try to view it on your PalmPilot, you're going to do a lot of scrolling to read each page.

Scrolling's disruptive and pulls a user's attention away from your document. Unless your content is really of interest to the user, there's a chance that he or she will stop reading it. If a person stops in the middle of your first eBook, the chances aren't very good that he or she will purchase subsequent titles. The moral of the story? Scroll and lose sales, or size your documents properly and get repeat business.

When you create an eBook for an eBook reader that doesn't reflow, see whether your authoring tool lets you choose the size of the page. The following steps show you how to optimize a PDF document for viewing on a Pocket PC:

1. **After you create your document in Microsoft Word, change your document margins by choosing File⇨Page Setup.**

   The Page Setup dialog box appears.

2. **Click the Margins tab.**

Make sure the Apply To option is set to Whole Document. Also, set all the margins (top, bottom, left, right, and gutter) to 0. The header should be set to 1.2" from the edge. The footer should be set to 0.1" from the edge. The Mirror Margins and 2 Pages Per Sheet options should *not* be selected. Last but not least, select Left for the Gutter Position option. Your settings should look like those shown in Figure 8-9.

Figure 8-9:
To resize a document to fit on a smaller screen, you must reset the page margins in the Page Setup dialog box.

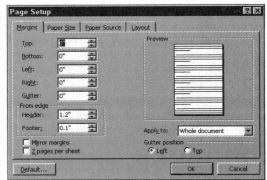

3. **Before you close the Page Setup dialog box, click the Paper Size tab.**

In the Paper Size drop-down list, select Custom Size. Set the Width option to 3" and set the Height option to 4.5". The Orientation option should be set to Portrait and set the Apply To option to Whole Document. After you make these changes, click the OK button. See Figure 8-10 for an example of how the page settings should look.

Figure 8-10:
You need to change the page setup by using the Page Setup dialog box.

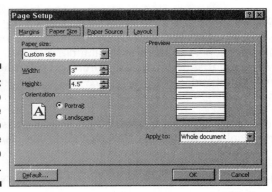

Because Acrobat makes some modifications to the layout of the page and the Primer reader makes adjustments as well, you may have to fiddle with the page size and margins to come up with settings that display properly on the Jornada's screen. When you create layouts for specific platforms, plan to spend a lot of time making adjustments and testing the final layout.

4. **You now need to change the indents for all paragraphs in the document. Select the entire document by pressing the Ctrl key while holding down the A key on the keyboard.**

   The entire document is selected.

5. **Drag the Right Indent button on Word's ruler to the right edge of the document. Drag the First Line Indent button to the left edge of the document. Drag the Left Indent button to line up directly under the First Line Indent button.**

   Figure 8-11 has callouts that show the names of each Indent button, in case you're not sure which is which.

Figure 8-11:
The Right
Indent, First
Line Indent,
and Left
Indent
buttons
allow you to
change the
indentation
of your
document.

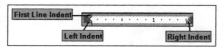

If you want more content to fit on each screen, go through the document and use a smaller font size than usual for your text and headings. If you use images in your document, you need to resize them to fit in the smaller page size.

Pocket PCs and other handheld devices have much less memory than desktop computers. Because each font you use in a document takes up memory, using multiple fonts can cause display problems on your handheld device. Shutting down applications or using less fonts can correct the problem. If you find your fonts aren't displaying correctly on your handheld device, go through the document and convert all the fonts to a single font type.

You can save the file with the new settings using Word's Save option from the File menu and then import the document into Acrobat. (You can save time if Acrobat is installed on the same computer you use for authoring.) When you install Acrobat, a Create Adobe PDF item is added to Word's File menu. This option lets you create the PDF file within Word.

6. **With the document open in Word, choose File⇨Create Adobe PDF.**

   The Acrobat PDFMaker 4.05 for Microsoft Word window appears.

7. **Click the General tab.**

   The Use Acrobat Distiller option should be selected and the Print via Distiller's Printer option should be checked. You want to select PressOptimized from the Distiller Settings drop-down list.

8. **Under the File Options section on the General tab, select Prompt for the PDF Filename, View the PDF File after Creating It, and Report Errors, as shown in Figure 8-12.**

Figure 8-12:
You can set the options for your PDF file from the Acrobat PDFMaker 4.05 for Microsoft Word window.

9. **Click the Output tab to change more settings in the Acrobat PDFMaker 4.05 for Microsoft Word window.**

   You can use the default settings shown on this screen, but make sure that Fit Page is selected from the Destination Magnification drop-down list.

10. **Click Apply to save the settings and click the Create button to start converting your Word document into a PDF file.**

If you convert documents for a variety of eBook readers, it requires additional effort for each title you sell, but you'll be able to offer documents that are optimized for a variety of screens. This helps your eBooks stand out from the competition.

Headings: The key to organization

Imagine how this book would look if there were no headings to break up all the text. The information would all look the same and you'd be forced to read page after page of text without clues as to where one section ended and another started. If you picked up the book in a bookstore, you would probably flip through some of the pages to get an idea of how the information was organized and what the book contained. Without headings, the dense-looking pages would soon overwhelm you and you'd put the book back on the shelf, and look for something user-friendlier.

Headings help organize the text and make pages look more pleasing by dividing separate sections of content. Hopefully, you used an outline to create your text, and the outline headings became the headings in your final draft (for more on outlines, see Chapter 5). But if you didn't use headings this way, you can still add them to your text: Review each page and determine what the two or three main points per page are. These points can be inserted into the text as headings. You may need to move paragraphs around and do additional editing to get the text to flow from point to point, but after reworking the document, you'll have text that's better organized and more comprehensible.

It's more difficult to add headings to your content if you're working on fiction, which doesn't lend itself well to headings. But, if you're working on interactive fiction (where the user can choose where to go next), you can use links instead of headings as a way to break up the text.

Breaking up text with numbers and bullets

If you're writing a work of nonfiction, numbered and bulleted lists can be used effectively to break up text on the page and give the reader's eyes a point of reference. Lists or bullets are easy for the audience to scan, absorb the information, and move on to the next section of content, so they support the way people read onscreen. Remember to keep each list item short — no more than two or three lines of text. You don't need to create entire sentences for each list or bulleted item; phrases are preferable because they're easier to read quickly.

Guiding your audience's eye with icons

Although you may not be aware of it, the *...For Dummies* books are great examples of how to chunk content effectively. I've always been a fan of how they incorporate the *...For Dummies* graphics as points of reference to let you quickly search out the tips, warnings, and technical stuff on each page.

If you're working on a book-length document, you can come up with standard icons that can be included within the body of text. Try to limit your common icons to no more than four so you don't overwhelm the user.

Here's a list of some icons that you may want to include in your document:

- Tips, Tricks, Cool Stuff
- Warning, Caution
- Remember
- Check This Out
- Exercises to Try
- Additional Information, Background Information
- List of Related Material, List of Links
- Additional Help
- Of Note

While you write the text for your eBook, include a paragraph that says *"<Insert Of Note icon here>"* every place you want to include an Of Note icon, for example. After you finalize all the text, search for small graphics that will be used as your icons and replace the text string with the appropriate image. Look at clipart collections with license agreements that let you distribute the art with an eBook. Clipart libraries often contain lots of images that are small and perfect for using as icons.

Using Links Effectively

eBooks have a big advantage compared to printed books because they let you link to different sections of a document or to different documents. There's a golden rule about repeating information in an eBook text: *Never repeat when you can link.* It's better to take someone to the original reference than to summarize or paraphrase the same content. (See Chapter 7 for more on linking to other documents and to Web sites.)

When you include links to external documents or Web pages, you need to determine whether your audience will have access to the external content. Including links to the Web in your eBook can be a risk. Although many eBook readers allow you to access Web sites, your audience may not all be connected while they read your eBook. You should test how gracefully your eBook reader handles a broken link. You want to make sure that your audience knows that they need to be connected to the Internet before the links work; otherwise, they may assume that your document is incomplete.

Before you include a link in a document, you need to give your audience a reason to click the link. When a link is available, you're asking your audience to make a decision: stay with the current document and keep reading, or follow the link to a different section of the same document (or to a new document).

You can tell the user why he or she would be interested in clicking a link in a few ways:

- **If the link is textual, the text should describe what the link is:** If I include Billy Bob's Catfish Web site as a link in my eBook, the audience has a pretty good idea of what the link is about before they click it.

- **Group links under a summary heading:** If the heading is *The 20 Best Catfish Web Sites,* the audience has an idea of what the links are focused on before they click. ***Note:*** Don't use a generic heading, like *More Information.* It just isn't descriptive enough.

- **With image links, the picture caption should include information about the link:** If I include a catfish picture with a link in my document, the caption could read "Click the catfish to jump to *Billy Bob's Catfish* Web site, where you can get some of the best catfish-catching tips around!"

- **With image maps, include a caption that explains how the user can find the different links associated with the image:** An example of a caption that would work for an image map of the United States would be "Click any catfish shown on the map to find the best fishing sites in each state."

Laying Out the Perfect Page

Let me admit something to you: When it comes to graphic design and page layout, I'm no expert. But, even though I'm far from talented in the design and layout fields, I can still inform you about some of the basic design principles and show you how to cheat and create great-looking documents that are based on the designs of others.

Resembling Web pages

Web designers are pros at designing layouts that work well for onscreen reading. Unlike textual documents, most people don't print out a Web page before they read it. To get an idea of what works for your eBook, take a look at some of your favorite Web sites, and focus on the following points:

✔ **How has the designer provided navigation for the Web site?** Are the links to the main pages included in a navigational bar, in a banner across the top of the page, or some other way?

✔ **Is a *splash screen* shown before the first content page of the site?** A splash screen is usually decorative and highly graphical. It sometimes contains animations, in addition to graphics. You can use the concept of a splash screen as a cover design for your eBook.

✔ **How has the designer chunked the content for easy onscreen reading?** Is there good use of headings, lists, and bullets? Have tables been used to separate some sections of content from others?

✔ **When graphics are featured, do they add to the content, or are they just eye candy?** Although eye candy can be appealing, it's annoying to users with slow modems. Make sure that the images you include are there for a good reason.

✔ **How many different fonts are used on the Web page?** Although they may be in different sizes, usually only a handful of fonts are used.

✔ **How many different colors are used on the page?** Is there a dominant color? This may or may not be relevant to you, depending on whether the eBook reader you're designing for supports colors.

✔ **How much white space is on the page?** *White space* is a section of the page where no text or images exist. Well-designed Web pages include lots of white space to help break up the page for easier onscreen reading.

Cheating (just a little) with templates

Even if you study well-designed Web pages or other eBooks, it's not easy to come up with a well-designed page layout. The good news is that you don't have to do it by yourself. Plenty of templates are available that can help you get started. The templates lay out the page for you; you just need to add your own content.

If you plan on using a template, you should author your eBook with Acrobat (which preserves formatting) or save your document to HTML before you import your document into an authoring tool. Most desktop-publishing packages let you save to HTML format after creating a document (although some of the formatting may be lost in the conversion).

Microsoft Word contains many templates for different types of documents. To use one of these templates for your eBook design, follow these steps:

1. **Choose File⇨New.**

   The New dialog box appears and shows many different templates listed under each tab shown in the window. Some of the best tabs to look through for eBook styles include Publications, Reports, and Business Planner templates.

2. **Select a template by clicking the template icon.**

   You see a preview image of the template design in the pane on the right-hand side of the window.

3. **Make sure that Document is selected in the Create New option. Click the OK button.**

   Word creates a new document with the template you selected.

4. **Customize the template by replacing the sample content with your content before you import the file into your eBook-authoring tool.**

If you're designing an eBook for a handheld eBook reader, steer clear of using templates for page layout. Because the screens are so small, you don't have much room for margins, large fonts, and the other elements that make the templates look distinctive. You're better off keeping the design as simple as possible for small screens.

Colorized eBooks

If your eBook will be viewed on an eBook reader that displays colors, you have more options for designing your document. If you're used to working on black-and-white documents, it may be difficult to design a color document. Here are some pointers to keep in mind when you work with color:

- ✔ **If you include a number of color images in your eBook (especially photographs), keep your text black to make the images catch the audience's eye:** If you want to use color for the top-level headings, select the color that's predominant in your images. For example, if there's a lot of blue in your photos, use blue for the top-level headings.

- ✔ **Use no more than two colors for the document headings:** These colors should be from the same primary color family. For example, you can use a deep blue for the top-level headings and a lighter blue for the second-level headings.

- ✔ **Select a primary color as a theme and use a variant of this color every time you feature color in your document:** Using a single color theme makes the document look more consistent and professional.

✔ **Use color consistently:** If one top-level heading is shown in dark blue, all top-level headings should be dark blue. When the user's eye scans the document, he or she will associate dark blue with a text heading and get a feel for the structure of the document.

✔ **Colors can serve as a navigational cue for your users:** A different strategy from the previous bullet, this use of color helps your audience identify different sections of the document by using different colors. Section One of the document could have all chapter titles and headings in dark blue, while Section Two could feature dark green, and Section Three could feature red. Having all the chapters in a section feature the same color scheme makes it easier for users to tell what section of the document is open.

✔ **Make sure that your icons feature the same three colors, two of the colors being black and white:** Making your icons the same colors help pull together the look of your document.

✔ **Colors are powerful — show restraint when you add them to your document:** Unless you're designing your document for children, it shouldn't look like a rainbow. If it does, reduce the number of colors used to make the document seem more professional.

✔ **Colors have emotional context, so select a color palette:** Red is associated with excitement, while blues and greens are calming. For an ultra-professional look, go with corporate blue. For a fun document, play around with reds and oranges.

If you design eBooks that will be read on a PC, remember that monitors and graphics cards vary in how many colors are displayed onscreen and the resolution that's used to display them. Just because an image looks great when it's displayed on my monitor and graphics card combination doesn't mean it'll look the same on your screen. To make sure your images look good to your entire audience, set your monitor settings to the lowest common denominator for your reading audience. You want to set your display to 256 colors and 640 x 480 pixels. If the image looks good at this setting, it will look good on every setting.

Picking Fonts for Your eBook

Using different fonts in your eBook is a way to add visual interest to your content (especially if you don't plan to use colors or images in your text). The key to using fonts well? Show restraint when you pick the fonts you want to use. Keep these pointers in mind when you add fonts to your document:

✔ **Use only two or three fonts per document.**

✔ **Change the font size or style to add additional interest to your document:** For example, make some words **bold** or *italic*.

✔ **Use a mix of serif and sans serif fonts:** *Serif* fonts are fonts with small extensions on the ends of the letters; they are easier to read. *Sans serif* fonts don't have extensions on the ends of the letters. Generally, your body text should be in a serif font and headings should be in sans serif.

✔ **Top-level headings should be larger than subsequent headings:** For example, level-one headings should have a slightly larger or bolded font, while second-level headings should be a bit smaller. Third-level headings should be even smaller than second-level headings.

✔ **If you use color with fonts, don't increase the font size or make the font bold:** The color draws the reader's eye; adding to the size of the font causes a garish effect.

✔ **Use common fonts:** Some authoring tools (such as Acrobat) automatically bundle the fonts you need; others don't. Make sure you use commonly available fonts in your eBooks, unless you can bundle the fonts with the document.

✔ **Screen resolution affects the readability of fonts onscreen.** Unless you design an eBook specifically for a handheld eBook reader, use larger fonts to improve the readability of your document on all screens.

Creating a Professional-Looking Cover

A professional-looking cover is an important element that your document must have. It adds visual interest to your eBook and catches the reader's eye. Therefore, the cover should be prominently featured on all of your marketing materials. It should be shown on all the Web sites where you market or sell your eBook. Designing a professional-looking cover helps your eBook stand out from the competition, and may increase your sales.

Size requirements

The size of your eBook's cover depends on your eBook-authoring tool. Table 8-1 shows the sizes that are required by different eBook readers.

Table 8-1	Size Requirements for eBook Covers	
Authoring Software	*eBook Reader*	*Cover Image Size (in Pixels)*
Adobe Acrobat	Acrobat/Glassbook Reader	813 pixels wide x 1,050 pixels high. This creates a cover image that's approximately 8.5" x 11".
ReaderWorks Publisher	Microsoft Reader	Requires multiple cover images: a library image (99 x 132 pixels), cover image (510 x 680 pixels), cover page image (108 x 680 pixels), Pocket PC library image (90 x 45 pixels), and the Pocket PC cover image (480 x 240 pixels).
Reader Add-in for Word	Microsoft Reader	Although it lets you create LIT files from Word documents, it doesn't let you modify the eBooks with custom images. A default cover image is used, which features the Word logo.
RocketWriter	Rocket eBook	A good size for images is 400 x 300 pixels, although the Rocket eBook allows you to scroll over larger images. Because the eBook reader shows images in black and white only, color images don't look great when included in Rocket eBook files.
SoftBook Personal Publisher	SoftBook Reader	It converts pages from Word, so any image that fits on an 8.5" x 11" Word document works as a cover. If the image is too large, the SoftBook Personal Publisher resizes the image to make it fit.

Unfortunately, each authoring tool requires a differently sized image, which means that you need to produce a different cover image file for each eBook file type you want to support. You may want to invest in software that quickly lets you resize, crop, and recolor images. I use the Microsoft Photo Editor (because it came bundled with my copy of Microsoft Office), but many good tools are available. If you want to test the software before you buy it, go to www.zdnet.com or www.cnet.com and search for image-editing shareware that you can download.

A cover's purpose

A cover should attract the audience's eye and tell them something about the content. At a minimum, the cover should contain the title of the book and the name of the author. If you're trying to establish a brand of eBooks, the title should also contain the branding or name of the publisher. (An example of strong branding is the *...For Dummies* line of books. All of them contain the yellow and black cover with the *...For Dummies* guy smiling on the front.) The advantage of establishing a branded cover is that people will come to associate your eBooks with the brand and will pick your cover from a list of others.

Tips for creating a great cover

Although you're trying to attract the user's eye, you don't want to give the user a headache by making your cover too gaudy. Stand out, but don't be garish.

Here are some tips to help you create an eye-catching cover:

- ✔ Save the neon colors for a '60s retrospective book.
- ✔ Colors that look good on your monitor may look different when they're viewed at a lower resolution.
- ✔ Make sure that the font you use for the eBook title is large enough to be read at a variety of resolutions. If the audience can't read the title, they won't buy the eBook.
- ✔ Test your cover by doing a search on Amazon.com or BN.com. Create an image that's the same size as the thumbnails shown on these sites. Compare your cover to those that are professionally done, and make improvements based on your comparison.
- ✔ Less is more. Keep your cover simple, but dramatic, by using large text with a shadow effect applied against a background of contrasting color.
- ✔ Use a simple background image with the title over the image — but make sure you can read the title.
- ✔ Use red, white, or black to draw the reader's eye to your text.

If you have no design sense, ask a design or fine arts student at your local college to do your cover as a freelance project. You'll get an inexpensive cover and the student will have another item to put in his or her portfolio.

Chapter 9

ePublishing in Multiple Packages

* *

* *

*W*hen you think of ePublishing, you probably think about the distribution of eBooks over the Internet. You can ePublish a lot more than just eBooks, however. If you ePublish only full-length eBooks, you miss an opportunity to make more revenue. After you create a document of any length in one kind of format, you can expand or contract your work to create a new *package* for a different audience. For example, you can turn a full-length eBook into a series of articles, and you can lengthen an article into a comprehensive how-to manual just by adding instructional text.

Why do I use the word *package* instead of talking about different kinds of formats? In other chapters of this book, when I mention formats, I refer to file formats, such as Microsoft LIT files. So, to help reduce confusion, I use the term *package* when I discuss documents packaged in different lengths, like articles and manuals. Clear as mud, right?

As you develop a market for a certain length of work, you have the opportunity to sell other packages based on the same core content, but to tailor that information to different audiences. You can also play around with different marketing strategies. For example, you can give away free booklets in order to build up a list of people to whom you can advertise full-length eBooks. Or you can offer a free article as a way of saying "thank you" to the customers that buy your manual.

In this chapter, I focus specifically on nonfiction. If you write fiction, you can still create different packages, such as a short story, novella, serial novel, or a full-length novel. With the exception of a novel that's packaged for serial distribution, it's hard to reuse fictional content in different packages — although a short story can sometimes be expanded into a longer work.

Choosing a Package for Your Work

With so many package options, it can be hard to know what form your new project should take. I hate to disappoint you, but the choice isn't entirely up to you. Outside factors, especially the amount of time that you have to work on your project, can influence what you decide to create. You should also consider your target audience, and the amount of information that you have about your topic when you design a package.

Determining how deep to explore your topic

The longer the work, the more in-depth you should go — this is the general rule to follow when determining how detailed your work should be. For example, if you write a short article (about two to five pages), you can't get too detailed about the topic unless you write with a narrow scope. An exception to this rule is a book-length work that serves as an overview or introduction to a discipline. In this case, the information that you present may be general, but you'll cover many topics.

Meeting your audience's expectations

The more someone pays for your package, the more they expect from it. A large precedent exists for getting free content from the Web, so if you want to charge for your document, you need to provide more value to your readers. This is especially true if you hope to sell shorter works (like articles and booklets, which most readers are accustomed to getting for free). Before you price your articles or booklets, research the quality of the free content that is available on the Web. If you want to sell any copies, you need to provide a greater value in the form of exclusive content, timely content, or content that helps people make or save money.

Calculating how much time you can devote to writing

Before you determine how much time you can devote to writing, you need to ask yourself how committed you are to a particular project. This is especially true if you are going to ePublish. Without an editor waiting to get the manuscript that you promised, it can be easy to put off writing.

Before you begin working on an ePublishing project, draw up a personal contract with deadline dates for specific sections of the document. For example, if you're working on an article, commit to deliver the outline by June 4, the first draft by July 1, and the fully edited version by July 15. Give your contract to a friend and ask him or her to make sure that you meet your commitments. In addition to putting deadlines in the document, put rewards in as well. The reward can be simple (no need to spend all your profits before you make them), but it's important to give yourself a reward for achieving your goals. If you promise yourself a hot fudge sundae, make sure you get a hot fudge sundae. (Forget about the diet for one day — you earned it!)

Here's how to calculate how much time you can work on a writing project each day:

- Calculate how many hours you spend in an average week at work. Many people actually spend more than 40 hours a week working. Make sure that you include any overtime, time you spend answering work-related e-mail at home, and your mealtimes.

- Calculate how many hours you spend in a week commuting to and from work.

- Add up how many hours you sleep each night and multiply the number by seven.

- Determine how many hours a week you spend preparing food, eating meals, and cleaning up after meals. Add this number to the tally that you're keeping.

- Figure out how many hours you spend a week on household chores like shopping, cleaning, taking care of the yard, and laundry.

- Figure out how much time you spend with family and friends. Although you can cut back on this number a little, make sure you spend enough time caring for the people who care for you. Some people will be more understanding than others. (As my six-year old daughter so eloquently puts it, "Aren't you done with that stupid book yet?")

- Mark down the time you spend on other responsibilities (like walking the dog, cleaning out the fish tank, or taking the cat to the vet).

- Finally, include the downtime that you need. This varies from person to person. Some people need to watch their favorite TV show at night. I need to read for half an hour every night before I go to bed, or I can't get to sleep.

Add up all the hours, subtract the total from 168 (the total number of hours in a week), and divide by 7. This is roughly the amount of time you can spend writing each day.

In one week, for example, if you're at work for 54 hours, sleep 56 hours, spend 6 hours preparing and eating meals, spend 5 hours cleaning, spend 20 hours with loved ones, and need 3 hours of downtime, that adds up to 144 hours a week. This gives you 24 hours a week to write, which is roughly 3½ hours a day.

The type of document that you write depends on how much time you have to write, how quickly you're able to produce a fully edited product, and how quickly you need to get something done to meet a deadline. If you want to publish something in a week or two, you should work on an article or booklet. If you have a few months to spend on a project, you can tackle an eBook or a manual.

Something's gotta give

When you write something, no matter what size it is, you need to juggle between the amount of time you have to work on the project, and any help you can get from others to complete your work. (For example, you can get editorial help, ask other writers to ghostwrite some of the text, or find someone else to do your laundry.) You also need to decide when something's good enough to publish, even if you want more time to do a better job.

No writer ever thinks his or her work is good enough. As a writer, you may have difficulty completing a project because you know it always has room for improvement, but keep this in mind: No one ever achieves perfection, so try to let go of your project when it's good enough to be published.

If you work on a deadline, and you can't get more time to complete your project, you need to add more resources or let the quality slip. Because you don't want the quality to suffer too much, here are some suheaggestions for adding more resources:

- ✓ **Hire a copy editor:** An editor can help you look for typos and mistakes in grammar.

- ✓ **Hire a housekeeper for a week or two:** If you don't have to clean, you have more time to focus on writing.

- ✓ **Send your laundry out.**

- ✓ **Hire a babysitter to supervise your children:** Go to your office and write instead of going out to a movie.

- ✓ **Hire a kid in the neighboorhood to walk your dog.**

Getting your hands on more resources may sound great, but if your budget is outta extra cash, here are other suggestions for getting more time to write:

- ✓ **Let the house stay dirty for a while:** If you don't invite friends over for a week or two, no one has to know that you've become a pig — plus you'll save the time that you would have used for entertaining.

✔ **Don't watch TV:** I feel very *tired* (lazy) after I get my kids to bed. The last thing I want to do is write when I could watch TV. Unfortunately, TV is a big waste of my time, so it's the first thing I give up when I need room in my schedule.

✔ **Let the gardening go:** Tell yourself that you're cultivating a wild look, and spend more time staring at the monitor instead of staring out the window.

✔ **Eat more take-out:** Then eat these take-out meals on paper plates with plastic utensils so clean-up is a snap.

✔ **Trade time with your spouse:** "Give me a week where you take care of all household chores, and I'll return the favor when I'm finished with the manuscript." (If you don't have a spouse you can trade with, see if a friend is interested in a similar arrangement.)

✔ **Call in sick from work:** Don't try this one too often, or you'll have more time than you planned for writing.

No matter how much time you're able to create in your schedule, try to make the time count by actually writing when you're scheduled to write. Writing isn't checking your e-mail or surfing Web sites.

Writing Articles and eMatter

An *article* is a short reference piece (several paragraphs to several pages in length) that's usually featured in newspapers, magazines, Web sites, and other periodicals. The beauty of writing an article is that it's a quick process compared to the effort involved in writing a manual or full-length eBook. The articles you write can be published as *eMatter* on MightyWords.com. (See Chapter 12 for more information on how to do this.)

Writing articles

If you don't have time to write a full-length eBook, you can still become an author — just write articles instead. Some of the reasons why articles are written include the following:

✔ **It's a great way to get known as an expert in a certain area:** I wrote many articles on the subject of multimedia before I was asked to write a chapter on multimedia for another author's book. Then I was asked to write my own book about multimedia. Without those early articles that I wrote for free, I would never have written (and been paid for) my first book.

✔ **You're short on time:** Writing an article is what to do when you want to write about a certain subject, but you don't have the time for a lengthy work.

✔ **The topic is new:** Writing an article is a great way to publish a document about an up-and-coming topic before the competition. In this case, you can quickly publish an article, become acknowledged as an expert on the topic and then take your time working on something longer.

✔ **To promote the ePublication of a longer manuscript:** Suppose you just published an eBook about southern cooking and you want to promote it. Your next step is to write as many articles about the subject for as many publications as possible, because each article is a chance to promote the eBook to a new audience.

The advantages of writing an article

The biggest advantage to writing an article: It doesn't take as long as writing dozens, if not hundreds, of pages for a longer work on the topic. Still, writing a quality article does take time because you need to make every word count (which means that you need to spend a lot of time editing it).

If you're a prolific article writer, you can quickly develop a large backlist of material to sell. You can also combine different articles into eBook anthologies, which can be sold at higher prices.

The disadvantages of writing an article

One disadvantage of writing an article instead of a longer work is that you don't have the opportunity to go deeply into a topic or include extraneous information. You pretty much have to give the facts and nothing but the facts, ma'am. For people who don't know when to shut up (like me), keeping it short and sweet is harder than filling pages.

Another disadvantage to writing an article? You can't charge as much as you could for a longer work. And when you do ePublish it, it's not easy to sell as many copies. People are just not used to paying for short documents. However, as consumers become accustomed to buying content from Web sites like eMatter.com and Contentville.com, it will be easier for you to make a profit (but for now, don't quit the day job to sell articles full time).

Tips for writing a great article

Because articles are short, they usually focus on one primary idea or topic, whether it's about how to do something, a comparison of different products, or telling the readers about something that happened.

Here are a few things to keep in mind when you write an article:

- ✔ **Use the inverted pyramid method to organize your information:** Start with the most important concept in the first paragraph, include supporting information in later paragraphs, and leave the supplemental material for the end. (See Chapter 5 for more information about how to structure your content.)

- ✔ **Focus on the five *W*s of journalism:** Who, what, when, why, and where. After you write the article, review it to make sure you address each question.

- ✔ **Write a short introduction:** Unless you write a news story, your article should include a short introduction that specifies the article's purpose. The introduction can be as short as a single sentence, but it should let the audience know why they should be interested in reading the rest of the article.

- ✔ **Stick to the point:** When you find yourself straying from the primary purpose of the article, stop and focus directly on the topic again. Articles are too short for rambling.

- ✔ **Triple-check your facts:** When possible, confirm a fact with more than one source. This is especially important when you want to include a rumor in your article.

- ✔ **Try to fit a lot of information into a fairly small package:** A great way to display a lot of data is to show it in a table (which can take the place of many paragraphs of explanatory text). Tables can often explain things in a cognitive way that's easier for the reader to understand.

Writing Booklets

Booklets are often given away as a promotional tool to gain attention for another product that you're trying to sell. Booklets also establish your credibility as an expert on a topic. Although they're used as a form of advertising, you need to make sure that the booklet contains real value if you want it to be read.

Booklets are usually short — no more than 10 to 15 pages in length and written in a direct style. The information in booklets is presented in short sound bytes of information that are focused on a specific topic. Booklets aren't meant to be detailed documents; they give just a short overview of the subject, often in the form of bulleted items.

The Part of Tens chapters in this book contain the type of content that works well in a booklet.

Booklets are designed to target a specific audience. For example, parents of toddlers would be interested in a booklet called *Ten Tips to Get Your Toddler Off of the Pacifier,* and people hunting for a new job may want *101 Phrases to Make Your Resume Stand Out.*

Printed booklets often have highly visual elements that are designed to catch the reader's eye. Although your booklets will be "printed" digitally, you should still incorporate images and layouts designed to get your reader's attention, especially if you plan to distribute the booklet by e-mail.

What to focus on when you write a booklet

Before you create a booklet, keep the following tips in mind:

- ✔ **The headline is the most important line in a booklet:** People decide whether a booklet is worth their time based on the headline. Make your headline short and use it to let the audience know what the booklet can do for them.

- ✔ **Write an introduction:** The introduction should explain the problem that the booklet solves and tell the reader how the information in the booklet provides the solution.

- ✔ **Use images and layout to provide visual interest:** If you don't have a graphic arts background, look for a professional to help you. As an alternative, you can use a desktop-publishing program (many provide templates that you can use as a starting point), or you can collect brochures to use as inspiration for your own design.

- ✔ **Bulleted information should be short, but long enough to provide value to the audience:** Booklets can be written about any topic. The writing style is often light-hearted, but this depends on your topic.

- ✔ **The pitch to get readers to buy your longer content should go at the end of the booklet:** People disagree about whether a subtle approach is more effective than a direct one. Both approaches can work, however, so you should match your pitch to what you think will be most effective with your audience.

Creating a professional-looking eBooklet

The following steps use Microsoft Publisher 2000 and Adobe Acrobat 4.0 to create a well-designed booklet. After you finish creating your document, I show you how to convert it to an eBooklet that can be distributed in PDF format:

1. **Open Publisher from the Windows Start Menu by choosing Programs⊏>Microsoft Publisher.**

   Publisher displays the Publisher Catalog, which shows all the layout templates available.

2. **Under the Wizards pane (on the left side of the screen), click Brochures.**

   The Brochures list of templates expands to show the available brochures.

3. **Click one of the informational brochures by either clicking Informational in the pane, or by clicking one of the template thumbnail images, as shown in Figure 9-1.**

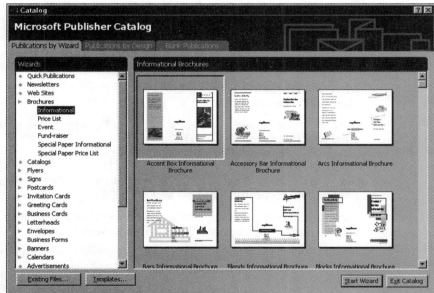

Figure 9-1: You can click any of the Microsoft Publisher brochure designs to start the Brochure Wizard.

4. **Click the Start Wizard button.**

   You can make changes to the layout of your brochure by using the Brochure Wizard options in the left panel. You can customize the text shown in the brochure by clicking the text shown in a frame. This action highlights the text, which you can replace by typing in the material to be used in your brochure.

   You can replace the images used in the brochure by clicking the right mouse button and choosing the Change Picture option from the context menu.

Working with frames takes some getting used to. Most desktop-publishing programs use frames of content (which can be resized or moved around the screen), including Microsoft PowerPoint. If you have never worked with frames before, you should review the Publisher Tutorials (which you can access from Publisher's Help menu).

5. Review the first screen of the brochure and update all the content to suit your needs.

You can look at the content on the second screen of the brochure by clicking the page navigation icon, shown at the bottom of the screen. (The icon looks like a little page with one corner turned down.)

You can add new pages to the booklet that you're creating by choosing Insert⇨Page. The Insert Page dialog box appears, giving you the option to put the new page before or after the current page. You can also create a blank page, a page with a single text frame, or a page that's a copy of an existing page.

After you add the page, you may notice that a new icon has been added to the page navigation icon at the bottom of the screen.

6. After you customize the template, choose File⇨Create Web Site from Current Publication.

Note: Because Adobe Acrobat can't import Publisher files, you need to save your Publisher files to HTML.

The Convert to Web Site dialog box appears.

7. Select the Use the Web Site Wizard to Automatically Create a Web Design with Hyperlinks option and click OK.

A Publisher dialog box appears and asks whether you want to save your current publication before it's converted to Web format.

8. If you want to save the print version, click Yes. If not, click No to continue the conversion process.

Publisher saves your booklet to a layout that has been designed for Web pages. Although the layout is different, all of your content has been preserved (see Figure 9-2).

Before you save your booklet, check the settings under Web Properties (which can be found under the File menu). On the Site tab, make sure that Microsoft Internet Explorer or Netscape Navigator 3.0 (or later version) is selected. The remainder of choices shown in the dialog box can be left as is.

9. Save your document by choosing File⇨Save As Web Page.

A dialog box appears, asking you where the file should be saved. Select the folder to save the files to. You may want to create a new folder for the files; this way, it's easier to keep all the files together for conversion to PDF. Don't worry about naming the individual files — Publisher manages this step for you.

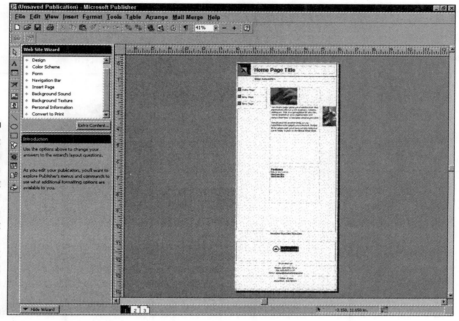

Figure 9-2:
The design
looks
different
after you
convert the
document
to a Web
site, but
the content
remains
the same.

10. **Publisher saves all the Web site files to the Booklet directory.**

11. **Close Publisher and then open the folder where you saved the Web site files for your booklet.**

    The files consist of two types: image files and HTML files.

12. **Open Adobe Acrobat from the Windows Start Menu by choosing Programs⇨Adobe Acrobat 4.0.**

    The Acrobat program opens, but no files should be open. If the program window opens in *maximized* format (filling the whole screen), resize the window by clicking the Restore button. Resizing the window moves it so you can see the Acrobat program and the folder containing your booklet Web files.

13. **Select all the files in the booklet folder by clicking the first file shown. Hold down the Shift key and click the last file shown. All the files should be highlighted.**

14. **Drag the highlighted files into the Adobe Acrobat Window.**

    Adobe converts these files to PDF format.

    After all the files are converted, Acrobat displays the first page of the booklet that you created, as shown in Figure 9-3.

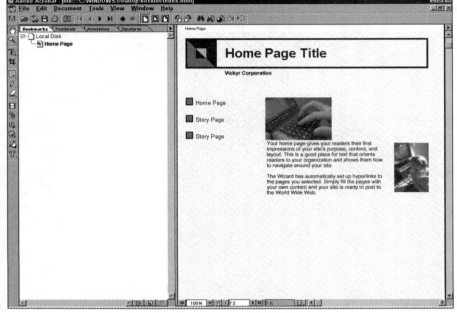

Figure 9-3:
After you
convert the
image and
HTML files
to PDF
format, the
first page of
your booklet
is displayed
in Acrobat.

You may get an error message when you convert some of the image files. Don't worry about it though — just click the OK button to let the conversion process continue.

15. **To display the second page, click the link for the second page in the booklet's navigation bar.**

    After you click the link, the second page displays under the list of local disk bookmarks (shown on the left pane of the Adobe Window).

16. **Click the link for the third page in the navigation bar to display the third page. Continue clicking the links for all the pages shown on the navigation bar.**

17. **After all the pages are opened in Acrobat and the bookmarks are added to the file, choose File⇨Save As to save the book in PDF format.**

    When the Save As dialog box appears, make sure that the Optimize option is selected before you name and save the file, as shown in Figure 9-4.

Figure 9-4:
You can use the Acrobat Save As dialog box to name and save your new eBooklet in PDF format.

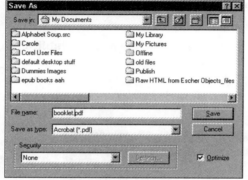

18. **Name and save the new PDF file.**

    This new file is an eBooklet that can be distributed by e-mail. An advantage to converting the booklet to PDF is that the file is compressed, so it is much smaller than the sum of the original image and Web files that you saved from Publisher.

    Before you close Acrobat, a dialog box appears, asking whether you want to save the original versions of the image and HTML files as separate PDF files. Click No in each dialog box.

Writing and Designing Manuals

Manuals are instructional documents that cover a topic in depth. A manual on how to use Microsoft Publisher, for example, offers step-by-step information about how to use the features of Publisher. At the end of the manual, the user should have an understanding of how to use the product and should know where to get information about specific commands or features.

In general, manuals are no less than 50 pages in length, but no more than 100 pages. Because a manual provides instructional information, you should include illustrations to help your readers understand how to follow the steps that you describe.

You can use Microsoft Word 2000 and Adobe Acrobat to create an eBook-style manual. Although you still have to go through the work of writing the content, the following steps take the work out of formatting your manual:

1. **Open Microsoft Word and choose File⇨New.**

   The New dialog box appears.

2. **Click the Publications tab and select the Manual publication template by double-clicking the icon.**

   Make sure that the Document option is selected under the Create New panel, as shown in Figure 9-5, and click OK.

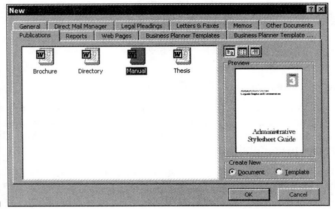

Figure 9-5:
You can use Word's Manual template to create a manual-type eBook.

A new manual opens, as shown in Figure 9-6. The manual is already formatted, so all you need to do is replace the sample text with your text.

The sample document contains great information about the type of content that should go into a manual, and how to replace the text with your own information. Print out a copy to read before you begin customizing the document.

3. **After you enter all the text for the document, save your manual as a Word document.**

4. **Open Adobe Acrobat from the Windows Start menu by choosing Programs⇨Adobe Acrobat 4.0.**

5. **Choose File⇨Open and select Microsoft Word (*.doc) from the Files of Type drop-down list in Acrobat's "Open" dialog box.**

6. **Select the manual document that you saved in Word and open it by clicking the Open button.**

   Adobe's OpenAll Transform Status window opens and shows you that the Acrobat distiller is converting your Word document to PDF format. This process may take a few minutes.

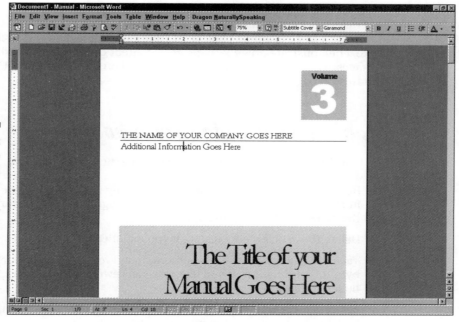

Figure 9-6:
After the
Word
template
opens
a new
manual, you
can replace
Word's
sample text
with your
text.

7. **After the distiller finishes, your manual is displayed in Acrobat. Save the file by choosing File⇨Save As.**

   Make sure that the Optimize option is selected before you name and save the file.

Reusing Your Content Effectively

You can get a lot of mileage out of your material by delivering the information in multiple packages. This is pretty simple to do after you know how. For example, you can create booklets out of your eBooks to be used as marketing material. Or, you can create articles from manuals and publish them to get attention for the other content you sell. I think of this as the "serving leftovers" style of publishing.

Because you don't want your audience to get bored with the same content, make sure that you create new packages for different target markets. If you distribute a booklet for teens, write articles designed for parents. If you create a manual for auto mechanics, write an eBook for people who want to know what mechanics do to their cars.

Sometimes, it's easier to show than tell. To illustrate the differences between an article, a booklet, a manual, and a full-length eBook, I formatted Chapter 1 of this book as an example of each. In addition to showing what each package is like, I demonstrate how the same core content can be reused in different packages. The example packages can be found on the CD-ROM that comes with this book.

Making an article into a booklet

The following tips can help you convert your article into a booklet:

- ✔ Rewrite the article's introduction, especially if it's lengthy. The new introduction should be no more than a paragraph or two that details the benefits offered by the booklet.
- ✔ Delete the article's conclusion, if you included one.
- ✔ Take the main point of each paragraph and rewrite it as a short "sound byte" of information (if you like, you can rewrite each paragraph as a bulleted item).
- ✔ Figure out the target audience of your booklet and make sure that each bullet point addresses the interests and needs of that group.
- ✔ In the back of your booklet, write material that advertises other documents that you sell. Make sure to provide the title of each document, where it can be purchased, and the price.
- ✔ Write a bio that tells the audience about you and your qualifications.
- ✔ Write an eye-catching headline.
- ✔ After you write the text, format the document so the layout is appealing and include graphical elements. (This is easy if you use a template from word-processing or desktop-publishing software.)
- ✔ Save the document in eBook format by using eBook-authoring software.

Expanding a booklet into a manual

The following tips can help you convert your booklet into a manual:

- ✔ Rewrite the booklet's introduction to explain the purpose of the manual. The introduction should include an overview of each section that is included in the manual.
- ✔ Each bulleted item can become a separate chapter. When you write each chapter, the information doesn't have to target the needs of a specific group; it's fine to include more generic material.

- ✔ In addition to chapter titles, include the headings and subheadings within each chapter. Each subhead should contain at least a paragraph of text.

- ✔ The focus of each chapter should be to explain to the reader how to perform a task or series of actions. Try to give step-by-step instructions when possible.

- ✔ If you have pictures that demonstrate how to perform tasks for your audience to follow, include these within the text of the manual.

- ✔ After the manual's text has been written, add a Table of Contents and an Index.

- ✔ Revise the booklet's advertising blurb to give a list of other documents that you ePublish and your Web site address. (The focus should be on the other titles you offer, but it shouldn't read like an advertisement.)

- ✔ Include a bio that tells the reader about you and your qualifications.

- ✔ The booklet's headline can become the title of the manual. If appropriate, use the words *Handbook, Manual,* or *Guide* in the title.

- ✔ After you write the text, format the document so the layout is appropriate for a manual. If you're a formatting novice, use a template from word-processing or desktop-publishing software.

- ✔ Save the document in eBook format by using eBook-authoring software.

Expanding a manual into an eBook

A manual more than 100 pages long is not really different from an eBook. If you want to expand your manual into an eBook, you can include the following:

- ✔ In addition to the how-to steps, you can add stories and real-life examples, which make the eBook more fun for your audience.

- ✔ If your manual contains terms that may be unfamiliar to the reader, include a glossary.

- ✔ Include more advanced topics that may be of interest to the audience after he or she masters the basics described in the manual.

Chapter 10

Building a Simple eBook

*W*hen programmers learn a new programming language, "Hello World!" is usually the first application they learn how to code in the language. This program simply displays the words "Hello World!" onscreen after the program runs.

In this chapter, I show you how to create a "Hello World!" eBook. By following the steps in this chapter, you can create a simple eBook, incorporate an image into your eBook document, and learn the basics of an eBook's construction. You will construct your "Hello World!" eBook using the Open eBook Publication Structure specification. This spec is becoming the standard for eBooks in the same way that *HTML (HyperText Markup Language)* became the standard for hypertext documents. HTML tags let the Web browser know how to display the document after opening a file. The OEB spec uses HTML and *XML* (eXtensible Markup Language) tags to let an eBook reader know how to display an eBook after opening the file.

If you have an interest in knowing why things work the way they do, this chapter teaches you how eBooks are built. Some knowledge of HTML is helpful, but unnecessary for working through the examples in this chapter. If you're only interested in getting your eBook built as quickly as possible, skip this chapter and jump ahead to Chapter 11, which shows you how to use different eBook-authoring tools.

Understanding the Open eBook Publication Structure Specification

In the past few years, a consortium of publishers, hardware manufacturers, and software manufacturers have worked together to create a standard for developing eBooks, hoping that a common standard would enable the eBook industry to grow. With a standard in place, authors and publishers can write to a common eBook format that is recognized by all eBook readers, and that works on different hardware platforms (including PCs, handheld devices, and eBook readers). The result of this group's work is the Open eBook Publication Structure 1.0 (called the *Open eBook spec* for short), which was released in September 1999.

Some of the companies working to support the OEB spec include the following:

- Adobe Systems, Inc.
- Andersen Consulting
- Barnes & Noble, Inc.
- Everybook, Inc.
- Glassbook, Inc.
- Houghton Mifflin
- IBM Corporation
- IDG Books Worldwide, Inc.
- iUniverse.com
- McGraw-Hill
- Microsoft Corporation
- netLibrary, Inc.
- Palm, Inc.
- Random House, Inc.
- RR Donnelley & Sons Company
- Simon & Schuster
- SoftLock.com
- Time Warner

To get more information about the specification, go to the Open eBook Web site at `www.openbook.org`. You can see formatted eBook samples at `www.openebook.org/samples.htm`.

A standard based on HTML and XML

The Open eBook spec defines a set of tags that, when included in a document, tell the eBook reader how to structure and display the information. At the simplest level, you can write your text, include these tags, save the file, and *voilà!* — you've built an eBook. By adhering to a standard set of XML tags, publishers and authors can deliver their material in a single format that's recognized by all OEB-compliant devices.

The spec requires all conforming eBook readers to support XML, CSS, JPEG, and PNG files. If you create a document that supports these formats, and if you don't include any additional media types, then your eBook will be viewable on all eBook readers that support the spec for basic eBook documents. The rest of this chapter shows you how to build an OEB-compliant eBook, even if you're far from being an XML expert.

Expanding on the spec

The companies listed in the consortium are committed to supporting the basic Open eBook spec, but some companies are going beyond the spec to bring expanded functionality to eBooks.

OEB documents versus extended OEB documents

The Open eBook Publication Structure 1.0 specification describes the difference between basic OEB documents and Extended OEB documents. Basic OEB documents completely adhere to the requirements, tags, and document structure as described in the spec. Extended OEB documents meet the OEB common requirements, but may add elements and attributes not defined in the spec. These elements or attributes could be rich media types, such as video or sound, or external style sheets. Extended OEB documents work on common OEB readers, but the spec requires that a down level or fallback version of the file must be provided in one of the supported formats. In English, this means that if you want to include QuickTime movies in your eBook, for example, you need to provide a JPEG image to represent the movie for those eBook readers that don't support QuickTime.

Digital Rights Management

Members of the Open eBook Forum, the group that helps define the specification, are also involved with defining a proposal for how the spec can be expanded to include Digital Rights Management. This proposal is designed to protect publishers' rights to ensure that they are paid when someone reads the content of an eBook. This group leads the efforts to define a set of tags that allow an eBook to be encrypted, and to determine which sections can be viewed for free and what content needs to be paid for before someone can view it.

To find out more about the efforts of the Digital Rights Management Working Group, see its proposal and charter at `www.openebook.org/drm_wg_proposal.doc`.

Analyzing the Major Parts of an OEB File

In order for an eBook to conform to the OEB spec, several components need to be included in the eBook package. A standard eBook package has an OPF extension (Open eBook Package File), and includes the `package` identity, the `metadata` elements, the `manifest` element, the `spine`, the `tours` element, and the eBook guide. These items are defined in the following sections.

Package identity

An eBook may be composed of a number of separate files — these files are referenced by a `package` element. Another way to think of a `package` element is an XML document that contains references to all the other `package` elements that comprise the eBook.

Each `package` element must have a unique identifier, which helps to differentiate that eBook package from all others. You can think of the `package` identity as a unique name that you give your eBook to make sure that it can't be confused with any other eBooks.

Here's an overview of what the XML for an OEB `package` looks like:

```
<package>
     metadata
     manifest
     spine
     guide
</package>
```

Metadata elements

The metadata elements are data that applies to the entire eBook publication. You won't need to include all this information, but usually metadata elements include the following:

- ✔ eBook's title
- ✔ Creator (the primary author of the eBook)
- ✔ Subject
- ✔ Description
- ✔ Publisher
- ✔ Contributor (list of information about other people that contributed to the creation of your eBook)
- ✔ Publication date
- ✔ Type of eBook (a novel or poem, for example)
- ✔ Format
- ✔ ID (an ID for the file that can be referenced from the package element)
- ✔ Source (if the publication was derived from a prior source)
- ✔ Language
- ✔ Relation (how auxiliary files relate to the overall package)
- ✔ Coverage (the time or place that the eBook's content covers)
- ✔ Rights (the copyright notice and related information)

Here's an example of how the metadata elements appear in an eBook:

```
<metadata>
   <x-metadata>
     <meta name="price" content="USD 29.99"/>
   </x-metadata>
</metadata>
```

Manifest

The manifest is a list of all the files that go into the eBook. For each item listed in the manifest, you need to include an ID, a link to the file, and a specified MIME media type (which is another way to define what type of file the identified item is).

Here's an example of how the `manifest` appears in an eBook:

```
<manifest>
    <item id="intro" href="introduction.html"
        media-type="text/x-oeb1-document" />
    <item id="chap1" href="chapter1.html"
        media-type="text/x-oeb1-document" />
    <item id="chap2" href="chapter2.html"
        media-type="text/x-oeb1-document" />
    <item id="toc" href="tableofcontents.xml"
        media-type="text/x-oeb1-document" />
    <item id="image1" href="view.jpg"
        media-type="image/jpg" />
</manifest>
```

Spine

After the `manifest`, the eBook needs to have a `spine`, which defines the primary reading order for the publication. The `spine` tells the eBook reader which file should be shown first when the eBook is opened, and the order in which files should be displayed so the eBook reader's next-page function works properly. The `spine` only lists text files (`text/x-oeb1-document` media types), and it works by referencing the ID numbers given for each text file in the `manifest`.

The `spine` doesn't need to list all the text files that are contained in the eBook because some files may not need to be accessed through an eBook reader's next page/previous page feature. Files accessible through hyperlinks, for example, don't need to be listed in the eBook `spine` element.

A sample `spine` looks like this:

```
<spine>
    <itemref idref="toc" />
    <itemref idref="c1" />
    <itemref idref="c2" />
</spine>
```

In this sample `spine`, the eBook reader knows to display Chapter 1 immediately after the Table of Contents, and Chapter 2 immediately after the last page of Chapter 1.

The tours element

The spine provides the primary way to navigate through an eBook, but a tour can provide a suggested or additional method of navigation. An eBook doesn't need to contain a tour (and not all eBook readers support this option).

Each tour must be named with a unique tour ID. In addition to the ID, the tour element lists the title and links for the documents to be featured in the tour.

If you want to include a tour in your eBook, it's formatted like this:

```
<tours>
<tour id="tourSeattle" title="Tour of Seattle">
    <site title="Seattle Center"
            href="SpaceNeedle.html" />
    <site title="Puget Sound"
            href="Psound.html" />
</tour>
<tour id="tourRedmond" title="Tour of Redmond">
    <site title="The Microsoft Campus" href ="campus.html"
    />
    <site title="The RedWest campus" href="Redwest.html" />
</tour>
</tours>
```

eBook guide

The *eBook guide* lists any reference elements that may be included in the eBook. Like the tours element, guides aren't required, and may not be supported by all eBook readers. *Reference* elements are the sections of a publication that may be included to help a reader navigate through the information.

To create a guide, you need to provide the title, links, and reference type for each document to be included. Reference types can be one of the following:

- cover (which includes the book cover, jacket information, and so on)
- title-page (a page that includes the title, author, publisher, and similar metadata)
- toc (Table of Contents)
- index (the type of index included at the back of most non-fiction print books)

- ✔ glossary
- ✔ acknowledgements
- ✔ bibliography
- ✔ colophon (an inscription placed at the end of a book, or a publisher's emblem or trademark placed on the title page)
- ✔ copyright-page
- ✔ dedication
- ✔ epigraph (the motto or quotation shown at the beginning of a book that helps set the theme)
- ✔ foreword
- ✔ loi (List of Illustrations)
- ✔ lot (List of Tables)
- ✔ notes
- ✔ preface
- ✔ other (if you need to include a reference not shown in this list, the name of the reference must begin with the string other)

Complying with the OEB spec

To be compliant with the OEB spec, an eBook must meet the following minimum requirements:

- ✔ The eBook must include a single, well-formatted OEB package file (OPF) that meets the OEB requirements listed in the OEB spec.
- ✔ The metadata element of the package file must contain at least one dc:Identifier and at least one dc:Title element; the dc:Identifier should correctly reference the unique-identifier attribute of the package.
- ✔ If an extended value must be used to specify the dc:Contributor, the value of the role attribute must begin with an oth. string.
- ✔ The package file must include a single manifest, which lists each file incorporated in the eBook.
- ✔ The manifest must define a recognized MIME media type for each file used in the eBook publication.
- ✔ If you want to define your own unique reference type to be included in the guide, the value of the type attribute must begin with an oth. string.

If this seems like a bunch of meaningless jargon to you, hang tight. It'll all start to make sense when I show you, step-by-step, how to build an eBook.

Creating a Word Document

You probably already use a version of Word to write most of your documents, so it makes sense to build your first eBook using a tool that you're comfortable with. Although I start this chapter by promising to show you how to create a "Hello World" eBook, you actually need a little more text than just the words "Hello World."

1. **Open Word 2000 from the Windows Start menu, or by clicking the Word icon.**

   Word opens a new blank document.

   Although this may seem like a fine time to start working on your next novella, save the actual writing for another time. Instead of focusing on the words, I want you to concentrate on how to format a document correctly.

2. **Close the blank document that was created when you launched Word. Open an existing document by choosing File➪Open.**

   You can either open the sample HelloWonderland.doc file that's provided on the CD-ROM that came with this book, or open a document file that you have already created.

   If you work with an existing document, make sure that the text includes section headings formatted using Word's document styles. (Not sure what I'm talking about? Keep reading — I explain it all in the next section.)

Formatting your text using Word styles

You can just start typing in Word, but when you create a document that's over a page or two in length, you want to incorporate *paragraph styles.* These styles help organize the structure of your document and make it visually appealing to readers.

A *paragraph style* is a set of formatting characteristics that are named and applied to a section of the content. If I decide that my document headings should have a bold font, I can go through the text, highlight each heading, and then apply bold character formatting to each. But for a long document, this gets tiring, page after page. It would be easier if I created a style called *Heading 2,* so that the bold formatting is automatically applied whenever I add a Heading 2 paragraph to my document, as shown in Figure 10-1.

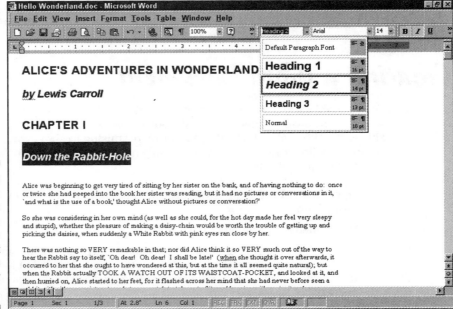

Figure 10-1:
You can
use Word's
paragraph
styles to
format
headings
in your
document.

To apply a paragraph style to text in your document, follow these steps:

1. **Make sure that the cursor is in the paragraph that you want to format by clicking somewhere within that paragraph.**

2. **Select the style that you want from the drop-down style control, which you can access from Word's Formatting toolbar.**

   In this example, I use the `HelloWonderland.doc` document. I click the Alice's Adventures In Wonderland line at the start of the document, and then I select the Heading 1 style.

   The document's title is updated. The font is now Arial and 16-point size, and the font style becomes bold.

3. **You can change another paragraph to a different style by selecting another type of style from the style control drop-down list.**

   I select the paragraph that reads By Lewis Carroll and choose Heading 2 from the style control. The font changes to 14-point size, and the font style becomes italicized and bold.

4. **Go through the remainder of the document and apply style formatting to all the paragraphs.**

The paragraph styles that come with Word's Normal template are useful — but only a few exist. To really customize a document, you have to create and save your own styles.

Creating new paragraph styles

For a simple eBook, the paragraph styles that come with Word's Normal template are enough to get you started, but when you create longer documents, you will want new styles. Word provides a very simple way to create new styles:

1. **Type the text for the paragraph that will be formatted using the new style.**

2. **Choose the font, the font size, and the font style to be used with the new paragraph style.**

   The easiest way to choose a new font is from the drop-down font list in the Word formatting toolbar. By clicking the down arrow, you can scroll through a list of all the fonts installed on your system.

   You can select the size of the font from the font size control, which is located to the right of the drop-down font list control box. You can type a number directly into the control box, or click the down arrow to choose from the different sizes available.

   You can select a font style by clicking the Bold, Italic, or Underline buttons in the formatting toolbar. You can also see more options by choosing Format➪Font. Under Effects, you can choose from all the effects associated with a different font.

   Just because you have the Alleycat font on your computer doesn't mean that everyone reading your eBook has the same font installed. Some eBook authoring tools let you embed fonts, so that everyone reading your eBook can see things the same way you do. Other authoring tools only work with the fonts installed on a reader's system. You should check the documentation that came with your authoring tool; if you are not able to embed fonts, you should only use *safe fonts* — fonts that are available on most computers. You can find a good list of safe fonts at `www.efuse.com/Design/web_fonts_ basics.html#WebSafeFonts`. If a font is considered safe for a Web page, it'll be okay for inclusion in your eBook.

3. **After you select the formatting for the new style on the formatting toolbar, click inside the Style box and type over the existing style name to give a name to the style that you just created.**

4. **Press Enter to save the new style name.**

   In the case of the Wonderland document, I created some new styles called Title, Author, Body, and Footnote.

I also updated the font used in the Heading 1 and Heading 2 styles by changing the font to Verdana. Here's how I did it:

1. **Select a paragraph formatted in the style that you want to change.**

2. **Choose the font, the font size, and the font style to be used with the modified style.**

3. **Try to reapply the style to be changed. (For example, if you used the Heading 1 style, but want to change the font to Verdana, change the paragraph to use the Verdana font, and then try to apply the Heading 1 style to the paragraph.)**

4. **A dialog box appears, asking whether you want to update the style to reflect the changes or reapply the formatting of the style to the selection.**

   To change the Heading 1 style to use the Verdana font throughout your document, select the Update the Style to Reflect the Changes option and click the OK button. The Heading 1 style is updated to use the Verdana font.

Another way to create a new style is to base it on an existing style and then make the necessary changes. To do this, follow these steps:

1. **Choose Format⇨Style.**

2. **Click the name of the style that you want to modify, and click the Modify button.**

3. **Click the Format button and select whether to change the font, paragraph, tabs, border, language, frame, or numbering for a particular style.**

4. **Click the Add to Template check box and click the OK button.**

5. **You can click the Organizer button in the Style dialog box to choose specific styles to save to a Word template.**

If you need to create different styles for different eBooks, creating a different template for each style helps you keep each group of styles together. You can create a template for children's eBooks and a different template for adult fiction.

Adding images to a Word document

You can add images in Word to be incorporated into your eBook. Follow these steps to do it:

1. **In Word, choose Insert⇨Picture.**

2. **Select the From File option.**

   The Insert Picture window appears, as shown in Figure 10-2.

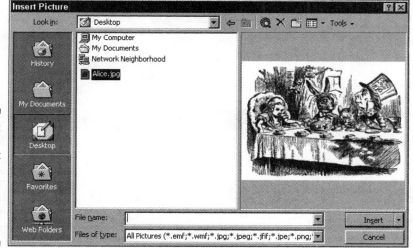

Figure 10-2: You can use the Insert Picture window to add an image to your eBook.

3. **Select the folder where the picture is located from the Look In drop-down list.**

4. **You can insert the picture by double-clicking the name of the picture, or by typing the image's filename into the text box and clicking the Insert button.**

   Word inserts the selected picture into your document. If you're working on my sample Hello Wonderland.doc file, you can add the alice.jpg image, as shown in Figure 10-3. (This image is available on the CD-ROM included in this book.)

Figure 10-3:
You can
spruce up
your eBook
by adding
an image,
such as
alice.jpg,
to your
document.

Converting Your Document to HTML

After you add images to your document, it's time to convert it from a Word file format to HTML. This is the next step in preparing a basic OEB document. Before saving your document as HTML, save a copy of the document in the .doc file format. That way, you have a backup copy in the event that you want to start over.

Setting your Web options in Word

Before you save your document as a Web page, you need to modify your settings in Word. To modify your settings to optimize the type of HTML that you produce for your eBook, follow these steps:

1. **In Word, choose Tools⇨Options.**

   The Options dialog box appears, as shown in Figure 10-4.

2. **Click the General tab.**

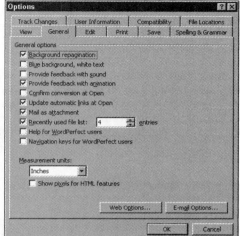

Figure 10-4:
The Options
dialog box
allows you
to modify
your
settings in
Word.

3. **Click the Web Options button.**

   The Web Options dialog box appears, as shown in Figure 10-5.

Figure 10-5:
In the Web
Options
dialog box,
make sure
that the
General tab
is showing
and both
Appearance
options are
selected.

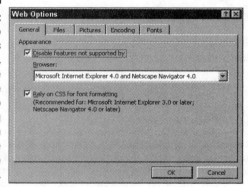

4. **Click the General tab.**

   Make sure that the Disable Features Not Supported By check box is
   selected, and the Web browser shown in the Browser drop-down list is
   Microsoft Internet Explorer 4.0 and Netscape Navigator 4.0. The Rely on
   CSS for Font Formatting check box should also be selected.

5. Click the Files tab.

Under the Filenames and Locations group, make sure that Organize Supporting Files in a Folder is unchecked, and make sure that Use Long Filenames Whenever Possible and Update Links on Save are checked.

In the Default Editor panel, make sure that the Check if Office Is the Default Editor for Web Pages Created in Office check box is selected, as shown in Figure 10-6. You can decide whether to select the Check if Word Is the Default Editor for all Other Web Pages option. If you plan on only using Word to author HTML files, check the option (otherwise, leave it unchecked).

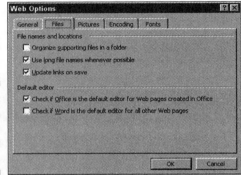

Figure 10-6:
The Files tab in the Web Options dialog box.

6. Click the Pictures tab.

Under the File Formats group, make sure that the Rely on VML for Displaying Graphics in Browsers option is unchecked. The Allow PNG as an Output Format option should be checked because PNG is one of the two image file formats allowed by the OEB spec.

You can decide how to set the options shown under the Target Monitor group. If you know your eBook will be displayed on a PC monitor, you can leave the screen size at 800 x 600. If you're creating an eBook that'll be displayed on a small screen (like that found on the Rocket eBook device), change the setting to display fewer pixels per inch. For this exercise in creating a simple OEB file, you can leave Word's default settings.

If you use Word to create many OEB documents, you may want to experiment with the screen size and the resolution (pixels per inch) that work best for your needs.

7. Click the Encoding tab.

Make sure that the Unicode (UTF-8) option is selected from the Save this Document As drop-down list, as shown in Figure 10-7.

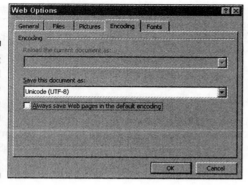

Figure 10-7:
You should
select the
Unicode
(UTF-8)
option in the
Encoding
tab.

Make sure that the Always Save Web Pages in the Default Encoding check box is checked if you plan to work on many OEB documents, because UTF-8 is the encoding recommended by the OEB spec.

8. **Click the Fonts tab, as shown in Figure 10-8.**

Because you're creating a simple OEB document, leave the default settings as is. If you create eBooks for international distribution, however, you may want to experiment with different character sets by changing these settings.

Figure 10-8:
You can
leave the
default
settings
shown on
the Fonts
tab as is.

9. **Click the OK button on the Web Options dialog box.**

Saving the document

You can save the document as an HTML file by choosing File⇨Save As Web Page from the menu. Give your file a name and make sure that Web Page (*.htm; *.html) shows in the Save As Type drop-down list.

Word creates a Web page — the file with the .htm extension. After you save your HTML document, open it in your Web browser by double-clicking the icon associated with your HTML file. The Web page that you just created is displayed in your Web browser.

Viewing the HTML source

After you confirm that you can open your Web page in your Web browser, review the HTML source code. You can do this by choosing View⇨Source in Internet Explorer.

You can also view the HTML source code by opening the Notepad program that comes with Windows:

1. **Click the Windows Start button and select Run from the menu.**

   The Run dialog box appears, as shown in Figure 10-9.

Figure 10-9:
You can launch the Notepad application from the Run dialog box.

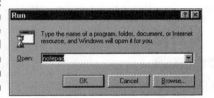

2. **Type** notepad **in the text box and click the OK button.**

   The Notepad application opens, as shown in Figure 10-10.

3. **Open the folder where you saved the HTML file created in Word.**

4. **Drag the icon associated with your HTML file into the open Notepad window.**

   This action opens your HTML file in Notepad. Now you can see what the source code looks like.

If you're familiar with basic HTML code, you may notice that Word throws in a lot of extra XML markup tags, along with the HTML for displaying the basic document. These XML tags allow Word to *round trip* your document. Round trip means that you can write a Word document, save it as HTML, view it in your Web browser, open the document again in Word to make editing changes, and then save it again as a .doc file, if you want. Figure 10-11 shows an example of what your HTML code may look like in Notepad.

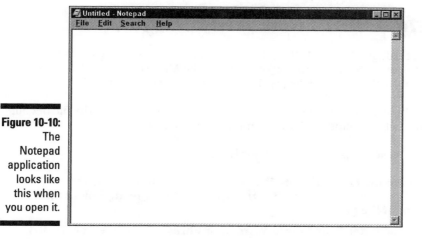

Figure 10-11:
The HTML
code for
your
document
looks like
this when
it's opened
in Notepad.
Word adds
extra XML
tags for
round-
tripping
between the
Word DOC
and HTML
formats.

```
Hello Wonderland.htm - Notepad
File   Edit   Search   Help
<html xmlns:v="urn:schemas-microsoft-com:vml"
xmlns:o="urn:schemas-microsoft-com:office:office"
xmlns:w="urn:schemas-microsoft-com:office:word"
xmlns:dt="uuid:C2F41010-65B3-11d1-A29F-00AA00C14882"
xmlns="http://www.w3.org/TR/REC-html40">

<head>
<meta http-equiv=Content-Type content="text/html; charset=utf-8">
<meta name=ProgId content=Word.Document>
<meta name=Generator content="Microsoft Word 9">
<meta name=Originator content="Microsoft Word 9">
<link rel=File-List href="./Hello%20Wonderland_files/filelist.xml">
<link rel=Edit-Time-Data href="./Hello%20Wonderland_files/editdata.mso">
<!--[if !mso]>
<style>
v\:* {behavior:url(#default#VML);}
o\:* {behavior:url(#default#VML);}
w\:* {behavior:url(#default#VML);}
.shape {behavior:url(#default#VML);}
</style>
<![endif]-->
<title>ALICE'S ADVENTURES IN WONDERLAND</title>
<!--[if gte mso 9]><xml>
 <o:DocumentProperties>
  <o:Author>Victoria Rosenborg</o:Author>
  <o:LastAuthor>Lewis Carroll</o:LastAuthor>
  <o:Revision>2</o:Revision>
  <o:TotalTime>15</o:TotalTime>
  <o:Created>2000-06-27T14:54:00Z</o:Created>
  <o:LastSaved>2000-06-27T14:54:00Z</o:LastSaved>
  <o:Pages>5</o:Pages>
  <o:Words>1664</o:Words>
  <o:Characters>9485</o:Characters>
  <o:Company>IDG Books Worldwide</o:Company>
  <o:Bytes>136192</o:Bytes>
```

XML makes round-tripping possible. Round-tripping is useful if you plan to use Word as your primary HTML editor. If you're creating a simple eBook, though, you don't need to round-trip, so you can delete all those unnecessary XML tags.

Removing Unneeded XML Tags

Going through all the HTML code in your document to remove line after line of unneeded XML is a tedious job. Luckily, the Microsoft Office team has a nifty tool, called *HTML Filter,* which does the dirty work for you.

A side benefit of removing unnecessary XML is that the size of the file becomes smaller, which helps readers download your file faster!

Follow these steps to clean up your HTML file:

1. **Go to the Office Update Web site at** `http://officeupdate.microsoft.com/` **and click the <u>Search Office Update</u> link at the top of the page.**

2. **In the Enter Your Search Word(s) or Phrase textbox, enter** HTML Filter **and pick Exact Phrase from the Select Your Search Criteria drop-down list.**

3. **Click the Search Now! button.**

   The search returns a list of different results, as shown in Figure 10-12.

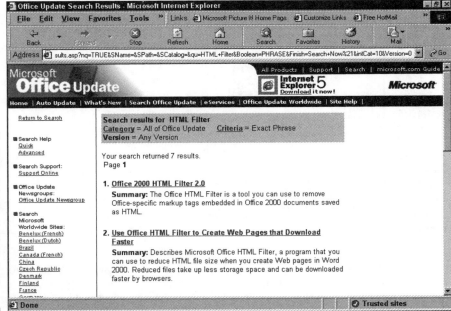

Figure 10-12: These results are returned when you search for HTML Filter on the Office Update Web site.

4. **Click the <u>Office 2000 HTML Filter 2.0</u> link.**

   This action takes you to a page where you can download the utility.

5. **Click the <u>Download Now!</u> link at the top-left corner of the Web page.**

   Follow the instructions given in the dialog boxes to copy the `Msohtmf2.exe` program file to a folder on your hard drive. The file downloads.

   Note: Shut down Word if you have it running.

6. **Double-click the `Msohtmf2.exe` file.**

   The HTML Filter installation program starts.

7. **To finish installing the filter, follow the instructions.**

Using the HTML filter to peel your files

After you install the HTML filter, you can use it to "peel" the XML markup from the file that you want to create for your eBook. To peel the XML tags from your file, follow these steps:

1. **Open your file in Word 2000.**

   In this example, I opened the Hello Wonderland document that I've been working on by right-clicking the file icon and selecting Edit from the right context menu.

2. **Choose File⇨Export To and choose the Compact HTML option.**

   The Export To HTML As dialog box appears, as shown in Figure 10-13.

Figure 10-13:
You can name your file and save it to a folder on your hard drive in the Export To HTML As dialog box.

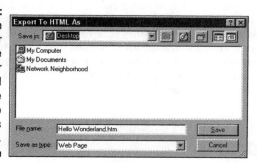

3. **Name your file and save it to the folder on your hard drive.**

4. **Open the HTML file in Notepad to view the HTML code without Word's additional XML markup.**

   The XML has been peeled from the HTML file, and you're ready to start creating the OPF file, which identifies the files that comprise your eBook.

After you use the filter to remove Word's XML markup, the round tripping tags are lost. If you want to make changes to the document, open the original .doc file and export it to HTML again, instead of trying to open and edit the Web page in Word.

Using other applications to create HTML files

If you're like me, most of your writing is probably done in Word. (Well . . . most of my writing is actually done in an e-mail program, but Word is a close second.) The steps I list in this chapter let you use Word to write and create the HTML files for your eBook. When you focus on getting the words down on-screen, it makes sense to use the program in which you're most comfortable.

If you prefer to use a different program to create Web pages (like Notepad, FrontPage, Dreamweaver, and so on), you won't need to go through the extra step of peeling XML tags out of the file. You can write in Word and copy the text into your Web-editing program, or you can just write in your Web-editing program.

Note: Be sure to use UTF-8 encoding when saving your HTML and to use PNG instead of GIF image files.

If you choose to copy text from Word, wait until you bring it into your Web-editing program to format headlines and other paragraph styles. Copying formatted text from Word into another editing program can have mixed results. If you choose to write within your Web-editing program, be careful about how you use tables to display your content. Although tables allow you to create a good-looking Web page when the page is displayed in a Web browser, an eBook reader may not have the same support for tables (or may have a much smaller screen that's unable to display the page properly).

Building the eBook

Now that you have an HTML file, you're ready to build your first eBook. What differentiates an eBook from a basic Web page is the eBook *package file*. This file bundles the other files associated with the eBook, provides a structure, and dictates the order in which the files should be read.

Creating an OPF file

A package file contains information for the metadata, manifest, spine, and guide associated with the eBook. All you need to create a package file is Notepad, although you can use any HTML editor as long as it doesn't add any extraneous tags to the text of the file. To create a package file in Notepad, follow these steps:

1. **Open Notepad to create a new, blank text file and add the following lines of code:**

   ```
   <?xml version="1.0"?>
   <!DOCTYPE package
      PUBLIC "+//ISBN 0-9673008-1-9//DTD OEB 1.0 Package//EN"
      "http://openebook.org/dtds/oeb-1.0/oebpkg1.dtd">
   ```

   The first line identifies the document as being an XML file and the remaining lines point to the eBook *DTD*. A DTD is a document-type definition and helps to define the common XML tags used in a specific document. In this case, two DTDs are used to define eBooks. A package DTD defines the tags needed to find the components of an eBook and how those components should be organized. The basic OEB document DTD defines the tags that can be incorporated into the eBook document.

   Although the OEB specification supports many HTML tags, not all *W3C-* recognized tags are supported. (W3C is the *World Wide Web Consortium,* the governing body that recommends tags that can be added to the HTML specification.) If you plan on creating many eBooks without using a specialized authoring tool, take the time to review the specification to make sure that readers can open your eBooks without problems.

2. **You can now add tags that specify the eBook package.**

   You need to give the package identifier (the part between the quotation marks) a unique name.

   Because I'm creating an OPF file for my Wonderland document, I add the following package tag to the file:

   ```
   <package unique-identifier="wonderlandebook">
   ```

3. **Identify any** metadata **tags that need to be added to your eBook.**

   These metadata tags help identify global information about your eBook (for example, the title, the author, and a summary of the publication). You want to add as many tags as possible because this information helps readers search through multiple publications to find an item that interests them.

   At a minimum, the metadata tag needs to have an identifier and a title element. The identifier needs to reference the unique identifier that you used in the package tag.

XML is a way for different groups to agree on a common set of definitions for a set of tags. Sometimes, two or more groups may use the same set of tags (but the use of the tags may vary). To avoid confusion, an XML document declares a *namespace*. A namespace is a prefix used with a colon before a tag to help identify whose definition of the XML tag should be used.

OEB documents used a group of XML tags with the *dc:* prefix. This means that the document recognizes `metadata` attributes defined by the *Dublin Core Directorate* (another standards group that works to define a common set of tags for digital documents).

`Metadata` tags that you can add to your `package` file include:

- `<dc:Title> </dc:Title>`
- `<dc:Creator> </dc:Creator>`
- `<dc:Subject> </dc:Subject>`
- `<dc:Description> </dc:Description>`
- `<dc:Publisher> </dc:Publisher>`
- `<dc:Contributor> </dc:Contributor>`
- `<dc:Date> </dc:Date>`
- `<dc:Type> </dc:Type>`
- `<dc:Format> </dc:Format>`
- `<dc:Identifier> </dc:Identifier>`
- `<dc:Source> </dc:Source>`
- `<dc:Language> </dc:Language>`
- `<dc:Relation> </dc:Relation>`
- `<dc:Coverage> </dc:Coverage>`
- `<dc:Rights> </dc:Rights>`

The following links need to be included in the `metadata` tag of your OPF file to ensure that the namespace declarations work correctly:

```
xmlns:dc="dc/elements/1.0/"and xmlns:oebpackage=
        "http://openebook.org/namespaces/
        oeb-package/1.0/"
```

The metadata section of my OPF file looks like this:

```
<metadata xmlns:dc="http://purl.org/dc/elements/1.0/"
        xmlns:oebpackage="http://openebook.org/
        namespaces/oeb-package/1.0/">
```

```
    <dc-metadata>
        <dc:Identifier id="wonderlandebook"
    scheme="adhoc">wonderland0627</dc:Identifier>
        <dc:Title>Alice in Wonderland</dc:Title>
        <dc:Creator role="aut" file-as="Carroll,
    Lewis">Lewis Carroll</dc:Creator>
    </dc-metadata>
</metadata>
```

4. Add the `manifest` **section of the eBook package.**

This lists every file that has been incorporated into the eBook. In addition to listing every file, the MIME media-type of each file must be specified in the `manifest`. (For more information about MIME media types, see the Web site `www.ietf.org/rfc/rfc1738.txt`.) See the warning at the end of this list to correctly add the names of the new image files to the `manifest`.

5. Add the single text type file to the `spine`.

You can use the item ID name that you assigned to a file in the `manifest` to reference the elements in the `spine`.

```
        In the case of the Wonderland eBook, I assigned
        the Hello Wonderland.htm file an item ID called
        doc, so this is the ID that I reference in the
        spine:<spine>
    <itemref idref="doc"/></spine>
        Because this is a simple eBook, I haven't
        included tours or guide sections, so the only
        thing left to do is to review the entire package
        before saving the file. Here's what my final
        package file looks like:<?xml
        version="1.0"?><!DOCTYPE package
    PUBLIC "+//ISBN 0-9673008-1-9//DTD OEB 1.0 Package//EN"
    "http://openebook.org/dtds/oeb-1.0/oebpkg1.dtd">
        <package unique-identifier="wonderlandebook">
    <metadata xmlns:dc="http://purl.org/dc/
        elements/1.0/"
        xmlns:oebpackage="http://openebook.org/
        namespaces/oeb-package/1.0/">
            <dc-metadata>
                <dc:Identifier id="wonderlandebook"
    scheme="adhoc">wonderland0627</dc:Identifier>
                <dc:Title>Alice in
    Wonderland</dc:Title>
                <dc:Creator role="aut" file-
    as="Carroll, Lewis">Lewis Carroll</dc:Creator>
    </dc-metadata>
```

```
            </metadata>
            <manifest>
                <item id="doc" href="Hello Wonderland.htm"
                media-type="text/x-oeb1-document" />
                <item id="ALice_Image"
                href="Hello%20Wonderland_image002.jpg" media-
                type="image/jpg" />
            </manifest>
            <spine>
                <itemref idref="doc"/>
            </spine>
        </package>
```

6. **Save your document in Notepad with an OPF file extension.**

   For the Wonderland eBook, I saved the package in a file called
   Wonderland.opf.

Word assigns a default name to any image file used in the creation of a Web
page, regardless of the image's original filename. The new names for each
image file need to be added to the `manifest`.

1. **Open the file in Notepad to find out the name of the image files used
   in your HTML file.**

2. **Choose Search⇨Find.**

   The Find dialog box appears, as shown in Figure 10-14.

Figure 10-14:
You can use
Notepad's
Find dialog
box to
search for
JPG and
PNG files
in your
HTML file.

3. **Type** .jpg **in the text box and click the Find Next button.**

   Make sure that you start searching from the beginning text of the file and
   that the Down radio button is selected.

4. **Each time you find a JPG file, copy the name of the file.**

The name of the .jpg file is contained between two quotation marks. In the case of the Hello Wonderland.htm file, the only JPG file is `Hello%20Wonderland_image002.jpg`.

Continue searching until you have found all the JPG files featured in the document.

5. **Repeat the same process, but look for all the .png files in the document.**

   After you search for all the PNG and JPG files, a list of image filenames are added to the `manifest`.

For the Wonderland eBook, you only created a single HTML file and a single image file to be listed in the manifest. The following lines are added to the package file:

```
<manifest>
<item id="doc" href="Hello Wonderland.htm"
media-type="text/x-oeb1-document" />
<item id="ALice_Image"
href="Hello%20Wonderland_image002.jpg" media-
type="image/jpg" /></manifest>
```

Testing Your Document

In theory, the great thing about standards is that when they're followed, a single file can be opened on a variety of eBook readers. Unfortunately, most of the readers on the market today don't provide support for basic OEB files — not yet, anyway. Until more companies start supporting the standard, it may be hard for you to view the OEB eBooks that you create.

Wait a moment . . . you didn't think I would take you through so much work just to tell you that your file can't be opened? I wouldn't do that to you! Luckily, the Opera 4.0 browser provides some support for basic OEB. You can see the `metadata` information shown in your package file and click links to the files listed in your `manifest`.

Downloading and installing the Opera 4.0 browser

Different versions of the Opera browser are available for multiple platforms, including Windows 95, Windows 98, Windows NT, and Windows 2000. To download and install the Opera 4.0 browser, follow these steps:

1. **Go to** www.operasoftware.com/download.html **and click the link associated with your operating system.**

2. **Download sites are shown, grouped by geographical location; click the appropriate link for the site closest to you.**

   Some of the links are for 4.0, while others are for 4.0 with Java. Opera recommends that you have a *JVM,* or *Java Virtual Machine* (code which allows you to run Java applets) installed on your system to make full use of the browser.

   If you are planning to use Opera as your primary browser, go for the Java version. But if you're only installing Opera to view your eBook files, don't bother. You can open OPF files without the JVM, and you save some time on the download.

   The File Download dialog box appears, as shown in Figure 10-15.

Figure 10-15:
The File Download dialog box asks you whether the file should run from the current location or be saved to disk. In this case, you want to select the Save This Program to Disk option.

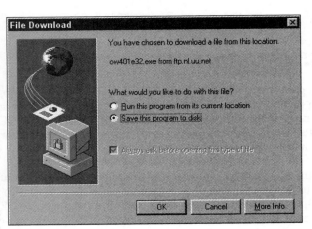

3. **Select the folder where you want to save the file.**

   The Opera executable (.exe) file downloads.

4. **Double-click the file to start the installation process.**

   Follow the instructions to install Opera.

5. **Double-click the Opera 4.0 icon on your desktop to start Opera.**

   Note: If an error message displays after you open the browser, warning you that you haven't installed the Java Virtual Machine, just ignore it. (It won't make a difference in your ability to open OPF files.)

   Close any windows open in the Opera browser before you attempt to open your eBook.

Opening your eBook

You can open the eBook that you created very easily. To open your eBook, follow these steps:

1. **Drag your OPF file over to the Opera browser.**

   The file opens in the browser and you're able to see your eBook's metadata, as shown in Figure 10-16.

2. **Click the links to open the files associated with your eBook.**

Figure 10-16: The Hello Wonderland eBook package is shown in the Opera 4.0 browser. You can click the **Hello Wonderland. htm** link to open the Web page in the browser.

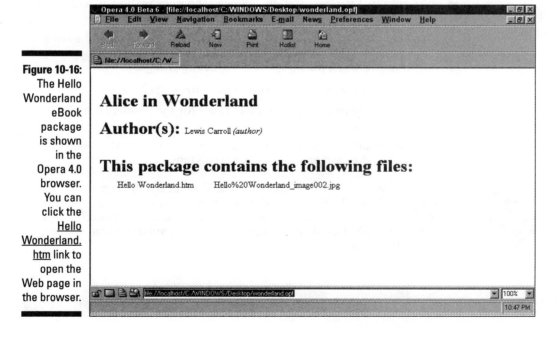

Correcting any problems

You've carefully created your package file and, with great anticipation, moved it over to the Opera browser and — ta-da! — nothing happens. Before you tear your hair out in frustration, here are some things to check:

✔ Does every tag have a corresponding end tag? If you have a `<manifest>` tag, is there a `</manifest>` tag to go with it? HTML can be forgiving about formatting errors, but XML is picky. Check and double-check your code to make sure you haven't forgotten an end tag somewhere.

✔ If you still can't spot any errors, try dragging your OPF file into the Internet Explorer browser. If your XML is well-structured, the browser displays the contents of the file. If there's a problem somewhere, Internet Explorer displays the number of the line containing the problem to help you troubleshoot.

If you try to open the OPF file in Internet Explorer, make sure you are online. Because external style sheets are referenced in XML, Internet Explorer needs to link to these style sheets to display the OPF file properly.

✔ Make sure that you've carefully followed the rules on how to make your eBook OEB-compliant. Here are some things to look out for:

• Forgetting to include one of the following in the OPF file: the required metadata, the manifest, or the spine; or forgetting to wrap everything between the `<package></package>` tags.

• Forgetting to include all your files in the `manifest`.

• Forgetting to include the MIME types for the files listed in the `manifest`.

• Forgetting to include either the `identifier` or `title` elements within the `<metadata></metadata>` tags.

If all else fails, you can try the OEB Validator Tool, available from Brown University and NuvoMedia. The tool is available at `www.stg.brown.edu/ service/oebvalid/index.html`. In addition to helping you identify errors in your XML, the site has plenty of good information about converting your HTML to OEB format.

Chapter 11

Using Authoring Tools to Create eBooks

· ·

In This Chapter

▶ Selecting an authoring tool

▶ Building eBooks for various eBook readers

▶ Testing your eBook's format

· ·

*1*n this chapter, I demonstrate different software packages that you can use to author your eBook. I try to use shareware or freeware as examples in the creation of content, but you may need to purchase software to build the final document. In addition to telling you the software that you need to create eBooks, this chapter shows you the basics of using different authoring tools to create a simple eBook.

Most of the software packages that I mention in this chapter are in the beta phase of development or are a Version 1.0 product. Because of this, you may run into a bug or glitch when you create an eBook. If you notice a problem, contact the Web site of the software publisher to report the issue and find out whether a *workaround* (a set of alternate steps you can take to achieve a desired result) is available. You should also offer to sign up as a beta tester of the next version release. eBook technology is in its infancy and you can help your own publishing efforts by keeping up with authoring tool improvements as they become available.

Competing Document Standards

Before you can determine what software to buy, you need to decide what eBook formats you want to support. I hope that a single standard emerges in the future, but until that day comes (if it ever does), three standards seem to stand out from the rest: Adobe Acrobat Reader, Microsoft Reader, and the Rocket eBook. The following list summarizes the three standards:

- ✔ **Adobe Acrobat Reader:** Acrobat has the largest installed base of users. Acrobat has the advantage of being cross-platform, which means that versions of this eBook reader exist for Windows PCs and for Macintosh. Additionally, the GlassBook Reader opens Acrobat files.

- ✔ **Microsoft Reader:** The Microsoft Reader will be featured on the new eBookMan devices, and the reader is bundled with every Pocket PC device. Microsoft offers a free Word add-in that enables you to create eBooks from Word documents. Because of these efforts, and because the reader's patented ClearType technology improves the experience of reading onscreen, the Microsoft Reader is emerging as an important standard.

- ✔ **Rocket eBook:** Two new versions of the Rocket are planned: one will be offered at a price designed to be competitive with the eBookMan, and the other version will be a high-end model with a color screen. RCA has a large launch planned for the product, designed to increase sales before the Christmas 2000 selling season. For this reason, it's a good idea to offer a version of your eBooks in the Rocket eBook format.

Another standard may yet show up and be the clear winner, but for today, place your bets on these three formats. Additionally, you need to store your *source files* (the content files you use to create eBooks) in a style that makes it easy for you to convert your document from one format to another.

So many options . . .

As with any major new technology, companies compete to own the standard in order to make the most profit. Although Company X may give the reader away for free, authors need to buy the authoring tool in order to create eBooks, and publishers have to pay a royalty on every eBook sold. Owning a major technology standard is like having a license to print money, so everyone wants a piece of the action.

Too many standards can hurt an emerging market. Publishers won't publish eBooks unless enough people have installed readers. People won't install readers unless enough titles are available to make the download and installation worthwhile. So if the market is fragmented among five or six readers, it's possible that eBooks may never become a product in every household.

In an effort to help the eBook industry, a number of publishers and hardware and software manufacturers have joined the Open eBook Consortium. This group works to create an *OEB* standard for eBooks. With a single standard (instead of different competing formats), publishers can save files in a single XML-based format that can be read by a variety of readers and hardware `devices. The work of the OEB Consortium resulted in functional specifications for supporting the first release of the standard. To date, the readers on the market aren't able to read OEB files that adhere to the standard, but a number of authoring tools are able to import OEB files.

Creating and storing your eBook source files

For now, using Microsoft Word is the best way to author the text for your eBook files because a number of authoring tools let you import Word documents. HTML is also a good way to store your document files. HTML makes it easy to create links within a document, and many authoring tools can convert HTML to their proprietary eBook format.

Another good format for source files is the OEB format, which lets you include metadata information about the document (metadata includes the title, name of the author, the publisher, copyright information, and so on) along with the source content files. For more information on the OEB file format, see Chapter 10.

The best way to store your image files is in JPEG format. JPEG is a very common image file format; many of the images found on Web pages are JPEG images.

Table 11-1 shows the file formats that can be imported into the authoring tools for the three most popular readers. This table also shows the file formats that the authoring tools can export to.

Table 11-1	Import and Export Formats for eBook Authoring Tools	
eBook Software	**File Types It Imports**	**File Types It Exports**
Adobe Acrobat 4.0	Adobe Acrobat, Adobe FrameMaker, ASCII text, HTML, WordPerfect, Microsoft Excel, Microsoft PowerPoint, Microsoft Word, PostScript, and image files (GIF, TIF, PNG, JPG, JPE, BMP, and PCX)	Adobe Acrobat (PDF), PostScript, and EPS
Microsoft Reader Add-in	Word documents, HTML, and image files (JPG, GIF, PNG,BMP, and TIF)	LIT files (Microsoft Reader)

(continued)

Table 11-1 *(continued)*

eBook Software	File Types It Imports	File Types It Exports
ReaderWorks Publisher	Text files, Microsoft HTML Document 5.0 files, Open eBook Package files, and image files (JPG, JPE, GIF, and PNG)	LIT files (Microsoft Reader)
The RocketLibrarian	Text files, HTML files, and Rocket eBook (RB) files	Rocket eBook (RB) files

Creating the largest audience for your work

Producing your eBooks in just one file format is cheaper, but to make money from your ePublishing efforts, you need to support a few of the most common formats. I have Adobe Acrobat on my work and home PCs, but Microsoft Reader is my favorite. I love reading on my Pocket PC while I commute to and from work. After you try a number of readers for handheld devices, you may find that Microsoft Reader has the best readability because of its ClearType technology.

Preventing eBook piracy

Digital Rights Management (DRM) is a methodology for encrypting files so that only a purchaser of the eBook receives a key to allow him or her to unlock and read the encrypted file. DRM software acts like a wrapper around your file and prevents unauthorized access of the eBook content. Some DRM software works so that only the user of the computer the file was downloaded to can open the eBook. Other DRM software makes the user enter a password before permitting access to the file. Although there are a number of companies that offer DRM solutions (including Reciprocal, OverDrive, and Lightening Source, among others), these solutions can be costly and are not designed for the needs of a small ePublisher.

Even if you pay a vendor to provide you with DRM technologies, there's no guarantee that a hacker won't be able to crack the encryption (as Simon and Schuster discovered when bootleg versions of Stephen King's *Riding the Bullet* began showing up on the Web 48 hours after the eBook was released). If you have sensitive data that must be secured, the least expensive solution is to use Adobe Acrobat to create secure files.

After you invest in software for the different authoring tools that you need, it only takes a little more time to offer multiple reader formats. If you want to stand out from other small ePublishers and reach the largest possible audience for your work, you should publish in at least three eBook formats.

Software That You Need to Build eBooks

If you want to create eBooks for the Acrobat Reader, the Microsoft Reader, and the Rocket eBook, Table 11-2 lists the software that you need to get started. I did a quick search on Microwarehouse.com to give you a rough idea of the prices for each software package. The prices may change, or you may be able to get a better price by shopping around. You may be able to cut some corners by not getting these packages or by supporting your eBook on a single eBook reader, but if you're serious about the business of ePublishing, I recommend you get all the software mentioned here.

Table 11-2	Software Shopping List for Creating eBooks	
Software	*Approximate Cost*	*Where It's Available*
Adobe Acrobat 4.0	$230	Most software distributors
Microsoft FrontPage (optional)	$130	Most software distributors
Microsoft Office 2000/ Small Business Edition	$430 (only $210 for the upgrade from an earlier version of Office)	Most software distributors
Microsoft Office HTML Filter	Free	`officeupdate.` `microsoft.com/` and search for *HTML filter*
Microsoft Reader Add-in for Word	Free	`www.microsoft.` `com/reader`
OverDrive ReaderWorks Publisher	$120	`www.overdrive.` `com/readerworks/` `software/` `publisher.asp`
RocketLibrarian	Free	`www.rocket-ebook.com/` `Readers/Software/` `index.html`
Softbook Personal Publisher	Free	`www.softbook.com/` `enterprise/` `personal.asp`

In addition to the software listed in Table 11-2, you may want to buy other software tools, such as image-editing software, software to zip and compress files, FTP software for transferring files, an HTML editor, and so on. To save money, go to ZDNet.com (www.zdnet.com) and search for shareware downloads to meet these needs. If you find that you use a tool often, you can purchase it after the evaluation period has ended.

Adobe Acrobat 4.0

Of all the eBook readers available, Acrobat is the only one that's designed to retain the look of a page that has been formatted for print. If you build an eBook from a document that was originally created for print, Acrobat lets you retain the fonts and layout created for the printed version. Because of this, Acrobat documents look best when displayed on larger screens. If you want to build eBooks that look best on handheld devices, you should consider authoring for the Microsoft Reader, which runs on Windows desktops or Pocket PC devices.

Getting and installing the software

Although the Acrobat Reader is free and can be downloaded from Adobe's Web site, the Adobe Acrobat 4.0 software, which is what you need to author Acrobat documents, must be purchased. The software can be obtained through any retailer that sells computer software. The list price on Adobe's Web site is $249, although you may be able to find a discount if you shop around.

Building an eBook with Acrobat

After you install the Acrobat software, you're ready to begin creating Acrobat eBooks. However, Acrobat doesn't let you create the original content to be featured in the eBook. Instead, it acts as an integrator, letting you pull in content from different sources and distilling the results into an integrated document.

Before you create a simple eBook with Acrobat, you need to organize the text, images, and any other content that you plan to use. Copy everything that you need into a single folder so you know exactly where to find your materials.

The following steps show you how to combine multiple documents into a single Acrobat file:

1. **Open Adobe Acrobat.**

2. **Open a Word document in Acrobat by choosing File➪Open.**

The Open dialog box appears.

3. **In the Files of Type drop-down list, choose Microsoft Word (*.doc). Then click the name of the Word document that you want to open and click the Open button, as shown in Figure 11-1.**

Figure 11-1:
Select the
Word file
that you
want to
open by
highlighting
the filename
and clicking
Open.

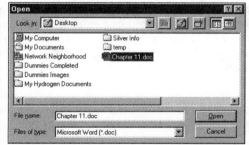

Acrobat opens the Word document and distills it to the Acrobat file format. Depending on the size of the Word document, this process can take a few minutes. After the file converts and is displayed in Acrobat, you can start to add content.

4. **Use the features of the Acrobat authoring tool to add images, links, and additional media. You can also password protect the eBook file.**

5. **After you finish working on your document, choose File⇨Save As to save the document as a PDF file.**

The Save As dialog box appears, as shown in Figure 11-2.

You can distribute this PDF file by e-mail or make it available for download from a Web site as an eBook.

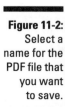

Figure 11-2:
Select a
name for the
PDF file that
you want
to save.

Using Microsoft's Reader Add-In for Word

Microsoft makes a free tool that lets you create files formatted for the Microsoft Reader. After you download and install the tool, you can create a Microsoft Reader file by clicking a single button in Microsoft Word 2000. This tool is useful, but you shouldn't use it to create files that will be sold to customers, because you can't add cover images. (For that, and other customization options, you need OverDrive's ReaderWorks software, which is described in the next section.)

The Reader Add-in tool is useful for creating a simple eBook draft and seeing how the eBook looks on a desktop computer or Pocket PC. After you're satisfied with how the document looks, you can create the final version with ReaderWorks.

Unlike Adobe Acrobat, which has both Macintosh and Windows versions, the Microsoft Reader Add-in requires the Windows platform. To be able to use the add-in, you need the following:

- ✔ Microsoft Word 2000
- ✔ A Pentium 75 (or higher) processor
- ✔ One of the following operating systems: Microsoft Windows 98 or 2000, Windows NT 4, or Windows Me
- ✔ 16MB of RAM
- ✔ 1MB of free space on your hard drive
- ✔ Microsoft Internet Explorer 4.01 (with Service Pack 1 or later version)
- ✔ A VGA or higher resolution monitor
- ✔ A video card that can display more than 256 colors

Downloading and installing the software

The Microsoft Reader Add-in for Word can be downloaded from www.microsoft.com/reader/info/selfpublish.htm. At this Web page, click the <u>Click Here to Download the Read In Microsoft Reader Add-in for Microsoft Word</u> link and follow the instructions on the series of Web pages that take you through the download process.

After the file downloads to your hard drive, make sure that you close down any running copies of Microsoft Word *before* you install the software.

You can install the add-in software by doing the following:

1. **Double-click the WordRMR.exe file to start the installation wizard.**

2. **Read the Introduction screen and click the Next button.**

   The License Agreement appears, which you are required to read. If you agree with the terms of the agreement, click the I Agree button and then click the Next button.

3. **You're asked to confirm whether you want the Add-in tool installed. Click the Next button to continue.**

   After the files for the tool are copied to the correct location on your hard drive, you have the opportunity to read the tool's release notes. You can scroll through the notes or click the Next button to continue.

4. **The installation is complete. Click the Close button to close the Wizard window.**

You need to start Microsoft Word 2000 before you can use the Add-in tool. From the Windows Start menu, choose Programs➪Microsoft Word. The Word application opens.

After you install the Add-in tool, Word's File menu features a new Read menu item. A Read button is also added to Word's standard toolbar. The Add-in wizard copies a special Reader template (WordRMR.dot) to your computer's hard drive as a part of the installation process. This template loads every time you start Microsoft Word.

Make sure that you don't accidentally delete this template or you won't be able to create LIT files. You'll have to reinstall the tool.

Optimizing a Word document for the Add-in tool

The Microsoft Reader LIT file format doesn't support all the formatting that can be incorporated into a Word file. The following list gives you tips to improve the look of your eBooks when you covert them from a DOC file to a LIT file:

✔ Use Word's Style feature to ensure that the formatting you select for headings, body text, and so on gets converted properly. (See Chapter 10 for more information on using styles.)

✔ Page breaks in Word documents are preserved when the document is converted. Section breaks are converted to page breaks in LIT files.

✔ After you open a Word document, but before you convert the file to the reader format, set your document's margins to a width of four inches. This is pretty close to the Microsoft Reader's layout, so it lets you see where lines break in the document.

Although changing to a page width of four inches helps you determine how the document looks on the desktop version of Microsoft Reader, the Pocket PC version may look different because of its smaller screen.

✔ Replace any tabs with spaces or use Word's indented paragraphs feature.

✔ Although the desktop version of the Microsoft Reader supports converted tables, the Pocket PC version cannot display tables of any type. Because of this, you should convert all tables to text if you plan on supporting both platforms.

✔ If you added a Table of Contents to your document, these convert to a series of links when the document is formatted as a LIT file. Unfortunately, the Pocket PC version of the Reader can't display the Table of Contents. It shows an error message where the Table of Contents page should be displayed.

✔ ClearType fonts are designed to work with Microsoft Reader's ClearType technology and to produce great readability on LCD monitors (the type of monitors found on laptops and flat-panel screens). If you plan on using these ClearType fonts, use Berling Antiqua, Frutiger Linotype, or Lucida Sans Typewriter as the normal text style for your eBook.

✔ If you save your source document in HTML format instead of DOC format before converting it to Microsoft Reader format, the formatting is retained, but some problems may result.

✔ The Add-in tool can work with images formatted as JPEG, GIF, PNG, BMP, or TIF files. The desktop version of Microsoft Reader can display JPEG, GIF, and PNG files (bitmaps and TIF format files are converted to GIF format when the document is converted). The Pocket PC can only display JPEG images. If you're trying to create an eBook that displays properly on all eBook readers, you should convert all your image files to JPEG before you convert the Word document to LIT format.

Microsoft Reader either does not support the following Word features, or they may cause you problems. When possible, edit your document to remove these features before you attempt a conversion to the LIT file format:

✔ Drop caps

✔ Equations and fractions

✔ Forms

✔ Headers and footers

✔ Nested tables

✔ Non-English fonts

✔ Right-to-left text (may appear reversed)

✔ Some paragraph border attributes (may not be displayed)

✔ Table of Contents

✔ Tables with rows longer than the recommended four-inch page width

✔ Template files (DOT) (can't be converted)

✔ Widow and orphan control

Printing to an eBook

After you optimize your document for conversion and while it's still open in Word, you can easily convert the file:

1. **Choose File⇨Read.**

   The Read in Microsoft Reader dialog box appears.

   Your document must be saved before the conversion can begin; the Add-in tool does this automatically before the file converts.

2. **Enter the eBook's title in the Title text box, enter the name of the author in the Author text box, and enter the filename to be used when saving the file in the Filename text box, as shown in Figure 11-3.**

   In the same dialog box, you can decide which Microsoft Reader library to send the eBook file to. If you want to send the file to a synchronized handheld device, select Reading Device Using Synchronized Files and select your device from the drop-down list. If you want to save your eBook to your desktop, select This Computer, and from the drop-down list, select a location in which to copy your file. You can also click the Browse button to find a different folder to save your files to.

3. **Click the OK button in the Read in Microsoft Reader dialog box.**

   A message lets you know that the file is being converted. After the conversion, a dialog box appears and tells you the name and location of the eBook. You have the option of opening the new eBook in Microsoft Reader by clicking the OK button, as shown in Figure 11-4.

Figure 11-3:
Enter the
title, author,
name, and
location of
your eBook
file in the
Read in
Microsoft
Reader
dialog box.

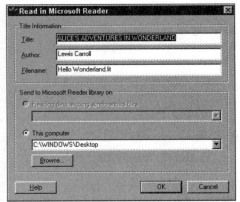

Figure 11-4:
You can
click the OK
button to
launch
Microsoft
Reader and
see your
newly
created
eBook.

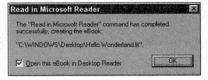

OverDrive ReaderWorks Publisher Software

You can create LIT files by using OverDrive's ReaderWorks Publisher. The software lets you add cover images to the LIT files that you create. Additionally, the software lets you customize the title's information, specify what page to jump to when the user clicks the Begin Reading link, and designate a copyright page.

Publisher also lets you specify the eBook's metadata (basic descriptive information about a title). Metadata includes information like title, price, name of the contributors, and so on. (For more information on the metadata that can be included in an OEB file, see Chapter 10.)

Getting and installing the software

OverDrive's ReaderWorks Publisher Software can be purchased directly from the company's Web site (www.overdrive.com/readerworks/software/publisher.asp) for $119. For $149, you can purchase free upgrades to the software for a one-year period. Click the <u>Download Publisher Now</u> link and follow the Web site's instructions to download and install the software.

To install and use Publisher, you need Windows 98 or 2000, Windows NT 4, or Internet Explorer 4.01 (or later version), and a copy of Microsoft Reader installed on your desktop.

Building an eBook with Publisher

You can build Microsoft Reader eBooks after you install the Publisher software. Unlike the Microsoft Reader Add-in tool, Publisher requires files in HTML or OEB format to create an eBook. All the files to be included in the eBook — even the cover images — should be copied to the same directory on your hard drive before you compile the LIT file.

Follow these steps to create an eBook with Publisher:

1. **Open the Publisher program.**

   The Publisher application displays a splash screen and then opens the Quick Start–ReaderWorks Publisher dialog box. You have the option of creating a new ReaderWorks Project, converting an Open eBook Package file to LIT format, or opening an existing ReaderWorks Project.

2. **Select the option that you want and click the OK button.**

   I want to create a new project, so I select the Blank ReaderWorks Project option and click the OK button.

3. **In the ReaderWorks Publisher window, click the Add button to add source files to be used in the creation of your eBook.**

   Note: ReaderWorks Publisher accepts text files, PNG image files, GIF image files, Microsoft HTML Document 5.0 files, and JPEG image files as valid source documents.

   The Add Source Files dialog box appears.

4. **Select the folder that contains your source files for the eBook.**

Publisher requires all source files to be in the same folder. Highlight the files to be used and click the Open button, as shown in Figure 11-5. The source files are listed in the Publisher Source Files window, and the folder that contains your source files is listed as the Source Folder.

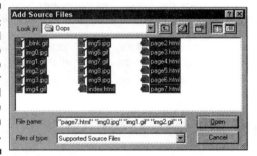

Figure 11-5:
Select all the files to be used to build your eBook and click the Open button.

5. **Click the Properties icon (located in the left pane of the ReaderWorks Publisher window).**

The Properties page appears, as shown in Figure 11-6. Click each of the properties that you want to define for your eBook and enter a text entry in the text box. If you're unsure about what a specific property is, look in the Notes section of the screen.

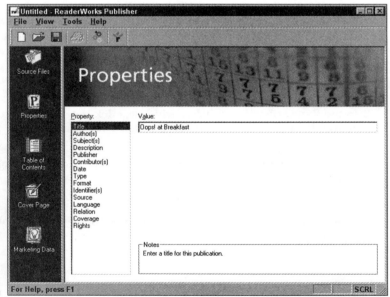

Figure 11-6:
You can set the properties associated with your eBook on the Properties page.

6. **Click the Table of Contents icon (located in the left pane of the ReaderWorks Publisher window).**

   If you want to include a Table of Contents with your document, check the Include Table of Contents option. If you have a Table of Contents defined as an HTML file (containing links to the sections of content in your eBook), click the Ellipses (. . .) button to select the name and location of the file. If you'd like to have a Table of Contents generated from your content, click the TOC Wizard button.

7. **Click the Cover Page icon (located in the left pane of the ReaderWorks Publisher window).**

   This page lets you define the cover-page images that can be used in your eBook. Image files can be in JPG, JPE, GIF, or PNG formats.

   To associate an image file with a cover type, click the cover type and click the Ellipses (. . .) button to select the name and location of the file.

8. **Choose File⇨Build eBook.**

   Publisher displays a warning, stating that the Pocket PC version of the eBook reader doesn't support the Find feature in a publication created from multiple files. If you hope to market to Pocket PC readers and need the feature, rework your source files into a single large HTML document. If you see the warning message, click the OK button.

   The Build eBook Wizard dialog box appears.

9. **In the Filename text box, enter the filename to be used when saving the file, as shown in Figure 11-7. Click the Next button.**

   The Wizard will compile your eBook automatically.

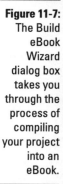

Figure 11-7:
The Build
eBook
Wizard
dialog box
takes you
through the
process of
compiling
your project
into an
eBook.

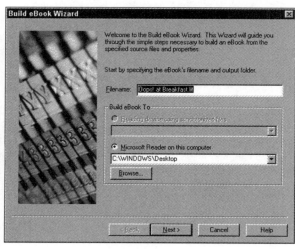

In the same dialog box, you can save the file to a handheld device or to your computer. Select the Reading Device Using Synchronized Files option to send the file to a handheld device. Select This Computer and pick a location to copy your file to if you want to save your eBook to your desktop. After you make your selection, click the Next button.

10. **After Publisher compiles your eBook, click the Finish button.**

11. **Before the Publisher application closes, a dialog box appears, asking you whether the eBook project file should be saved. Click the Yes button to save the file.**

    The Save As dialog box appears.

12. **Select the name and location in which to save your file, and click the OK button.**

    Note: ReaderWorks Publisher files are saved with a .rwp extension.

13. **Launch Microsoft Reader (if it's not already open) by choosing Start⇨Microsoft Reader.**

    Your eBook appears as one of the titles listed in the Microsoft Reader library.

14. **Click the title to open your eBook.**

RocketLibrarian

The RocketLibrarian tool is used to create eBooks for the Rocket eBook Reader. Although the eBooks you create are displayed on the Rocket's hardware device, you can also download and install a software-only reader on your desktop. This eBook reader mimics the look of the Rocket device and lets you test the eBooks built with the RocketLibrarian tool.

Getting and installing the software

The RocketLibrarian authoring tool is free and may be downloaded from the Rocket eBook Web site at www.rocket-ebook.com/Readers/Software/index.html. Two versions of the software exist — one designed to run on Macintosh computers, and the other designed for PCs. To run the software on Windows, you need the following:

- ✔ A PC with a 486 (or higher) processor.
- ✔ One of the following operating systems: Windows 95 or 98, or Windows NT 4.0.
- ✔ 16MB of RAM.

✔ 10MB of free space on your hard drive.

✔ An available serial port for connecting the Rocket eBook device. *Note:* You can still create Rocket eBooks if the device isn't connected, but you should download and install the eRocket software to display the files that you create.

✔ Internet access and a Web browser.

You should also download and install a copy of the eRocket application. This software-only version of the Rocket eBook Reader lets you read un-encrypted RB files. Go to the Rocket eBook Web site at `www.rocket-ebook.com/ eRocket/register.html` to register and download a copy of the software. After the file copies to your hard drive, double-click the filename to start the Installation Wizard. This wizard shows you how to install the eRocket software.

Building an eBook with RocketLibrarian

After you install the software, you're ready to create a Rocket eBook. The following steps take you through the process:

1. **Open RocketLibrarian.**

   The authoring tool displays a splash screen and then opens the main RocketLibrarian window. The pane on the right lets you organize the eBooks already installed on your Rocket device. (You can also download more eBooks from within the RocketLibrarian window by clicking the Browser tab and going to the Rocket eBook Web site.)

   If you don't connect your Rocket eBook to the serial port of yor computer before launching the RocketLibrarian software, you see an error message when you first start the program. Don't worry about this error message — just click the OK button. You're still able to build Rocket eBooks with the software.

   The left pane in the window is where you create an eBook, as shown in Figure 11-8.

2. **Choose Title⇨Import File Using RocketWriter.**

   The Open dialog box appears.

3. **Select the file to be used and click the Open button.**

   Note: You can import ASCII text files, HTML files, or Rocket eBook files.

4. **In the Create Personal Title dialog box that is displayed, enter the eBook's title in the Title text box, and enter your name in the Author text box.**

   If you included images or links in your files, you can select the Include Images or Follow Links check boxes to preserve these elements in the Rocket eBook edition of the document.

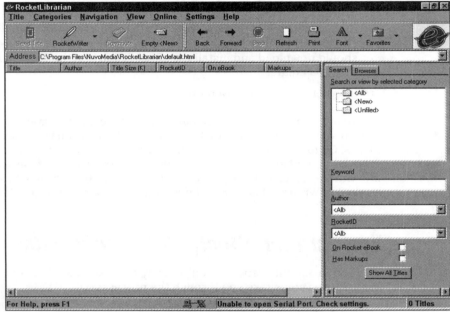

Figure 11-8:
The left
pane of the
Rocket-
Librarian
window
allows you
to import
files to be
converted to
RB format.

5. **After you enter the document information, click the OK button.**

   The eBook that you just created appears as a line entry in the left pane of the RocketLibrarian window, as shown in Figure 11-9. The properties that you just set for the file are displayed along with the file's size.

6. **Right-click the filename to display the context menu. Select the Export to File option.**

   The Save As dialog box appears.

7. **Select the name and location for the RB file that you're saving. Click the Save button.**

   The file is copied to your folder.

8. **Open the eRocket Reader.**

   The eBook reader displays the most recently opened eBook.

9. **Drag the icon for the file that you just saved into the eRocket Reader.**

   The Rocket eBook file that you just created displays in the eBook reader.

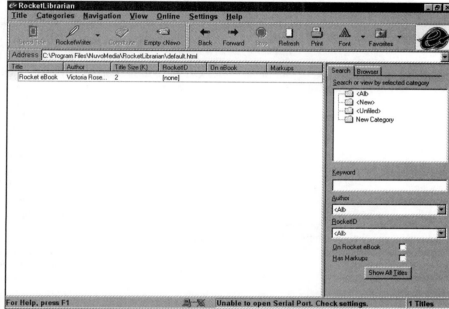

Other Authoring Tools

Many eBook readers are available. Table 11-3 lists some additional authoring
software that you can download for free from the Web and the types of eBook
that each tool creates.

Table 11-3	More eBook-Authoring Software		
Name of Tool	**Supported Reader**	**To Download a Copy**	**Notes**
Peanut Press MakeTool	Peanut Press Reader	`www.peanutpress.com/`	Must have the Java Virtual Machine installed on your computer.

(continued)

Table 11-3 *(continued)*

Name of Tool	Supported Reader	To Download a Copy	Notes
SoftBook Publisher	SoftBook Reader	`www.softbook.com/ enterprise/personal. asp`	Gemstar International Group acquired SoftBook in January 2000. This is the same company that acquired the Rocket eBook, so it's unclear whether SoftBook Readers will continue as a stand-alone line of devices.
Night Kitchen's TK3	TK3 Reader	`www.nightkitchen. com/downloadtools/`	The TK3 Reader and authoring software are in beta. You must apply to be part of the beta program before you can download and install the authoring tool.

Testing Your Formatting

After you create your eBook, you need to test it to make sure that no problems occur when the file is opened. The following tips show you what to test for:

- ✔ **Test your file on every version of the readers that you want your eBook to support:** For example, if you want to create an eBook for Microsoft Reader, you must test your eBook on both the desktop and Pocket PC versions of the reader.

- ✔ **Make sure that you look at every page of text:** Proofread the entire document even if you already did so before you converted the file. You want to make sure that all the characters and formatting have been properly converted and that new errors haven't been introduced.

- ✔ **Test your file on all operating systems supported by your eBook reader:** If your eBook reader runs on the Windows platform, this means testing on Windows 95, Windows 98, Windows NT, Windows 2000, and Windows ME. Because you probably don't have that many PCs lying around the house, you should ask friends and family to be beta testers for you.

- ✔ **Test how your eBook looks at different screen resolutions and at different font sizes:** You may be surprised how different your eBook looks if you change the resolution from 600 x 800 pixels to 1,024 x 768 pixels. You may also be surprised at how your eBook looks with a larger font.

- ✔ **Change the color settings on your PC:** This can be done from the Windows Start menu (choose Start➪Settings➪Control Panel and click the Display icon). In the Display Properties dialog box, click the Settings tab. The Colors drop-down list offers different options for changing the number of colors displayed on your monitor. Select a different color setting and click the Apply button. A dialog box appears, asking whether you want to restart your computer with the new color settings or change the settings without restarting the machine. Select either option and click the OK button.

Don't change to a different color setting unless you know your graphics card is capable of supporting that number of colors: If your graphics card can't support the new number of colors, your screen becomes unreadable and you won't be able to see anything clearly enough to change the settings back. Check with the documentation that came with your PC or graphics card if you're not sure what it can (and can't) support.

- ✔ **Test every link:** If your eBook contains links to external content that's displayed with a Web browser, make sure to test the link with a variety of browsers.

- ✔ **Check the overall size of your eBook:** If the file size is over 1MB, you need to see whether you can reduce the size of the file by compressing the images or removing images that aren't critical to your content.

- ✔ **Check the resolution of color images that are converted for display on a black and white screen:** Make sure that the images look good. If they don't, you may want to convert the files before you compile them into a final eBook.

- ✔ **Make sure that the eBook's layout works on smaller screens (if your eBook reader displays on non-PC devices):** If necessary, redo the layout in Word, and change the page width to mimic the size of the smaller screen. After you redo the layout, convert the document to your eBook format.

The ePublishing
For Dummies
Online Directory

The 5th Wave By Rich Tennant

"You want to know why I'm mad? I suggest you download my latest novel called, 'Why an Obsessive Control-Freak Husband Should Never Pick Out Bathroom Tile Without Asking His Wife First'."

In this directory . . .

This Online Directory contains many of the Web sites I found helpful while I researched for this book. If you look through the listings, you find the following:

- ✔ How to find an agent online
- ✔ How to research online
- ✔ Web sites where you can download an eBook reader
- ✔ How to get online help with designing interactive products
- ✔ Web sites dedicated to the topics of reading and authoring eBooks
- ✔ Web sites that offer help for writers

About This Directory

A number of the Web sites in this directory have *micons* (mini icons) listed after the Web site's URL. These micons give additional information about each site's features. The following list shows the meaning of each micon.

🛒 Lets you purchase eBooks and other content.

$ A subscription fee is needed to access all the services.

📇 Requires registration and log in before accessing all services.

↘ Has files that can be downloaded.

↖ Lets you upload your content to be ePublished.

☞ Has a chat room you can participate in.

📋 Has a bulletin board where you can leave messages.

Agent Information

Here are a couple of Web sites that should help you find information on getting a literary agent to represent you.

LiteraryAgent.com

www.literaryagent.com

LiteraryAgent.com has (what they claim to be) the most comprehensive database of literary agents available on the Web. You can search through the database free of charge. The site also lets agents create individual home pages; if you're interested in more information, you can look at any agent home pages accessible from the LiteraryAgent.com Web site.

WritersNet Guide to Literary Agents

www.writers.net/agents.html

WritersNet is a support site for authors. The site offers a database of literary agents, which is helpful because it contains contact information only for those agents that don't charge a reading fee. You can search for an agent by name, agency, location, or area of literary specialization.

Clipping Services

Here's a list of Web sites that can help you track specific topics or companies when articles are published in periodicals or on the Web.

Dow Jones

www.dowjones.com

$ 📇

One of the most popular clipping services is DowJones.com, where you can do a business search from the front page. By typing in a word, phrase, or symbol, you can elect to search through the newswires and the DowJones.com index of 2,000 top business Web sites; or search through 250 news and business publications, including *The Wall Street Journal*. Any headlines that you retrieve are free, but it costs $2.95 to purchase the full text of the article. ***Note:*** Before you pay Dow Jones to retrieve an article, you should go to the Web site of the periodical that originally published the article. Sometimes, you can read the article for free by going directly to the source.

eWatch

www.ewatch.com

$

A comprehensive Web-clipping service is eWatch.com. This service allows you to define a keyword(s) and be notified by e-mail when that word appears on one of the sites that it monitors. eWatch monitors thousands of publications on the Web — more than 63,000 Usenet and Electronic Mailing Lists, hundreds of public discussion areas on AOL and CompuServe, and finance/investor bulletin boards on Yahoo!, Motley Fool, and Silicon Investor. This level of research is expensive — the cost of the service, for 1 to 10 users, is $3,600 a year.

Excite NewsTracker Service

www.excite.com

Excite offers a free NewsTracker service to users who register at the site. With this service, you can define a keyword and NewsTracker will search through more than 300 online newspapers and magazines available on the Web. *Note:* The results from NewsTracker aren't e-mailed to you, but they can be viewed from the Excite Web site.

GotMarketing.com's Infowatch Service

www.gotmarketing.com

$

A newcomer to the Web is GotMarketing.com's Infowatch Service, which scans 400 Internet news sites for articles. It currently has over 2,800,000 Web-based news clippings that can be searched. At $100 per month, the service is expensive, but they do offer a 30-day free trial to help you decide if the service meets your needs.

TVEyes.com

www.tveyes.com

An interesting free service to subscribe to is TVEyes.com. You can enter your e-mail address and keyword of interest into a form, and TVEyes.com e-mails you whenever that keyword is mentioned on TV. If you register with the site, you're allowed to enter additional keywords in the search form to create a more personalized search.

Dedicated Reading Devices

The following Web sites are the official sites for each type of eBook reader. You can go to these Web sites for product support and to get information about new versions of your eBook reader.

Everybook

www.everybook.net

The Everybook Reader is in the process of completing redesigns on the product to compete with the laptop PC market. With its two high-resolution color screens, the Everybook Reader is the Rolls Royce of dedicated reading devices. The new version allows you to type notes and surf the Web.

Franklin eBookMan

www.franklin.com/ebookman/ default.assoftp

Franklin Electronic's new eBookMan multimedia reader and content player is scheduled for release at the end of 2000. From the Web site, you can get more information about the three versions of the device. Because the eBookMan will incorporate the Microsoft Reader, you can download and read any Microsoft Reader-compatible files and create your own LIT files with the Word Add-in tool.

Rocket eBook

www.rocket-ebook.com

The Rocket eBook Web site gives information about the eBook reader, along with links to let you purchase a reader, bestsellers in the Rocket eBook format, and periodicals. In addition, contests are often given so you may try to win an eBook reader — if you're not ready to purchase one for yourself.

SoftBook Reader

www.softbook.com

Because the SoftBook Reader comes with an internal modem, you can connect to this Web site to download new eBooks by using the eBook reader. This site also contains a link to let you download publishing software, so you can save your own documents to the SoftBook file format for viewing on the eBook reader.

Design Help

These Web sites focus on the topic of good interactive design. Although they focus primarily on Web site design, some information is relevant to eBooks as well.

Jakob Nielsen's Personal Web site

www.useit.com

Recognized as one of the top experts on Web design and software interface, Jakob Nielsen was Sun Microsystem's guru on Web design until he started his own consulting firm. His personal Web site is a collection of useful tips and pointers on how people interact with digital content.

Web Design Group

www.htmlhelp.com

This group was founded to promote the creation of non-browser-specific, well-designed Web sites. This site offers good material on a wide range of Web-related topics. Be sure to look at the section of the site that covers design elements.

Web Pages That Suck

www.webpagesthatsuck.com

The name says it all. By studying examples of what not to do, you can learn to create better interactive designs for your products. This site has been a cult classic for years.

eBook Newsletters

You can go to these Web sites to sign up for *eZines* (e-mail newsletters) that focus on the topic of eBooks.

Barnes & Noble Insider

www.bn.com

This eZine is designed to help BN.com sell more books, but it offers interesting insight into which books that B&N thinks will become bestsellers. It currently offers over 70 newsletters. To sign up, go to the Web site and click the bn.com Insider link.

ebookNet.com eZine

www.ebooknet.com

This eZine focuses entirely on eBook and ePublishing topics. When you sign up for the newsletter, you get information about new developments in ePublishing technologies, news about the growing eBook industry, and information on eBook best-sellers.

TipWorld

www.tipworld.com

This Web site provides free newsletters on a wide range of topics, including everything from operating systems to news and gossip. The Books and Writing section offers a plethora of eZines.

eBook Publishers

The following Web sites belong to better-known eBook publishers and distributors. If you're looking to download eBooks, these sites offer a wide variety of titles.

BN.com

www.bn.com

Barnes & Noble has made a large effort to become one of the primary distributors of eBooks on the Web. BN.com offers titles in three primary formats: Adobe Acrobat (PDF files), Rocket eBook (RB files), and the Microsoft Reader (LIT files) formats.

BookLocker

www.booklocker.com

BookLocker offers many eBooks in multiple categories. All titles are sold in PDF format, so the Acrobat Reader is required to read the eBooks that you purchase. BookLocker reviews eBook proposals from authors, but it no longer accepts titles in the categories of poetry, creative writing, or children's books.

Bookmice

www.bookmice.com

Bookmice is a small ePublisher that offers titles in PDF and HTML file formats. eBooks can be downloaded from the site, but they're also available on CD-ROM. If you don't have a copy of Adobe Acrobat, Bookmice offers to convert any text files to PDF format for $100 per title. The cost of conversion includes colorizing titles and subtitles, creating bookmarks from chapter headings, and adding hyperlinks to your Web site or other sites that you mention within your text.

DiskUs Publishing

www.diskuspublishing.com

In addition to eBooks, DiskUs offers audio books that can be purchased from its Web site. It also offers free titles for you to download. Title formats are available as PDF, HTML, PRC (a format used by PalmPilots), Rocket eBook, SoftBook, and Microsoft Reader files.

eBooks.com

www.ebooks.com

eBooks.com is a newly launched Internet eBookstore. It hopes to be to eBooks what Amazon.com is to printed books. The site originated in Australia.

iPublish.com

www.ipublish.com

iPublish.com, sells eBook versions of the books published by Time Warner Trade Publishing. The site, which launches early in 2001, also lets you submit manuscripts that will be evaluated by other site members. The best submissions will be reviewed by the iPublish editorial team.

MightyWords.com

www.mightywords.com

MightyWords.com is featured as a place to purchase eMatter articles, but I also include it as a place to publish your own work. If you're looking for eContent to read, MightyWords.com features unique content from top authors, in addition to articles authored by experts in specific topics.

NetLibrary

ww.netlibrary.com

NetLibrary is like an online version of the local branch of your public library. After you register on the site, you can check out eBooks to read for a limited period of time. While an eBook is checked out, you're the only one that can read it. Other readers will be informed of a date when the title will be available again. When it's time for you to return the eBook, you're no longer able to view the title onscreen, and other people are able to check it out.

Peanut Press

www.peanutpress.com

Peanut Press titles are only available for PalmPilots, personal digital assistants with the Win CE OS, or Pocket PCs. Peanut Press titles are available from bestselling authors like Judith Krantz and Peter Straub.

eBook Web Sites

The following Web sites focus on the subject of eBooks and eBook publishing. They contain great information if you're new to eBooks or if you are looking for contacts with experience.

EbookNet.com

www.ebooknet.com

This site offers news about eBook developments and how the major publishing houses are developing eBook editions of print works, and features chats and a great message board. It also lists eBook publishers by the eBook formats that they support, which is useful when you're trying to find a title that works with the eBook reader you use.

Web-Source.net

www.web-source.net

This site is devoted to providing information on eBooks, Web-developer resources, Web design techniques, eMarketing, and promotional information. It takes a bit of patience to look through this site, but some useful information can be gained if you persevere. But be forewarned that much of the content on this site is thinly disguised advertising that is designed to get you to buy the author's content.

Finding eZines

Not sure where to go to sign up for e-mail newsletters that are focused on your topic of interest? The following Web sites represent dozens of newsletters that you can sign up for. I also include a couple of my personal favorites.

EduPage

www.educause.edu/pub/pubs.html

This eZine is published by EDUCAUSE, an international nonprofit association dedicated to transforming education through information technologies. EduPage focuses on technology, as it applies to education.

InfoBeat Inc.

www.infobeat.com

InfoBeat offers eZines on entertainment, finance, fun, news, sports, and weather. What's really nice about InfoBeat is that you can customize the newsletter content to fit your interests. When you subscribe to the sports eZine, you can decide to get information on baseball and football, but not hockey.

Standard.com

www.standardservices.com/newsletters/

This Web site provides coverage of the Internet economy. You can subscribe to a number of newsletters: Analyst Bullpen, Beat Sheet, Box Office, Daily News, Intelligencer, Intelligencer Europe, Internet Architect Spotlight, Market Movers, Media Grok, Metrics Report, and many more.

General Search Engines

Here's a list of some of the most popular search engines that you may want to try while you research for your eBook.

AltaVista

www.altavista.com

AltaVista is great when you're searching for a specific phrase or very targeted information. AltaVista searches through the text of the articles, and ranks them on a variety of factors, including domain names. After you're comfortable doing Boolean searches, AltaVista helps you find information on specific companies or individuals. AltaVista offers an added benefit when you do a search: It offers links to related searches when it returns your search results. Some of these may be what you were searching for, or can add depth to your research. *A word of caution:* Searches on AltaVista are case-sensitive. Typing *dog* into the search form produces different results than if you type *Dog*.

AOL.com

search.aol.com

With 22 million people using AOL for Internet access, if you're researching a competitor, do a search to see how high your competitor's Web site is ranked. AOL has an Open Directory Project, where 19,000 volunteer editors have categorized over 1,200,000 Web sites, with 3,000 Web sites added every day. When a user does a search on AOL, it searches through the Web sites in its directory before it searches the rest of the Web.

Ask Jeeves

www.askjeeves.com

When you're not exactly sure what you're looking for, try asking Jeeves. Ask Jeeves is useful when you're not comfortable with, or can't be bothered doing, Boolean searches.

Google.com

www.google.com

Instead of editorial placement in a directory, or ranking a Web site based on keywords, Google ranks Web sites according to how many other sites have linked to that site. In some ways, search results are a bit like a popularity contest.

Yahoo!

www.yahoo.com

The granddaddy of search engines, Yahoo! is the most popular search engine. Each site that gets added to the Yahoo! directory is evaluated by an editor who decides where the site should belong. When you search for a topic, you can search across all the sites listed on Yahoo!, or you can search within a directory, which makes it more likely that you'll find what you want to find.

Generic and Business Research Web Sites

Trying to do some basic research? These Web sites serve as a great starting point.

Company Sleuth

www.company.sleuth.com

Company Sleuth provides free information on publicly traded companies. The Web site provides stock quotes, news, insider trades, domain, trademark and patent registrations, analyst ratings, broker reports, and message boards.

Deep Canyon

www.deepcanyon.com

Deep Canyon compiles research available from a variety of sources (market research, industry analysts, and so on) and packages the information in reports, which it sells from its Web site. Most of these reports are expensive, but Deep Canyon does offer some free tools, like Competitor Alert or Research Alert, which can be of interest.

D-10 Generic and Business Research Web Sites

Dun & Bradstreet

www.dnb.com

Dun & Bradstreet offers comprehensive company information. Its Business Information Report (which you can purchase for individual companies) gives you summary financial information, information on any major corporate changes, public filing information, history, operational data, and the D&B rating.

Edgar Online

www.edgar-online.com

Edgar Online provides the Securities and Exchange Commission's filings for any company publicly traded on the Stock Exchange. The basic filing information is free, but you can also subscribe to the premium service, which gives real-time SEC filings, 144 Insider Transaction filings, and use of Edgar Online's *drill-down tools* (online tools that let you filter the information in a variety of ways).

10K Wizard Financials Online

www.10kwizard.com

You can easily search the Securities and Exchange Commission filings by using 10K Wizard Financials Online. If you know what you want to research, but don't know which companies to look at, this site makes it easy.

For example, say you want to find out which companies mention *online publishing* in their filings. You type the words **online publishing** into the Word Search online form, select the All Dates check box, and select Printing and Publishing from the Industry drop-down list. After waiting

patiently (it can take awhile), the 10K Wizards site returned a list of numerous companies with information about the stock symbol, company name, the type of form filed, and the date the form was filed. By clicking the company name, you can see text from the filing, in which the words *online publishing* are mentioned.

Fuld & Company's Internet Intelligence Index

www.fuld.com/i3/index.html

Fuld & Company specializes in providing large companies with corporate intelligence. As a free service, it provides an Intelligence Index, which lists over 400 links to some of the best informational Web sites that cover a variety of markets.

Hoovers Online

www.hoovers.com

Hoovers offers basic company information for free, but only subscribers to its premium content can access more detailed company info. A personal membership to access the premium content is $124.95 per year (or $29.95 per month).

Lexis-Nexis Group

www.lexis-nexis.com/lncc

Lexis-Nexis is one of the oldest providers of online information, and offers the largest database of legal and periodical data available. The information it offers is comprehensive, but can be expensive. Unless you can't obtain information anywhere else, you should probably try some of the other Web sites listed here first.

U.S. Census Bureau

www.census.gov

If you're looking for demographic data, the most logical place to go is the source: the U.S. Census Bureau. Although it takes time to sift through all the data, you can get profiles of social, economic, or housing characteristics for states, cities, counties, congressional districts, and more.

Vault.com

www.vault.com

If you're doing research on a company, be sure to check the Vault.com message boards. Vault.com encourages company insiders to post messages, and uses these to compile insider company profiles. Other Web sites can give you a financial picture of how a company is doing, but Vault.com tells you what the employees think.

Internet and Technology Sources

If you write about technology, these Web sites are valuable resources for looking up information or downloading shareware files.

AnchorDesk Briefing Center on ZDnet.com

www.zdnet.com/anchordesk/bcenter/ index.html

Part of the larger ZDNet.com Web site, this site is a one-stop resource for getting current information about technology. The Web site aggregates need-to-know data about a variety of subjects — including hardware, industry issues, Internet, networking, operating systems, software, and peripherals.

CNet.com

www.cnet.com

Similar to the ZDNet site, CNet.com is also a portal for technology. I find CNet's Web site to be easier to use than ZDNet. Try both sites and see which one provides you with the information that you need.

CyberAtlas at Internet.com

cyberatlas.internet.com

CyberAtlas provides statistics and Web-marketing information for anyone interested in how to market on the Web. Be sure to check out the Stats Toolbox section for up-to-date statistics on the Internet and technology industries. I find CyberAtlas of special interest because of its marketing orientation, but the rest of Internet.com is helpful as well.

Slashdot.org

www.slashdot.org

As hard on the eyes as an old copy of *Wired* magazine, Slashdot.org bills itself as "News for Nerds. Stuff that Matters." This is the ultimate insider's guide to what's going on in the technology industry.

ZDnet.com

www.zdnet.com

ZDNet is a portal for information on the technology industry. The amount of information offered on the site can be overwhelming. I recommend that you click the MyZDNet link to be taken to a page that offers a number of free services, like Web-based voice, e-mail, and fax services.

Newsgroups and Chats

These general newsgroups and chat Web sites help you find a community focused on your interests. Reading the message threads or attending chats on a regular basis can help keep you up-to-date on subjects that interest you.

Portal Web Sites

www.msn.com
www.aol.com
www.go.com

Most of the portal and other large Web sites have their own message boards and chats in which you can participate in areas that interest you. Go to the home pages of these sites and look for a Community or a People and Chat link.

Topica

www.topica.com

Topica is a free service that lists hundreds of e-mail lists so you can find, manage, and participate in topics that interest you. The Topica Directory is organized by topical area. You can elect to view the e-mail by having it sent to your inbox, or by viewing the e-mail threads on the Topica Web site.

Yahoo!

www.yahoo.com

To find forums and newsgroups in your area of interest, go to the Yahoo! Web site and click the <u>Chat</u> link.

To find newsgroups of interest, go to Yahoo!'s home page, select the <u>Computers and Internet</u> link, click the <u>Internet</u> link, and click the <u>Usenet Groups</u> link. Find a newsgroup that interests you and click the link to start participating. *Note:* This requires you to know the name of your Internet News Server, which you can find out from your Internet Service Provider (ISP).

Open eBook Initiative

If you plan to offer eBooks that are OEB-compliant, here's the site to keep you updated on the Open eBook Initiative.

Open eBook Forum

www.openebook.org

The Open eBook Forum (OEBF) is a group of hardware and software companies, publishers, and authors who are interested in creating a standard set of specifications for eBook readers, applications, and products. The purpose of the forum is to create and maintain common eBook standards and to promote the adoption of eBooks.

With a common set of standards for publishers, an eBook file will be accessible on different hardware and software platforms. This Web site's the place to find out what updates are being made to the spec and which companies are supporting the standard.

Places to Publish Your Material

If you want to distribute your eBook through an established ePublisher or distributor, these sites can help you.

1stBooks

www.1stbooks.com

1stBooks is a Web site where you can publish your own material in eBook or print-on-demand format. The site also lets you purchase the works of other authors. When you publish through 1stBooks, it provides worldwide distribution. Your book is made available through Barnes & Noble and Amazon.com.

MightyWords.com

www. mightywords.com

MightyWords.com lets you publish eMatter. When you publish eMatter through this site, you can set your own prices for the content and retain a 50 percent royalty for every sale that's made.

iPublish.com

www.ipublish.com

iPublish.com is the new eBook division of Time Warner Trade Publishing. The site, which launches early in 2001, lets you submit manuscripts that will be evaluated by other authors. Documents that receive strong reviews are evaluated by Time Warner editors for possible publication in either eBook or print formats.

Publishing Resources

Here are general Web resources to give you more information about the business of publishing.

Association of American Publishers

www.publishers.org/home/index.htm

The Association of American Publishers is the largest trade association of the book-publishing industry. The Web site can help you do research on what titles are being published.

NetRead

www.netread.com

NetRead is a business hub for the book-publishing industry. The site provides marketing tools, a publishing job board, business listings, news, and other information.

New York Times Books Bestsellers Lists

www.nytimes.com/books/yr/mo/day/bsp/index.html

The New York Times offers expanded book bestseller lists on its Web site. You can find the bestsellers for fiction, nonfiction, and advice for hardcover and paperback sales. The site also shows information on how well books are selling through independent bookstores, as compared to the chain stores like Barnes & Noble or Borders.

Note: When you look at the *New York Times*'s bestseller lists, pay attention to how many weeks each title has been on the list. If you want your eBook to sell for more than a few months, study the topics that have longevity.

PublishersWeekly.com

www.publishersweekly.com

Publisher's Weekly is the one magazine everyone in the publishing industry subscribes to. Like the printed periodical, the Web version covers industry news, bestseller lists, top author interviews, and early reviews of adult and children's books.

Simba Information Inc.

www.simbanet.com

Simba Information, Inc. is a research firm that publishes reports on the publishing and media industries. In addition to reports, Simba publishes newsletters that market intelligence and forecasts. Because their reports cost hundreds of dollars, Simba markets primarily to large corporate customers, but you can often find interesting (free) information by reviewing the press releases that they issue at `www.simbanet.com/press/index.html`.

Resources for Writers

Writing can be a lonely business. When you need support, turn to one of these Web sites.

Authorlink

www.authorlink.com

With something for everyone, this award-winning Web site's designed to serve the needs of authors, agents, editors, and publishers. In addition to many links to valuable information resources, Authorlink lets authors submit manuscripts to the ManuScript Showcase.

Weblications.net

www.weblications.net

This Web site offers a number of valuable articles for authors on topics like creating your own cover art, finding an agent, writing great query letters, and scams that authors should watch out for.

WritersNet

www.writers.net

WritersNet is a Web site that has a contact database of writers, editors, publishers, and agents. This is a good site to look through when you want to find an agent to represent you. The site also has plans to include a directory of open writing assignments.

Technology eZines

If you want to subscribe to e-mail newsletters focused on the topic of technology, then the following Web sites are for you.

CNet.com

www.cnet.com

This Internet and technology portal has a Web page that lets you sign up for eZines that can help you stay current, shop smarter, work smarter, and have fun. For subscription information, go to the CNet.com home page and click the <u>Free Newsletters</u> link.

Good Morning Silicon Valley

www.mercurycenter.com

This Web site is the *San Jose Mercury News's* daily update on what's happening in Silicon Valley and the technology industry. To subscribe, go to the Web site and click the E-mail Dispatches link.

Jesse Burst's Anchor Desk

www.zdnet.com/anchordesk/whoiswe/
  subscribe.html

Jesse Burst is a well-known columnist for ZDNet.com, who's been covering Microsoft and the technology industry for many years. His column offers insightful analyses, current technology news, new product information, and interesting shareware to download and try for free.

The Standard.com Media Grok

www.standardservices.com/newsletters

This award-winning daily report gives press coverage on stories written about the Internet economy.

Part IV
Profiting from All That Work

The 5th Wave   By Rich Tennant

@RICHTENNANT.

"You show a lot of promise in ePublishing. Your first novel was rich with gripping XHTML, breathtaking in its hyperlinks, and visionary in it's cross-browser platform."

In this part . . .

Although you may love writing, ePublishing is about making money and that's what this part is all about. If you want to profit from your efforts, Part IV shows you how.

Chapter 12 explains how you can build a Web site to sell your work or to submit your material to an online distributor.

Chapter 13 explains how to work with established eBook publishers and distributors, and how the experience differs from working with a print publisher. This chapter explains why you may want to work with an agent and shows you how to find one.

Chapter 14 covers the business fundamentals of starting your own ePublishing company. I help you identify the real cost of each eBook that you publish and how to price your titles. The chapter also shows you where to go to apply for an ISBN and how to copyright your material.

Chapter 12

Distributing Your eBook

· ·

· ·

*A*fter you write, package, and format your eBook, you need a way to get your product to the market. This chapter walks you through that process and gets you to the point where you can start selling your work. If you're not interested in acting as your own publisher and prefer to have someone else handle the details of distribution, jump ahead to Chapter 13, where I explain how to work with an ePublisher.

Distributing Your eBook

Compared to the struggle of writing and the work of marketing, distributing your eBook is relatively simple. You need a way to collect payment from people who want to buy your eBook and you need to deliver the eBook after you accept payment. Because you're dealing with a digital product, both parts of the transactions can be done over the Internet.

Letting potential customers learn about your product

When you market your eBook (see Chapters 15 and 16 for tips on marketing and publicizing your work), you need to send people to a place where they can purchase your eBook. Usually, this place is a Web site that you've set up for this purpose. If you don't have a Web site to sell the eBook, you should have a Web site where people can go to learn more about your product. On this marketing Web site, you should provide a link to a Web site where the eBook can be purchased. If you become an affiliate of a larger site that sells your products (a BN.com affiliate, for example), you get a percentage of the sale each time someone clicks the link to purchase your eBook. This is a pretty cool way to profit twice: once from the fee that you collect from the site's affiliate program, and a second time from the sale of the eBook itself.

Collecting payment

If you opt to sell your eBooks through your own Web site, you need a way to collect payment from customers. Although you can ask people to send a check, you probably won't get many sales that way (unless your product is so valuable that the information can't be obtained any other way).

E-commerce has become a source of instant gratification. If someone sees something they like, they want to buy it — right then and there. (If this weren't true, my American Express bill wouldn't be so high.) In the case of eBooks, the customer expects delivery of the product shortly after making the payment. If you can't satisfy the demand for "But, I want it now" buying, you lose the impulse sales that may make up the bulk of your profit.

Luckily, setting up a Web site to collect payments is fairly simple, thanks to sites like Microsoft Site Manager or Yahoo! Store. Later in this chapter, I take you through the step-by-step process to set up a Web site that allows you to collect payment for your eBooks.

Getting the eBook to the customer

After you receive payment, you can send the eBook to the customer in a number of different ways. The easiest way is to send an e-mail to the customer with the eBook attached. You can also set up a Web site to let the user download the eBook file. In the section "Securing Your eBook," I explain how to implement each method, and the pros and cons of each.

Collecting customer data for future marketing efforts

An important part of the sales transaction is collecting information from your customer, so you can contact them again in the future to market other eBooks. In addition to getting the customer's name and credit card information, make sure that you collect an e-mail address. This is important not only for future marketing, but also to contact the customer in the event that you discover a flaw in your product. If you realize that you included inaccurate information in an eBook, for example, you can send an updated eBook out *before* you get sued. If you discover that your eBook has inadvertently spread a horrible virus, you can contact your customers to warn them. (Or, you could just leave town in a hurry.)

Building an E-Commerce–Enabled Web Site in 15 Minutes

Many Web services are available for you to build an online store to sell products. Some of these sites don't charge you anything to build the store, but they put banner ads on the site that they create for you. Other services charge you a Web store setup fee, or a monthly hosting charge.

Check out these Web store services:

- **eCongo.com:** www.econgo.com
- **iCat Commerce Online:** www.icatmall.com/merchant/index.icl
- **Intershop:** www.intershop.com/
- **MerchandiZer:** www.merchandizer.com/
- **Microsoft bCentral:** http://sitemanager.bcentral.com/
- **Yahoo! Store:** http://store.yahoo.com/

Building a Web site with Site Manager

I used to work on Microsoft's bCentral team, so I'm most familiar with building a Web site using Site Manager. For this reason, I take you through the step-by-step process of creating a Web store with Site Manager. Although you may find some differences, the experience is pretty much the same no matter what store-building service you decide to try from the previous list.

bCentral.com's Site Manager service is supposed to go through a redesign in fall, 2000, so the steps and screens shown below may not exactly match the current version of the product.

1. **Sign up for bCentral's Web store service by going to** http://sitemanager.bcentral.com/ **and clicking the <u>Sign Up Now!</u> link.**

   A page appears, letting you choose from two different product offerings.

You can sign up for an entire year of the service and receive a discount, or you can sign up to pay monthly, with the first month for free. Select the offer that best meets your needs.

Before you sign up for Site Manager, make sure that you click the Member Agreement link to read the bCentral agreement before you proceed.

2. **Click the button that represents the offer that you want to sign up for, as shown in Figure 12-1.**

   If this is your first time signing up for a bCentral service, you're asked to create a user profile, which allows you to manage any service that you subscribe to.

3. **In the form shown on the Web page, enter your e-mail address, name, company information, address, phone number, and fax number, as shown in Figure 12-2.**

   You can indicate whether you want to receive bCentral newsletters, which provide information on how to improve and promote your Web site.

   You're also asked to provide a password to use the next time that you log on to bCentral.com.

   The password that you choose must be at least six characters long.

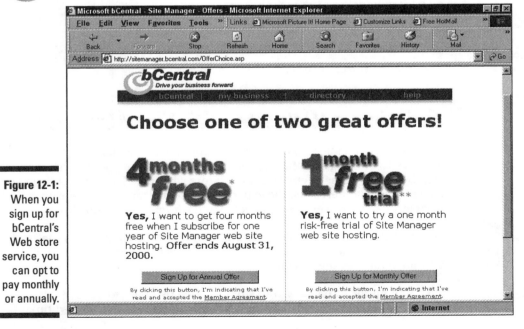

Figure 12-1:
When you
sign up for
bCentral's
Web store
service, you
can opt to
pay monthly
or annually.

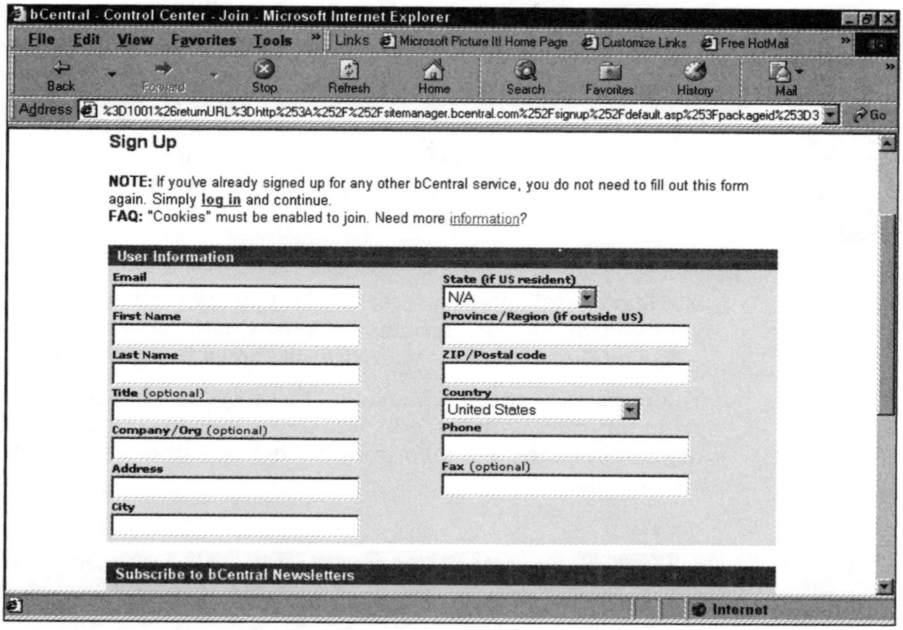

Figure 12-2:
You can create a bCentral account by filling out this simple form.

4. **After you set up your bCentral account, you're asked to enter your credit card information, as shown in Figure 12-3.**

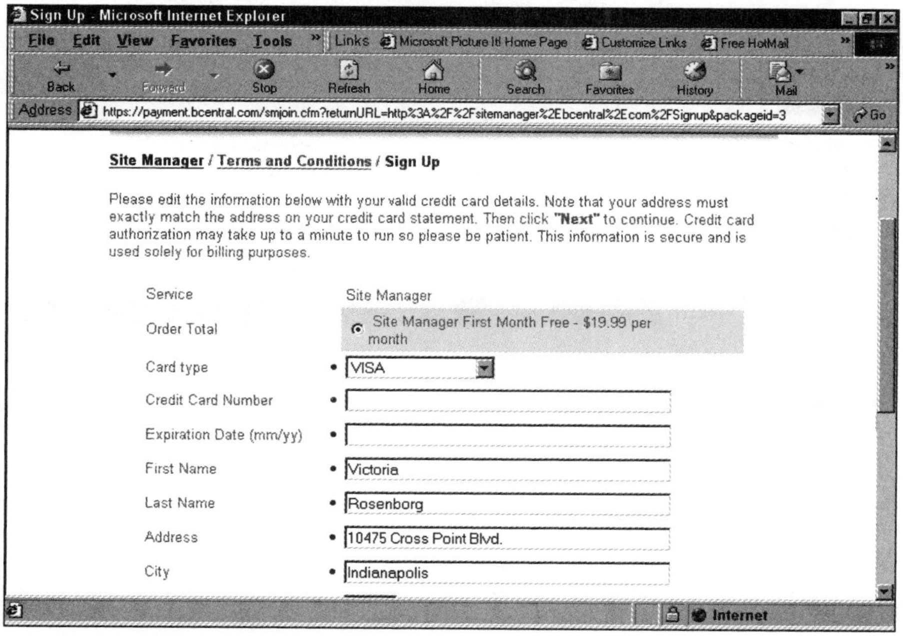

Figure 12-3:
On the bCentral Sign Up page, enter your credit card and billing information.

5. **After you pay for the service, you see an invoice page. Click the Continue button to start the process of building your Web site.**

   You see a page where you can name your Web site, as shown in Figure 12-4.

   Site Manager also lets you sign up for a custom domain name (for example, www.`YourDomainNameShownHere`.com), but not from this page.

6. **Click the Create Site button to start building your Web site.**

   Site Manager displays a screen to let you know when the home page of your Web site has been built. Click the Continue button to start customizing the content on your site, as shown in Figure 12-5.

   You're taken to the Site Manager Start page, as shown in Figure 12-6. From this page, you can edit, add new pages to, and customize the look of your Web site, and incorporate other bCentral services into your online business.

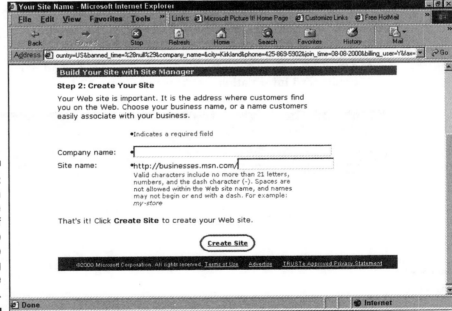

Figure 12-4: You can select the name of your Web site, prior to building your home page.

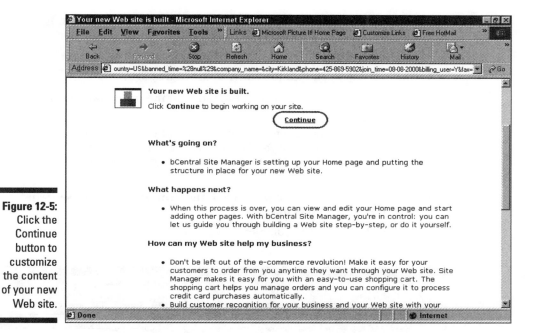

Figure 12-5: Click the Continue button to customize the content of your new Web site.

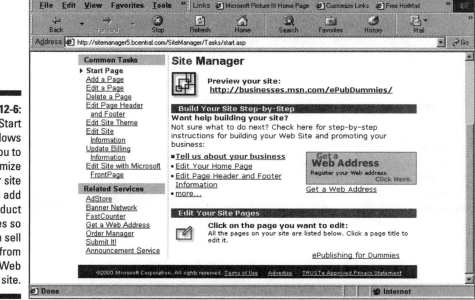

Figure 12-6: The Start page allows you to customize your site and add product pages so you can sell eBooks from your Web site.

7. **To preview what your Web site looks like, click the <u>Preview Your Site</u> link, which is located at the top of the Site Manager Start page.**

   The preview of your new Web site appears, as shown in Figure 12-7.

8. **Click the <u>Go Back</u> link to return to the Start page.**

9. **To edit your home page, click the name of the page that you want to edit.**

   Site Manager displays a form that you fill out to customize the content of your home page. You can also select the way your page should be laid out and whether to add an image to the page (see Figure 12-8).

10. **After you edit your Web page, click the Preview button to see what your Web page looks like.**

    Figure 12-9 shows the completed Web page.

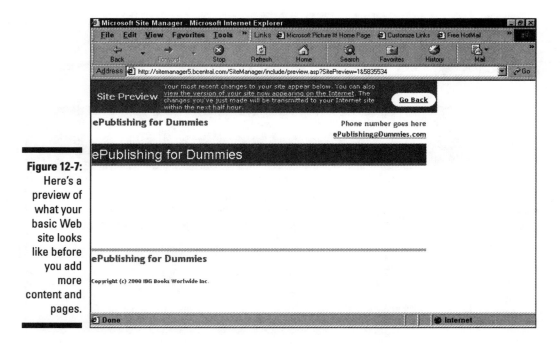

Figure 12-7:
Here's a preview of what your basic Web site looks like before you add more content and pages.

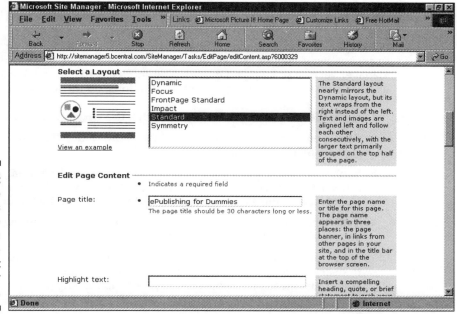

Figure 12-8:
Site
Manager's
Edit page
lets you
customize
the content
of your
home page.

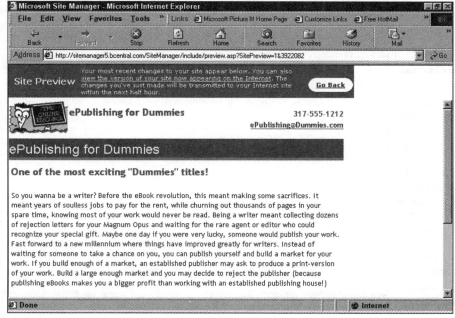

Figure 12-9:
After you
customize
the content
of your
home page
and click
the Preview
button, you
can see
what your
Web site
looks like.

Signing up for the Order Manager service

Before you add product pages to your Web site, you need to set up your site to accept secure online transactions. bCentral.com provides an Order Manager service to help you do this. The service is free for all Site Manager users. To set your site up for secure transactions, do the following:

1. **From the Site Manager Start page, click the <u>Order Manager</u> link.**

2. **After you review the information about the Order Manager service, sign up by clicking the <u>Sign Up Now!</u> link.**

3. **You're prompted for your bCentral.com e-mail address and password. (This is the information that you entered when you signed up for your bCentral account.) Enter the information and click the Log In button.**

4. **You're prompted for information in order to add a shopping cart to your Web site, as shown in Figure 12-10.**

   Enter your e-mail address, company name, and a password to allow you to decrypt the orders that come in. Don't let this decryption stuff scare you; it just means that you need to give an extra-long password that you have to remember when you want to look at your order page.

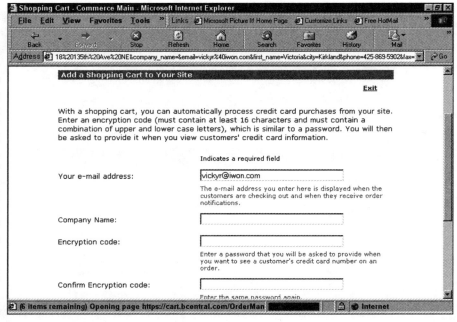

Figure 12-10: You must enter your e-mail address, company name, and a password containing at least 16 characters to add a shopping cart to your Web site.

5. **After you enter all the required information, click the Sign Up link.**

   Depending on what browser you use, you may see a warning dialog box asking you whether it's okay to send the information that you entered over a connection that may not be secure. If you get this dialog box, click the Yes button to continue.

   That's it! Now you're ready to take secure orders on your Web site.

You can make customizations like shipping costs in Order Manager, but you don't need to worry about shipping costs when you deliver an eBook, however, so don't change the default settings.

Adding product pages to your Web site

You can easily add Product pages to your Web site with Site Manager. To create a Product page for an eBook, follow these steps:

1. **From the Site Manager Start page, click the Add a Page link.**

   The Add a Page page appears.

2. **Select the type of page that you want to add to your Web site, as shown in Figure 12-11.**

Figure 12-11: Site Manager lets you add many different types of pages to your Web site, but if you want to sell eBooks, you need to add a Product page for each eBook title that you offer.

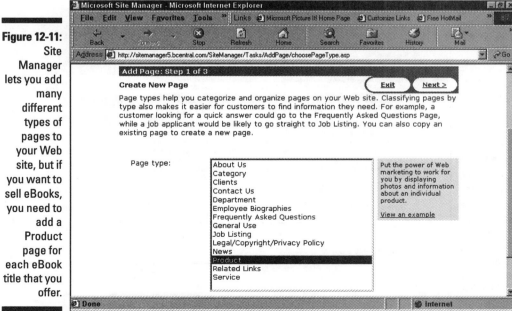

In this case, I'm adding a Product page, so I select Product from the list of page types.

3. **Click the Next button.**

4. **You're asked to give a name to the page, as shown in Figure 12-12.**

   This name will be shown in the list of links on the Web site banner, so keep it short.

   You also need to pick the *parent page* (the page that the new page gets linked to) of the new page.

   For my new Web site, I'm selling an eBook called *Dummies,* and it will be linked to the home page of my Web site, which is the only page that I've created so far.

   Click Next to move to the next screen.

5. **On this page, you can edit the content and layout for your new Product page.**

   The process of editing is the same as the editing process for your home page, but with a couple of differences:

   • You need to enter a product name.

   • You need to enter a price for the product.

   • You need to enter a SKU number. This is a number that the Order Manager uses to track the product when someone orders it.

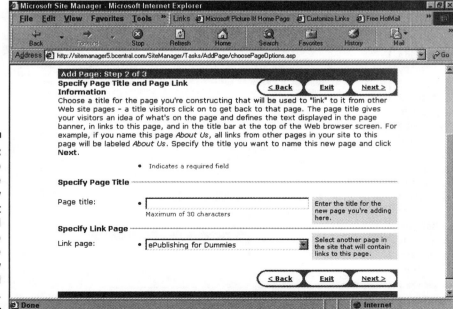

Figure 12-12:
You need to
name the
new
Product
page and
indicate to
which page
the new
page should
be linked.

TIP

You should enter the cover image of your eBook. You can also enter a small excerpt of the text in the Product Description text box.

6. **After you enter all the information for the eBook, you can see what the finished page looks like by clicking the Preview button.**

7. **If you don't have any additional changes, click the Save button to save your Product page.**

You can add other Product pages as you add new eBooks to your publishing list. Figure 12-13 shows what the final page looks like. After you get an order through the Order Manager page, you can deliver the eBook to the customer by sending an e-mail with the eBook as an attachment.

Accepting credit cards

When you sign up for bCentral's Order Manager, it encrypts the credit card information that the purchaser enters and allows you to view this data on the Process Order page. But it's still up to you to authenticate the credit card information and process the order.

Figure 12-13:
A user can order an eBook from your Web site by clicking the Add to Cart button.

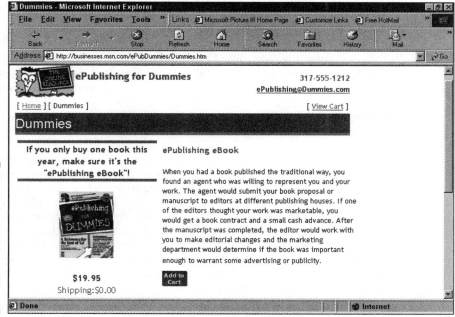

To do this, you must get a *merchant account* from a bank. A merchant account allows you to take credit card orders and process them. After the transaction has gone through, the bank sends you the proceeds of the order — minus their fee, which is usually a small percentage of the transaction. Traditionally, in order to get a merchant account, you needed to have a well-established business and a relationship with a bank.

Opening a merchant account has become much easier as a result of rising Internet businesses. Many companies will offer you a merchant account and will process your transactions online. bCentral has a partnership with Cardservice International. If you sign up for bCentral's Order Manager Web page, you can get credit card purchases processed automatically when someone buys an eBook from your Web site. The credit card number is authorized before the order is processed to protect you against fraudulent credit cards. Payments are automatically transferred into your checking account a few days after the transaction is completed.

The cost of the service is a flat fee of $19.95 per month, a $.20 fee for each transaction processed, and a 2.35 percent transaction fee. Although the cost is pricey, it's competitive with similar eMerchant services, and it greatly simplifies the process of taking an online order.

Securing Your eBook

Now you know how easy it is for someone to buy an eBook from your Web site. Unfortunately, unless you take steps to protect your eBook, someone can easily make illegal copies of your eBooks and send them to every friend and contact that they have on the Internet. Unless you hope to only sell a few copies, you need to think about how to secure your text to limit access to just the folks who have paid up.

Securing online content isn't easy, as many music executives discovered when Napster became a popular way for people to trade music files over the Internet. The book industry is just starting to learn the same lesson. When Stephen King released *Riding the Bullet,* it took hackers just 48 hours to figure out how to get past the decryption software. By the 49th hour, dishonest people were downloading bootleg copies from Web sites that posted the file. Because companies like Amazon.com were giving away the eBook for free as a promotional gimmick, having hackers crack the code wasn't a big deal financially, but the implications are troubling if the publishing industry (and you!) wants to profit from ePublishing.

Setting up for downloads

One method of securing files is to set up an area of your Web site where files can be downloaded, and put password protection on the server. Before a user can download the eBook file, he or she is required to enter a password to gain access to the area of the server where the file is located.

In fact, this isn't really more secure than sending a file out by e-mail (someone can share a password as easily as copying a file), but people tend not to share passwords as readily. Plus, it's easier to trace who is sharing passwords if you assign a unique password to everyone who purchases an eBook.

Distributing your eBook from an FTP site

A number of Web-hosting services let you host *FTP (File Transfer Protocol)* sites, even if your primary Web site is hosted someplace else. FTP is a way to share files with other people over the Internet. Files are copied to an FTP server and can be downloaded by anyone with FTP *client software* (client software is a software application that lets the user point to the location of the FTP server and name of the file to be downloaded). The FTP client application can be obtained as freeware from many Web sites, including cNet.com. The company that you select to host your FTP site should have a help page that tells you how to download, install, and use the FTP client software.

After you receive payment from a customer, you should send a confirmation e-mail that contains information on how to access the eBook file from the FTP site. You should include a *pointer* (the URL that's given to you by the hosting company) to the zFTP help page. If you think the help page is confusing or unclear (or even worse — not available), take the time to rewrite the help text in your e-mail so your customers are clear about how to access the file. These people paid for the right to read your eBook and you want to ensure that they don't encounter any barriers when they try to get the file.

The following list provides you with some *ISPs* (Internet Service Providers) that offer FTP-hosting services. In addition to reviewing these companies, you should talk to your current ISP to see whether it has FTP-hosting services available for you to use.

Unfortunately, Site Manager doesn't provide FTP-hosting services. If you use Site Manager to build your Web site, you need to work with a different ISP to provide separate hosting of your FTP files. As an alternative, remember that you can also e-mail eBook files to your customers.

✔ **Orphanage Services:** Provides an FTP-hosting account for $5 a month. See its Web site at www.orphanage.com/products/ftphost.shtml for more information.

✔ **NetBox:** Provides e-mail addresses for businesses and individuals. If you purchase a NetBox e-mail account for $1 a month (plus a $25 setup fee) you can add an FTP site for $1.50 (plus a $35 set-up fee). For more details, see `www.netbox.com/`.

✔ **Nvision.com:** (`www.n-vision.com/`) If you host your Web site with Nvision.com and purchase the Deluxe Server Package, you can create an unlimited amount of password-protected FTP accounts. (You can send the password for FTP access when you e-mail the customer.) The cost of the package is $80 a month with a $35 one-time set-up fee.

Password-protecting access to your FTP site

Some of the ISPs that you work with may offer password protection for your FTP site. If you decide to password-protect access to your site, make sure that you *don't* distribute your password to customers. (Your password is what you use to upload files to the site.) Your customers should have read-only access, as opposed to your personal access, which should be read-write access. This means that you have the ability to add and delete files to the FTP site, but customers can only download (read) the files. One advantage of password-protecting the FTP site is that a customer, after paying for the right to access the file, can copy the file to multiple platforms. If I buy access to an eBook formatted as an Adobe Acrobat file, I can copy it to both my desktop and my PocketPC. That way, I can keep reading a page-turner of a novel no matter where I am.

Ideally, you should create a unique password for each customer, giving that person access to a specific folder. And, you should create separate folders for each eBook that you sell. This way, a customer can use the password and get access to a single eBook in its folder, as opposed to getting access to all the eBooks on your list.

Creating separate passwords for each customer can be a lot of work, and tracking which password is sent for each payment that you receive can be even more work. If you start selling a lot of eBooks, you may want to create a single password for each eBook. Every customer receives the same password. Risky? Yes — because your password can be distributed over the Internet and people may stop paying for your eBooks because they can get an illegal copy for free.

One way to avoid this situation is to offer an added bonus (sent via e-mail) that is sent only to people who buy a copy of the eBook. The bonus should have real value that ties into the content of the original text. For nonfiction, content that is usually included in an appendix is great to send to someone as an incentive to pay for the eBook instead of copying a pirated version.

If your eBook becomes so popular that you're getting hundreds of downloads but not getting an equal number of payments, then it's time to distribute your content through a company like iPublish.com. iPublish.com can wrap your eBook file in a *DRM (Digital Rights Management) wrapper*. The wrapper is software that encrypts the eBook so only the authorized purchaser is able to unlock and view the file.

Distributing eBooks through e-mail

One of the easiest ways to distribute your eBook is to e-mail a copy to some-one after you receive payment. Don't worry if you have never attached a file to an e-mail before — it's a pretty simple process. Most e-mail programs (even free e-mail, like Hotmail.com) let you send files this way. For more info about how to use e-mail to send attachments, check out *E-Mail For Dummies,* 2nd Edition, by John R. Levine (published by IDG Books Worldwide, Inc.).

After you prepare the final version of your document, you should create an e-mail to send to your customer. This e-mail should contain the payment con-firmation and a "thank you" to the customer for the order. The eBook docu-ment should be sent as an attachment to this e-mail. A sample confirmation e-mail is shown in Figure 12-14.

To zip or not to zip? That is the question

Unless you include a lot of images or multimedia elements, most of the eBooks that you publish will be fairly compact in size (I'm talking about file size, not the length of your 1,200-page novel). When using authoring software, like Adobe Acrobat or the Microsoft Reader Add-in for Word, the authoring software compresses the file size for you when you save the file.

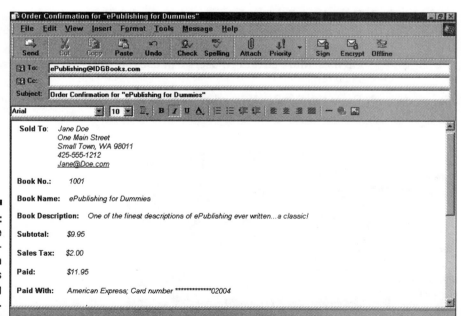

Figure 12-14: A sample order-confirmation e-mail looks something like this.

If you find that your files are becoming very large (anything over 250KB, for example) you may want to compress the file before you send it as an e-mail attachment. Some software programs compress the file into the smallest size possible. (I have no idea how these programs do their crunching magic; I just know that they work.) Of these programs, WinZip is one of the most popular for the Windows platform.

Although WinZip is a useful utility, your customers need a copy of the program to *unzip* (uncompress) the files. Remember to include information about this on the site where people purchase the eBook. If you distribute the eBook as an e-mail attachment, include instructions for unzipping the file within the body of the e-mail, along with the URL of a Web site where WinZip can be downloaded. This keeps your customers from getting confused and saves you the trouble of including the same information in a second e-mail (which you may have to send in response to questions about how to open the newly purchased eBook).

You can get an evaluation copy of WinZip from the Web site www.winzip.com. Follow the directions given on the Web site to download and install the file.

After you install WinZip, it's easy to create a *zipped* (compressed) file that contains the content of the original file. Just follow these directions:

1. **From the Windows Start menu, choose Programs.**

   The Programs menu contains a submenu called WinZip.

2. **From the WinZip submenu, select the WinZip program.**

   You can use the WinZip program in two ways: Novices can use the WinZip Wizard, which takes you through a series of screens to help you zip files. More advanced users can use the WinZip Classic version, which is faster.

3. **From the WinZip Wizard screen, click the Next button, as shown in Figure 12-15.**

Figure 12-15: The WinZip Wizard takes you through the process of zipping files, step-by-step.

The Select Activity dialog box appears.

4. **Select the Create a New Zip File option and click the Next button, as shown in Figure 12-16.**

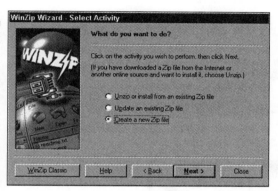

Figure 12-16: On the WinZip Select Activity page, choose the Create a New Zip File option.

The Choose Zip Name screen appears.

5. **Type the name of your new zip file in the File Name text box and click the Next button, as shown in Figure 12-17.**

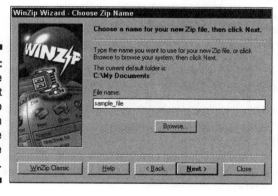

Figure 12-17: Name the zip file that you want to create in the Choose Zip Name dialog box.

You can change the directory where the new file will be created by clicking the Browse button. This allows you to browse to a new directory.

The Select Files dialog box appears, as shown in Figure 12-18.

6. **To select the files that you want to add, click the Add Files button.**

The Add Files dialog box appears. You can add the files to be zipped by clicking the name of the files. Multiple files can be selected by holding down the Ctrl key while clicking the filenames, as shown in Figure 12-19.

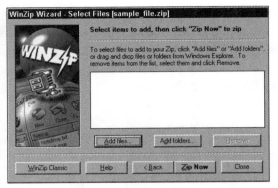

Figure 12-18: The Select Files dialog box is where you must pick the files to include in the zipped file.

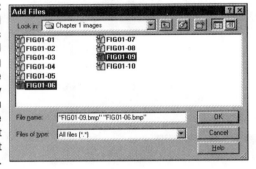

Figure 12-19: You can add multiple files to be zipped by holding down the Ctrl key while you click the files that you want to add.

7. **Click the OK button.**

You can see that the files have been added to the list shown in the Select Files screen. You can continue to add more files by repeating Steps 6 and 7, or you can zip the files by clicking the Zip Now button, as shown in Figure 12-20.

The WinZip program compresses the files and shows you a screen verifying that the operation is complete.

8. **Click the Close button to close the application.**

Unless you add images or sound files, don't expect WinZip to provide additional compression. Although it does a great job on text files, your eBook-authoring software has already compressed the text contained in the file. Experiment, but don't expect miracles. Nothing's going to shrink that 1.2MB monster into a petite little file. . . .

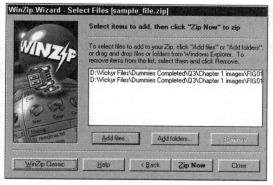

Figure 12-20:
When you're ready to compress the selected files, just click the Zip Now button.

Distributing eBooks through MightyWords.com

If you decide that setting up a Web site and taking credit card orders is just too much trouble — don't worry, you have other options. You can sell your eBooks through a distributor like MightyWords.com, or through an online bookstore like Amazon.com. Working with a distributor makes it much easier for you to get your eBooks to customers, but you have to pay the piper. Instead of keeping all the profits, you only get a percentage of the list price for each eBook that is sold.

If you plan on selling many eBooks, or if you want to become a publisher and offer a list of titles, then setting up your own Web site is cheaper. The only costs that you pay are the hosting cost and the costs associated with processing the credit cards. If you plan to sell a small number of titles, or if you think you'll only sell a few eBooks (because your magnum opus, *The Mating Habits of the Hummingbird,* has a limited audience), keep reading and I'll explain how to sell your work through another source.

MightyWords.com: A new market for your work

You can sell your eBooks and *eMatter* (digital documents that are longer than an article but shorter than a full-length eBook) on MightyWords.com. Listing your eMatter on this site costs $1 per file, per month. MightyWords.com pays authors a 50 percent royalty, which means that if you sell your product for $10, MightyWords.com sends you a check for $5 for every copy sold from their site. MightyWords.com accepts files submitted in Adobe PDF format, Microsoft Word 97 or 2000 DOC file format, Adobe Postscript format, and plain ASCII text files.

eMatter: Short but sweet

eMatter is a new vehicle for you to distribute your work and start to build an audience for your full-length eBooks. If you have very timely content or if you don't have enough time to pound out 200 pages on the keyboard, you can still write 10 to 50 pages and submit them for sale. If you find that some of your eMatter titles are selling well, you can take the time to develop these into full-length eBooks. You can sell these longer texts on your own Web site, but you already have an audience that's buying your work through MightyWords.com, so you may as well sell them through MightyWords.com.

eMatter can also be written as addendums to your full-length texts. For example, if you have an eBook that took you thousands of hours to write, you don't want to issue a revised version when you discover that your information is dated just a month or two after you published it. So instead of editing the manuscript, you can publish the new information as eMatter and point your readers to the document. In addition to providing updated information, this helps bring in extra revenue.

Submitting eMatter to MightyWords.com

If you go to the MightyWords.com Web site and click the <u>Publish eMatter</u> link, you find all the information you need to start publishing. The process is simple: You first need to register on the Web site by filling out a series of simple forms. After you create a user account, you're registered to purchase eMatter and are able to sell files on the site.

When you create a MightyWords.com account, you must provide credit card information. MightyWords.com charges $1 per month for each eMatter document that you post to the site. Your credit card is charged for this hosting fee.

You're also required to provide a Tax ID or Social Security Number. Uncle Sam requires MightyWords.com to send you a 1099 tax form if you earn more than $600 by selling eMatter on the site. The Tax ID or SSN is used when MightyWords.com fills out its portion of the form. If you're not comfortable giving this information when you create a user account, you can wait. MightyWords.com contacts you for the information after you reach the $500 sales mark.

If you have previously registered as a user at FatBrain.com (www.fatbrain.com), you can use your existing account information on the MightyWords.com site because FatBrain.com is the parent company of MightyWords.com.

You're also asked to agree to a Content Provider Agreement before your account can be created. Review this document carefully — it contains some useful nuggets of information, like when you get paid, in addition to the legal mumbo-jumbo that MightyWords.com's lawyers insisted be added to the agreement.

You must also include your name and a short biography (which is important in establishing credibility if you're not a well-known author yet). If you hope someone buys your treatise on how to manufacture widgets, you should use your bio to establish yourself as a widgets expert.

You should include an estimated page count, publication date, and list price. Not sure what to charge? Review MightyWords.com's minimum list price requirements based on file size. You can find this list at `http://ematter. fatbrain.com/ematter/support/faq_011.asp`.

Don't sell yourself short! The prices on MightyWords.com are the *minimum* prices that can be charged. You should do a search on the site for material that's similar to yours and see what the prices are. Your eMatter should be in the same price range as similar material, unless your document offers the audience a significant advantage.

You need to choose a subject category, which is where users will be able to find your document when they browse the site. To maximize sales, it helps to be as accurate and granular as possible when you choose a category. Don't just select Antiques & Collectibles when you could select Antiques & Collectibles/Books & Manuscripts. When potential customers browse the site, they look to purchase information of a specific nature. Although it's tempting to pick a broader category and hope more people see the blurb for your eMatter, your sales will actually increase if you try to focus on a more targeted group.

Finally, you're asked what type of file you'll be uploading to the site. MightyWords.com accepts files formatted as Adobe Acrobat (PDF) files, Adobe PostScript (PS) files, Microsoft Word (DOC) files, and ASCII text (TXT) files. Then you're done. (In reality, now starts the hard work of marketing if you hope to sell any copies, but at least you're done with the distribution process.)

Distributing eBooks through Amazon.com

Amazon.com has the Advantage Program for small publishers that allows them to list their books on the site and sell them . . . just like the big boys!

Unfortunately, Amazon.com doesn't currently sell eBooks (with certain notable exceptions like offering Stephen King's *Riding the Bullet* in eBook format). Because of this, if you want to sell eBooks through Amazon.com's Advantage Program, you need to copy your eBook files to CD-ROMs or floppy disks, and send several copies for Amazon.com to distribute. Amazon.com stores these in a warehouse and orders extra copies from you if it needs to fulfill new orders. You can find information on the Amazon.com Advantage Program by going to the home page of the site, and clicking the <u>Site Guide</u> link. This takes you to Amazon's Site Map; if you scroll down the page, you find a Special Resources section. Click the Advantage Program link to find out more about what Amazon.com offers small publishers and independent authors.

Copying eBooks to a CD-ROM that needs to be physically distributed misses the point of eBooks . . . almost as silly as a printed book about how to create eBooks. You can purchase a CD-ROM drive that allows you to read and write CD-ROMs, but burning CDs quickly gets expensive. In addition to the price of the drive (a good one usually costs between $300 and $500), each of the CD-ROM discs costs between 75 cents and a buck (depending on whether you buy in bulk). You need to create labels (more software, more supplies, more cost to you), plus jewel boxes or CD-ROM envelopes to ship the CDs. You need to provide installation instructions; these can be printed on a simple piece of paper that can be folded and slipped in the box or envelope, along with the disc. And you will need to pay for the postage to ship the discs to Amazon.com each time new inventory is needed.

A better solution is to create a zShop on Amazon.com for the purpose of selling your eBooks. Setting up a zShop is similar to setting up a Web store using the Microsoft Site Manager. The advantage to having a zShop: Your products will be listed on Amazon.com every time someone searches for a product that matches keywords entered in your product description. Because millions of people purchase products on Amazon.com, this can be a great way to promote your eBooks without needing to copy files onto CD-ROMs.

Working with BN.com

Through a relationship with iUniverse.com, Barnes & Noble has several programs available from its Web site to make it easier for authors to publish or reissue a book. From the BN.com home page, click the <u>Publish Your Book</u> link to get more information about the programs.

If you have a new manuscript, you should review the Writers Club and Authors Choice programs; authors who want to reissue out-of-print work should look at the Authors Choice Out-of-Print program and the iUniversity Press program, which was designed for new and out-of-print academic or training materials.

iUniverse.com provides templates that make it easy to submit text and graphics online, although it accepts mailed submissions as well. Currently, all books are issued as printed volumes, which can be sold through BN.com's distribution channel.

The program can be costly. For a first-time author who wants to submit a manuscript online, it costs $99 ($134 if you submit it by mail) to get the book printed. The book does not receive any editorial review or qualification, and you get one free copy of the book for the fee.

For eBook publishers who want to produce pBook versions of their text, the BN.com programs may be of interest, but BN.com is making a large investment in the eBooks arena. In the future, BN.com will probably offer a similar program (minus the $99 printing set-up fee) to allow authors to sell eBooks through the site.

Chapter 13

Working with an ePublisher

Not ready to become an ePublisher? Many new ePublishers are emerging that you can collaborate with to get your eBook published. Although each ePublisher has a different submission process, most work in the same general way. In this chapter, I show you how to look for an ePublisher, and I describe the advantages and disadvantages of working with one. I also show you how to find an agent that you can trust.

Even if you're convinced that you prefer to work with an ePublisher instead of going solo, I encourage you to read Chapter 12 (which covers how to distribute your titles) and Chapter 14 (which shows you how to ePublish your own content). When you see what's actually involved in ePublishing, you may decide to give it a try before you share your profits with someone else.

Contrasting ePublishing and Traditional Publishing

I used to have a recurring fantasy. It went like this: I write a brilliant and witty novel destined to be a *New York Times* bestseller. I submit the manuscript to a top literary agent, who recognizes a gem in the slush pile. The agent forwards the manuscript to a major publisher, like Warner Books, HarperCollins, Random House . . . I'm not picky. The editor signs me to a three-book contract and the bidding for the movie rights goes into the millions. Next thing you know, I'm a guest on *Oprah*.

Dissolve to real life. The problem with my fantasy is that I have a better chance of winning the lottery (another fantasy of mine). I may never publish a novel with Random House, but if I write well, the chances are good that an ePublisher will publish my manuscript.

Working with an ePublisher is different from working with a major print-publishing house. In the print world, an author gets an *advance* (an advance payment on royalties that the book is expected to make) after he or she signs the contract. The more copies the book is expected to sell, the larger the advance. After the book's publication, the author also gets *royalties* (a percentage of the sale of each book). Although the royalty rates vary from publisher to publisher, they're rarely more than 15 percent of the book's list price (and some publishers pay considerably less).

Because ePublishers are usually small companies, they don't pay advances when you sign an eBook contract. The good news, however, is that the royalties can be as much as 50 percent of the eBook's sale price. For authors willing to promote the sales of their eBook, the higher royalty rate may make an eBook more profitable than a printed book.

One of the reasons that eBook publishers can offer higher royalties is that they don't have the same production costs as print publishers. A print publisher needs to pay for printing, binding, packaging, warehousing, and shipping to retailers. In addition, print publishers accept *returns* (books not sold in the bookstore that are returned to the publisher). Because of this, publishing print books is expensive and risky. A print publisher can't print too many copies of a book unless it seems like a sure thing because too much revenue may be lost on the unsold books.

eBooks are much cheaper than printed books. Without the high production costs of printing books, an ePublisher can make a profit on a small number of sales (especially because no advance is paid to the author). For more information on the production costs involved in eBook publishing, see Chapter 14.

Because publishing eBooks isn't as costly as publishing printed books, many titles can now be published or republished that wouldn't have had a chance before ePublishing. These include the following:

- ✔ Niche books that don't attract a large audience.
- ✔ Books that are traditionally considered to be *mid-list titles* (quality books that aren't destined to be bestsellers, but are published by publishers specializing in literary titles). As publishing becomes more expensive and competitive, fewer mid-list titles are published (and fewer literary publishers exist to print them).
- ✔ Out-of-print books.
- ✔ Crossover books that span two or more genres, such as a romantic-horror story or a science-fiction mystery.
- ✔ Textbooks customized for a specific course.
- ✔ Digital books that take advantage of interactive elements like hyperlinks and media clips.

Experimental books are welcome

Some of the most successful eBooks are works that have been rejected by print publishers. This is because large publishing houses need to find hit books — mainstream stories that attract a large audience and generate revenue. In addition to book sales in the United States, publishers take an active role in selling the international rights, movie rights, and other book rights. Because the focus is on finding a mass market audience, the book industry, like the movie and TV industry, gravitates toward formulaic books that have proved successful in the past. If you think about it, how many books have been modeled after the John Grisham formula? In case you haven't read any good books lately, this formula involves a young, idealist lawyer who decides to fight the system, and in the process, wins a really big case in the name of justice.

ePublishers are in a much better position to take a chance on publishing experimental manuscripts. To have a successful eBook, an ePublisher must build a community of readers who feel involved in the text. To create this community, an ePublisher can publish an e-mail newsletter, create an online bulletin board, or host a chat.

Looking for an ePublisher

If you're interested in working with an ePublisher to distribute your eBook, keep these tips in mind while you search for one:

- ✔ **Identify ePublishers that focus on publishing titles in your genre or area of interest:** These ePublishers have contact with the key reading communities in your genre, and can help you promote your title.

- ✔ **Before you sign with an ePublisher, ask what type of promotional assistance the company provides for your title:** Don't expect a public-relations push or a book-signing tour, but a good ePublisher should help you participate in online chats and such.

- ✔ **Find out whether the ePublisher publishes an e-mail newsletter:** A company that reaches out to its readers on a regular basis will sell more copies than ePublishers who just put up a Web site and hope readers find it.

- ✔ **Find out how the ePublisher promotes his or her Web site:** They should have a well-defined plan for driving traffic to the site. No traffic, no sales. . . .

- ✔ **Find out whether the ePublisher can distribute your titles to other retail outlets:** A company that works with online bookstores, like BN.com and Amazon.com, will sell more copies of your title than a company that only sells through its own Web site.

✔ **If a company charges a fee to "evaluate" your manuscript, look for another company:** These companies make their money from evaluating the manuscripts of hopeful writers, not from ePublishing the manuscripts. If you're serious about getting published, look for a company that's serious about publishing your work.

✔ **Find out the formats in which your eBook will be offered:** Because nobody is sure which format will emerge as the standard for eBooks, find a company that formats your title in Adobe PDF, Microsoft Reader LIT file format, and RB (Rocket eBook) format.

✔ **Ask whether the ePublisher supplies *DRM* (Digital Rights Management) support:** With DRM, your eBook is encrypted and only a reader who purchases the right to read the eBook is able to open the file.

✔ **The ePublishing company should have a professional-looking Web site:** This means no garish colors, no irritating animated GIFs dancing all over the screen, the pages should be displayed quickly, and the site navigation should be easy for a user to understand.

✔ **Pay attention to how products are displayed on the site:** Does the potential buyer have a way to search or browse through the eBook catalog? Are the cover images clearly displayed? Is the right amount of information (title, author, price, page count, file-download size, supported formats, and short description) provided for every book on the site? Remember, if another author's title doesn't look good, your title may not look good, either.

✔ **Download an eBook from the site and review the production quality:** What fonts are used for the body text? What fonts are used for the headings? What colors are used? Review the images featured in the eBook (especially the cover image) to see whether images are shown at an optimal resolution. *Note:* Many ePublishing sites offer one or two free titles. Sometimes, a single chapter of an eBook is offered at no cost. Look for a freebie before you spend money to see the quality of an eBook's production.

✔ **If the ePublisher sells titles directly from a Web site, make sure that the site follows good e-commerce practices:** SSL security for protecting consumer's credit cards, a privacy policy that ensures that buyer information isn't sold, authentication of credit cards before the file is downloaded to the user's hard drive, and so on.

✔ **Look for an ePublisher that still accepts title submissions in your genre:** Because ePublishing firms are small, they may be swamped with manuscripts. If you're ready to publish a children's book, look for someone who can evaluate your manuscript soon (not a timeframe of six months to a year).

Getting an Agent

Why would you want to think about working with an agent? If you plan to ePublish your own work, an agent isn't really necessary unless you want to sell subsidiary rights to your work. But, if you plan to work with an ePublisher, an agent can make your life easier and give you more time to write. An *agent* works to sell your manuscript to an ePublisher and takes a percentage of the money you make. The best ePublishers are swamped with manuscripts; an agent who has connections and relationships with a number of editors can ask them to evaluate your work (and determine whether to publish it).

Although ePublishers are fairly new on the publishing scene, a few leaders will start to emerge from the pack in the near future. The best companies will attract the best authors and will offer the best editorial, marketing, and publicity support. The authors chosen to publish with these companies will have more sales and they will get better promotional opportunities. Because of this, more eBook submissions will come to these companies, and these companies will begin working with agents who can help editors identify the most promising writers.

Why it's better to have an agent

If you want to work with the best ePublishers, now is the time to establish a relationship with an agent. In addition to getting your work in front of editors, an agent can negotiate the best deal for you, and can work to sell subsidiary (and print) rights to your work. An agent generally takes 10 percent of the deal that you negotiate with a publisher, but a good agent is worth it.

I published this book using an agent. Working with my agent, Carole, has been a wonderful experience. She handled all negotiations, got two publishers interested in publishing this book, and negotiated on my behalf when I needed help during the proposal process. She reviewed my proposal and gave me valuable suggestions on how to improve it. She also gave me advice on how to promote my book after publication.

Getting an agent can be a catch-22. Many agents don't want to talk to you until after you publish a work (and how can you publish without an agent?). If you run into this conundrum, you can publish your first eBook yourself and contact an agent after you have a proven track record of sales.

Writing a query letter to your potential agent

To find an agent, you need to send out a query letter telling the agent about your background and the book that you want to write. Query letters used to be formal documents, but these days, a simple e-mail can be sufficient.

Like everyone else, agents are busy people. A query letter isn't the time to dazzle the agent with your mastery of prose. Keep it short, simple, and to the point (but remember to proofread and spell-check the letter before you send the e-mail).

Although your query letter should be short and sweet, make sure to cover these key points:

- ✔ Describe the book that you want to write in the first sentence of the e-mail.

- ✔ Let the agent know how you acquired his or her name.

- ✔ Let the agent know if some of your earlier work has been previously published.

- ✔ Explain why you're qualified to write an eBook about the topic you chose.

- ✔ Let the agent know your next logical step (for example, mention that you're willing to provide a writing sample and an outline for the eBook that you want to write).

If you decide to work with an agent, keep these pointers in mind:

- ✔ **Agents receive many unsolicited submissions:** Don't waste your time and efforts sending something to an agent unless you first send a query letter or e-mail and are then invited to submit a manuscript.

- ✔ **Look for an agent who has experience in brokering deals for digital content:** eBook authors get higher royalties but no advance. Make sure your agent knows the structure of eBook deals.

- ✔ **Look for an agent who has worked with other authors publishing in your genre:** This agent will have the editorial contacts that you want. It's pointless to find an agent who specializes in romance authors if you want to write a technical eBook.

- ✔ **Your agent should get your work in front of editors you'd never be able to get by yourself:** If your agent announces with delight that you have a deal to be published on MightyWords.com, look for another agent. You can be published on MightyWords.com just by going to its site, signing the author agreement, and uploading content.

- **An agent should never charge to read your work:** If someone charges you to read your manuscript, keep looking for a more professional agent.

- **Ask your agent to have the *digital rights* revert back to you after a period of time:** Digital rights allow you to publish the content in a digital format (like an eBook or online newsletter). If you negotiate for these rights, you can publish your work again after a period of time, or work with another ePublisher on a new distribution deal.

- **Ask your agent to make sure that you retain all print, international, and subsidiary rights to the work:** If you don't retain these rights, you should be getting more (advance and/or royalties) from the ePublisher.

- **At some point, your agent asks you to sign an author/agent agreement:** As with any legal document, review the terms carefully before you sign.

  Check with your accountant to see whether the fees paid to your agent can be deducted as a business expense.

- **Ask whether your agent will work to get any out-of-print titles reissued in eBook format:** This assumes you have out-of-print titles, of course.

Creating a proposal

If an agent agrees to represent you, he or she asks you to create a *proposal* for your eBook. A proposal is a short document that explains to an editor the content of your eBook, the target audience of your eBook, why you're qualified to write the manuscript, and a draft of the eBook outline. If your agent asks you to create a proposal, ask him or her for a sample so you can follow the agent's preferred format.

Even if you've already created the eBook, a short proposal is the best way to interest an editor. Ask your agent whether you should attach the eBook document to the proposal instead of the Table of Contents. With luck, the editor will start reading your manuscript and won't be able to put it down.

Finding an agent online

You can find a number of agents by simply surfing the Internet. Here are a number of methods to try:

- **LiteraryAgent.com** (www.literaryagent.com): This site has a large database of literary agents that you can search through for free. Some agents have home pages linked from the site. (You can find out more about an agent by looking at his or her home page.)

- **The WritersNet Guide to Literary Agents** (www.writers.net/agents.html): This Web site offers support for authors and a database of agents to search through. The Agents Guide lists only those agents who don't charge a *writing fee* (a cost that disreputable agents may charge for reading and evaluating your manuscript).

✔ **Your favorite writing support site:** Writers tend to be a generous bunch and you may get a lot of help if you post a question on a bulletin board, asking for suggestions to help you find an agent. I found my agent after another writer suggested that I contact her.

Contacting eBook Publishers Online

If you decide not to get an agent and want to contact ePublishers directly, here's a list of Web sites you may want to look at:

✔ **1stBooks.com** (www.1stbooks.com): This site is designed to support self-publishing, so it's technically not an ePublisher. But, from the site, you can publish your eBook. Any eBooks published through 1stBooks. com can be reformatted for print-on-demand distribution (your eBook will be printed at the time it's ordered). The distribution for these soft-cover editions is managed by Ingram Book Group, the world's largest distributor of printed books. With print-on-demand, your "printed" eBook can be made available through retailers like Barnes & Noble and Amazon.com.

✔ **BookLocker.com** (www.booklocker.com): This ePublisher features titles in various genres. Currently, BookLocker.com publishes in PDF (Acrobat) format only. The company no longer accepts proposals or queries in poetry, creative writing, or children's genres, but it does accept proposals for other genres.

✔ **BookMice.com** (www.bookmice.com): This small ePublisher offers eBooks formatted as PDF and HTML. In addition to letting customers download the eBook files from the Web site, BookMice.com can ship the content on a CD-ROM. BookMice also acts as an Acrobat service bureau; if you don't own Adobe Acrobat, it converts your text files to PDF for $100 per title.

✔ **iPublish.com** (www.ipublish.com): Although iPublish.com is a division of Time Warner Trade Publishing, the group acts like a small company (with the financing that a larger company offers). iPublish.com is devoted to creating a writing community; you can submit your Word manuscript by uploading it directly to the site.

✔ **MightyWords.com** (www.mightywords.com): This site supports self-publishing by authors. You can submit your document to MightyWords. com for a nominal fee. MightyWords.com does all document conversion and lists your title in its eBook/eMatter catalog. When someone purchases your eBook, MightyWords.com keeps 50 percent of the sale.

This is only a handful of ePublishers; many more are on the Web — with new companies being formed every day. If you want to keep current with the new organizations, or find ePublishers specializing in a specific genre, go to eBookNet.com (www.ebooknet.com). This Web site focuses on the eBook industry and contains a good listing of ePublishers. To find the comprehensive list of major eBook publishers, scroll down the home page to the Directory section, and click the <u>By Publisher</u> link under the Things to Read section.

Another good page to check out is eBookNet.com's Getting Published information. From eBookNet.com's home page, click the Getting Published link under the Writing eBooks section.

Chapter 14

Becoming Your Own ePublisher

*B*eing a publisher requires much more work than writing an eBook and letting someone else manage the marketing and distribution, but it can be much more profitable, too. You don't just get a percentage of the sale price of every eBook; you get to keep all the profits, and use these to launch new titles (which can create even more profits!). Before you decide whether to become an ePublisher, though, ask yourself whether you have the time and commitment to drive your own business. Being the owner means making hard business decisions and focusing on increasing profits. You need to keep detailed records about all of your business transactions, especially if you plan on publishing eBooks written by other authors.

Sound interesting to you? Keep reading. If owning your own publishing empire sounds like too much work (or just not interesting), I suggest that you look at distributing your work through Web sites like MightyWords.com (see Chapter 12) or work with one of the already established ePublishers (see Chapter 13).

Becoming an ePublisher

If you have set up a Web site to sell your eBook — congratulations! You're already an ePublisher. If you want to grow and start selling other titles, this chapter tells you a little bit about the business of publishing.

The advantages of becoming a publisher

If you currently sell your titles through a distribution arrangement with another company, you know the percentage that the company takes from the sale of every eBook. In some cases, the cut can be as high as 50 percent or more. Distribution and ePublishing companies justify this price because they *distribute* the eBook title (they receive payment and deliver the title after the purchase is transacted). ePublishers also provide some marketing support. Authors (especially authors of well-selling titles) question whether the support they're getting is actually worth the percentage that they're forced to pay.

You can easily set up your own Web site to sell titles. (See Chapter 12 for instructions on how to do this.) As an author, marketing your titles is something you need to take responsibility for, whether you publish yourself or are published by someone else. Unless your distribution service is providing you with valuable resources — like editing support, promotional support, or great product placement on the front page of the Web site — maybe it's time to go solo.

Figuring out whether ePublishing is profitable for you

The correct way to decide whether to ePublish is to sharpen up your pencil (or in my case, fire up the old spreadsheet) and start plugging in the numbers to make a good business decision. While you do the math, keep the following points in mind:

- ✔ **Figure out the *opportunity cost* of your time.** This is the time you put into your business that takes away from something else. If you plan on quitting your day job, it's easy to figure out the opportunity cost of your time. If you plan to work in your spare time, however, you have no opportunity cost to calculate (unless you give up a moonlighting job). When you determine the opportunity costs, don't forget to estimate what running your business will cost you in writing time — because you'll certainly have less. For example, if you made $4,000 from your last eBook, which took you 1,000 hours to write, then the opportunity cost of your time is $4 per hour. If you need to spend 100 hours a month to run your business, then the opportunity cost of your time is $400 per hour.

- ✔ **Determine any overhead costs needed to keep your business humming along.** Do you need to rent office space? Do you work at home but lease a high-speed data line? How much does it cost you to host your own e-commerce–enabled Web site? Anything else?

✔ **Do you need to add any capital equipment costs?** This may include the purchase of a new computer, scanner, graphics tablet, and so on.

✔ **Do you need to purchase new software?** To become an ePublisher, you will need to invest in the authoring software that converts Word or HTML documents to eBook formats.

✔ **Do you need to get professional support of any kind?** An accountant's usually necessary to help with tax preparation. You may need to calculate the cost of additional support services, as well.

✔ **Calculate the out-of-pocket costs for the services that you currently get from your ePublisher.** These services may include editorial support, marketing support, eBook cover design, and so on.

Other costs probably exist, but it isn't necessary to track every expense at this point (you need to track *everything* after you launch your new business; your accountant insists on it). Right now, you're just getting a rough idea of what it takes to start your own ePublishing effort. If you don't know the cost of everything, you can do some quick research on the Web. Look for firms that provide the services that you need and check out their prices. If a term sheet isn't available on the Web site, contact the company by e-mail and ask for price estimates.

After you collect all the numbers, you can enter them into a spreadsheet. You can just write down all the numbers on a piece of paper, but entering the content into a spreadsheet makes it easy to play around with the numbers. Figure 14-1 shows a sample spreadsheet that yours should resemble.

If you need to save some money, you can go with a cheaper editorial service or do some guerilla marketing instead of hiring an expensive agent.

After you enter all the data into a spreadsheet, you can quickly see whether it makes sense for you to stay with your current ePublisher or to go out on your own.

A copy of the spreadsheet shown in Figure 14-1 is available on this book's CD-ROM.

In addition to the costs of running your business, you will have individual book-production costs that vary according to how much you must spend to create each eBook. With ePublishing, you won't have the traditional (and expensive) costs of printing, binding, and shipping to a distributor, but you still have costs associated with hiring an editor and getting an artist to produce cover art.

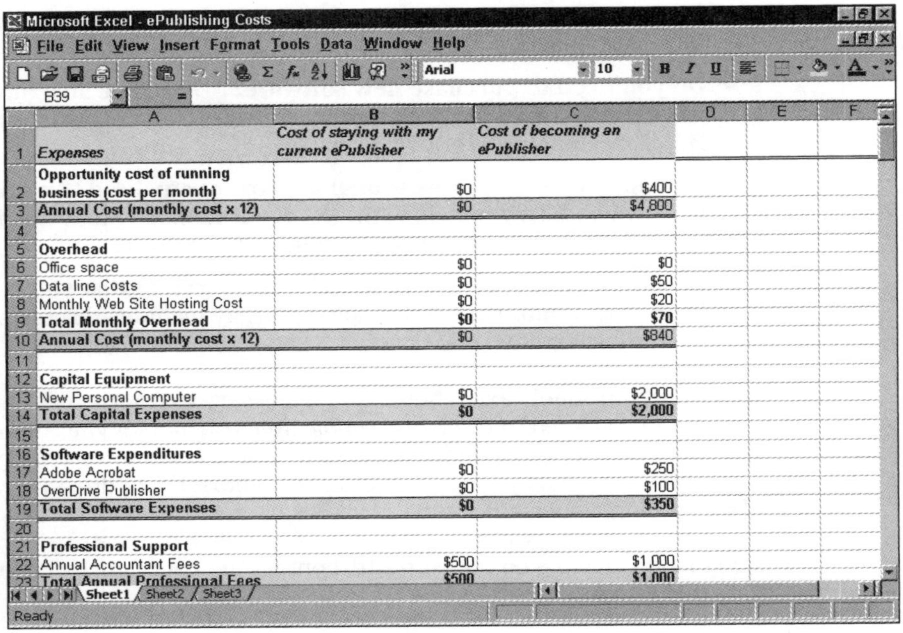

	A	B	C
1	*Expenses*	*Cost of staying with my current ePublisher*	*Cost of becoming an ePublisher*
2	**Opportunity cost of running business (cost per month)**	$0	$400
3	**Annual Cost (monthly cost x 12)**	$0	$4,800
4			
5	**Overhead**		
6	Office space	$0	$0
7	Data line Costs	$0	$50
8	Monthly Web Site Hosting Cost	$0	$20
9	**Total Monthly Overhead**	**$0**	**$70**
10	**Annual Cost (monthly cost x 12)**	$0	$840
11			
12	**Capital Equipment**		
13	New Personal Computer	$0	$2,000
14	**Total Capital Expenses**	**$0**	**$2,000**
15			
16	**Software Expenditures**		
17	Adobe Acrobat	$0	$250
18	OverDrive Publisher	$0	$100
19	**Total Software Expenses**	**$0**	**$350**
20			
21	**Professional Support**		
22	Annual Accountant Fees	$500	$1,000
23	**Total Annual Professional Fees**	**$500**	**$1,000**

Figure 14-1: You can use a spreadsheet to see if you can profit by leaving your current ePublisher to start your own ePublishing business.

Table 14-1 shows you rough estimates on what types of costs need to be calculated for producing your eBook. In fact, your eBook costs can vary tremendously depending on many factors, such as the quality of cover art you require, whether you need to pay development costs for audio, animation, or video, and how much effort you decide to put into marketing. In Table 14-1, I show you the cost of marketing — whether you ePublish yourself or through someone else. Notice that you will probably spend more if you do it yourself.

Table 14-1 Production Cost per eBook

Production Cost	*Cost of Staying with Current ePublisher*	*Cost of Becoming an ePublisher*
Editorial	$0	$200
Marketing	$300	$300
Annual book submission fee	$12	$0
Cover design	$0	$150
Total production cost per eBook	**$312**	**$650**

Now you need to estimate how many eBooks you want to produce in a year. For example, let's say I plan to launch three eBooks in 2001, and I'm trying to figure out whether I should continue to work with my current ePublisher or do it myself. To figure out what each book will really cost me, I divide my annual expenses by the number of eBooks I plan to publish. When I add this to the production cost per eBook, I find out what it really costs me to ePublish each title. Table 14-2 shows how I calculate this number.

Table 14-2	Real Cost per eBook for Three Titles	
	Cost of Staying with Current ePublisher	*Cost of Becoming an ePublisher*
Production cost per eBook	$312	$650
Number of titles per year	3	3
Annual production costs	$936	$1,950
Expenses per number of titles	$167	$2,997
Real Cost per eBook	**$479**	**$3,647**

Suppose I get 50 percent of the profits from each eBook that is sold through my current ePublisher, and suppose my eBook sells for $20. That means I get $10 per eBook sold. At this price point, I need to sell more than 48 titles to make back what it cost me to produce the title. If I ePublish the title myself and sell it at the $20 price, I need to sell more than 183 copies before I make a profit. But, as the publisher of the title, I can raise the price of the eBook (or figure out how to lower my costs). And if I expect to sell mucho copies of my eBook, it may be more profitable to ePublish titles solo.

If I produce more than three eBooks a year, however, the equation changes. Table 14-3 shows what the numbers look like if I produce ten titles in 2001. (By being hyper-productive, I hope to pay for that new computer!)

Table 14-3	Real Cost per eBook for Ten Titles	
	Cost of Staying with my Current ePublisher	*Cost of Becoming an ePublisher*
Production cost per eBook	$312	$650
Annual production costs	$3,120	$6,500
Expenses per number of titles	$50	$899
Real cost per eBook	**$362**	**$1,549**

This looks better. I only need to sell 37 titles to make back what it cost me to go with another ePublisher. If I ePublish the title myself, I only need to sell 78 titles before I turn a profit. If I raised the price of my eBook to $40, then I need to sell just 18 titles through somebody else or 39 titles myself before I make a profit. And if I decide not to purchase an expensive computer, I won't need to sell as many titles to be profitable before the year's end.

Making the move from author to publisher

I enjoy writing — when I can find the time to sit at my computer between dealing with the demands of my job and the demands of my family. But I don't enjoy bookkeeping. Writing is pleasure, but ePublishing is business. If you decide that you want the bigger profits that come from doing it all yourself, you need to be prepared to track all the finances that come with running a business. The purpose of this chapter isn't to tell you everything you need to know to run a small business (that would require an entirely different book!). But if you want to become an ePublisher, keep these things in mind:

✔ **Tax implications:** Tax-wise, owning your own business is different from working for someone else. Before you start your business, make an appointment with an accountant to find out what records you need to keep and how often you need to pay taxes.

✔ **Legal implications:** You should talk to a lawyer to find out whether the business should be incorporated, and how to protect yourself and your family's assets in the event that you get sued.

✔ **Sales tax:** Controversy surrounds the issue of whether Internet-based businesses should be required to charge sales tax on each purchase. Your accountant can guide you in this.

✔ **Publishing policies in different cultures:** The World Wide Web truly is worldwide. You'll be selling eBooks to people around the world. In the United States, the First Amendment protects your freedom of speech (you can write almost whatever you want, as long as you don't write something libelous or infringe on someone's copyright). Other countries, however, have more restrictive policies about what can be published. To date, no clear-cut guidelines exist about exporting editorial material over the Internet, but the issue is something to be aware of. You may want to talk to your lawyer about this, too.

One of the greatest things about ePublishing is that you can easily distribute eBooks by yourself with only a small capital investment. The need to consult accountants and lawyers may turn you off, but I encourage you not to skip these critical steps. Professional support can save you a lot of time, money, and heartache by helping you figure out the right way to run your business.

Two good reference guides to running a small business are *Small Business For Dummies* by Eric Tyson and Jim Schell, and *Starting An Online Business For Dummies* by Greg Holden. If you want to learn more about keeping the books for a small business, you can learn a lot from *Quicken 2000 for Windows For Dummies* by Stephen L. Nelson.

Setting a Price for Your eBook

After you calculate the real cost of producing an eBook, you can think about what to charge your customers. Remember, you need to focus on making a profit! You can do this by charging a lot for each eBook, thereby selling fewer titles, or you can charge a small amount for each eBook, and sell a large volume of titles.

Because eBooks are only just starting to sell well, you should try to keep your business costs down until you can accurately assess the market for your titles.

I can't give you a magic formula to help you determine what to charge for your eBooks. If the knowledge that your eBook offers is exclusive, highly targeted, or can help people make money — you can charge more. Or if you're an acknowledged expert or have a well-known name in your area of expertise, you can charge more. For example, Bob Vila can charge more for an eBook about house maintenance than your Uncle Frank who has been a carpenter for 30 years.

One of the great advantages to selling a product over the Internet is that you can easily change your price and see the immediate impact on sales. If your title isn't selling well at $12.95, drop the price to $9.95 and see if any change occurs in sales volume. Remember that it's always easier to charge less for something than to charge more. If you charge $19.95 for a title, you can put a "Special $13.95 bonus price — this week only!" notice on your Web site. People who were mildly interested in your title before, may now decide to check it out at the lower price. If you're not sure what to charge, start with the higher price and then lower it if you have to. You may find that the title is selling so well, you don't need to lower the price (and you'll be making more profit from each sale).

Ever wonder why stores charge $9.95 instead of $10.00? For some reason, the larger number serves as a psychological barrier. It seems silly, because I know I'm just saving a nickel, but it works. If you don't believe me, try it for yourself. Start by selling a title at a whole dollar price (like $5) and then lower the price by a nickel (or even a penny) and see what happens to the number of units that you sell.

Cheaper won't always sell more

Although more people are inclined to buy something at a lower price point, sometimes you can lower your prices too much. Before someone buys your eBook, he or she has to perceive you as a credible author. If you claim to be the greatest stock analyst that the market has ever known, yet you charge only $4.95 for *Making a* *Fortune in the Stock Market,* potential readers may see you as a charlatan rather than the expert that you are. Strangely enough, if you charge $39.95, you may sell more copies — especially if you include your bio and credentials in all your marketing materials.

Check the competition's prices

I'm chattering on and you're still waiting for help in figuring out a price for your eBook (enough theory, get to the point already). In Chapter 3, I show you how to research the competition for the topic of your eBook. Here I do a variation on the same research, but I focus on what the competition is charging. Once again, Amazon.com and BN.com are the best places to start.

To research your competition's prices, follow these steps:

1. **Go to** www.amazon.com **and type the topic of your eBook into the Search text box. Leave the All Products option showing and click the Go! button.**

   My hypothetical eBook is *Potty Training in Three Easy Steps,* so I use *potty training* as my topic. (This is wishful thinking on my part; the potty is actually a source of conflict between me and my three-year-old son.)

   I don't find any eBooks about potty training, so I look for printed books on this topic. When you price an eBook, expect to sell it for less than the price of similar *pBooks* (printed books).

   Amazon.com returns the top results for a search on potty training in four product categories: books, music, video, and zShops. Music and videos aren't really applicable when researching manuscript prices, so I focus on prices in the books and zShops section.

   When you research prices, make sure to use the All Products option when you begin searching. By searching for all products, you're able to find the books sold through zShops and auctions. These books may be the most helpful when determining a price for your product. Amazon.com doesn't have a dedicated eBook section, so most eBooks are sold through zShops.

2. Click the See all Results in Books button.

Amazon.com shows you the three most popular potty-training books. Two of these books are priced between $5 and $6, and the third book (a guide for parents) is priced at $12.55.

Under the top three sellers are the first 50 book results. Scanning through the list, I see prices ranging from $1.61 to $19.50. Scanning the prices gives me some idea of a range, but I know an easier way to do it — keep reading.

Right under the top three titles, Amazon.com shows me that the remaining titles are sorted by availability.

3. Click the down arrow in the drop-down list and select the Price: Low to High option, and then click the Go! button.

Amazon.com now ranks all the "potty training" books from the cheapest to the most expensive. By looking through the list, I notice that 17 of the books are priced between $5 and $6, and that 14 of the books are priced between $7 and $9. Because so many books are priced in this range, I can assume that my target market will probably buy potty-training books at these price points.

4. Click the More Results button to see the remaining books. These books are the most expensive.

Only one title is more than $20. The remaining books don't have a price listed because they're out of print. This research showed me that potty-training books are priced between $2 and $20 and most are listed between $5 and $9.

5. Use the Back button to go back to the Search Results page that shows how many results have been found in different Amazon.com product groups.

I click the Back button three times, until I'm back to the page that lists the results found in books, music, videos, and zShops.

6. Click the See All Results In button for one of the other product sections.

I click the See All 6 Results in zShops button. Of the six results listed, five listings are for the same product: a personalized potty-training book that sells for $8.95. (Maybe the author of this book created five separate products with the exact same name? We may never know the answer. . . .) The final product is a puzzle selling for $4.99. Because a puzzle isn't similar to the eBook that I want to sell, I ignore it.

To be thorough in your research, you should also take a look at the prices listed on the Barnes & Noble Web site.

Pricing eMatter compared to printed work

Pricing eMatter is tricky. You can charge per page, but with this method, longer eMatter documents may cost more than full-size books. Before you price your eMatter, you should do some research on MightyWords.com:

1. **Go to** www.mightywords.com **and type the topic of your eBook into the QuickSearch text box. Click the Go link.**

   Because of my new obsession with potty training (I'm so tired of changing diapers), I decide to look for any eMatter on the subject by typing *potty* into the QuickSearch text box. To my surprise, the query returns two results: an article by Gary Maddock priced at $2 for 10 pages, and an article by Amelia Taylor, priced at $15 for 24 pages.

   I don't know the credentials of either author, and considering the differences in cost for the two articles, I question how much value could be in a $2 article. I'm biased toward the more expensive article. But, because I want to be unbiased, I decide to do further research on both articles to see why they may be worth purchasing.

2. **Click the eMatter Title link to find out more about a specific article.**

3. **Click the Back button to return to the QuickSearch Results page and click the title link of a different article.**

   I click *The Consistent Parent Guide to Potty Training*, which is the title of the $15 article. The summary shows me that this article is focused on the content that I care about. But $15 for a 24-page article seems costly (many full-length books are available on the subject for less). MightyWords.com has certain minimum list prices, depending on the size of the file. But files under 5MB have a minimum list price of only $2 and this file is a mere 666KB.

4. **Click the Author Info link under the More Information column to see the author's bio and qualifications.**

   By clicking the Author Info link, I discover that the author holds a master's degree in special education and has extensive experience working with disabled children and adults. This author can charge $24 for her knowledge because she's a qualified expert in the field.

Copyrighting Your Work

Before you start distributing your document to the world, you need to take steps to protect yourself so others can't take credit for your work. In other words, you need to *copyright* your intellectual property. Applying for a copyright is pretty simple and can be one of the best investments you ever make.

Legally, a copyright gives an author the exclusive right to control the copying of a creative work. If you don't want anyone to copy or distribute your eBooks without your explicit permission, or if you want to ensure that you're reimbursed for any copies of your work that get circulated, you should learn a little about how copyrights protect your interests.

Why you should copyright your work

Technically, your ideas are copyrighted from the moment you write the eBook, even if you don't put a copyright notice on the document. Including a copyright notice with the text of your eBook helps remind readers that all the included content is copyrighted. Adding the notice strengthens your legal protection in the event that you need to sue someone who violates your copyright. To incorporate a notice in your text, you should add a copyright page to your document. This page usually goes after the title page, but before the first page of content. On the copyright page, add the following text near the bottom of the page: Copyright *(date goes here)* by *(your name goes here)*. You can also use the symbol © instead of the word *Copyright* in the notice.

I'm not a lawyer (and I don't even play one on TV). If you have questions about copyrights and copyright law, you should consult a lawyer who can give you information to meet your specific needs.

For even stronger copyright protection, you can apply for a *copyright registration* from the Library of Congress. A copyright registration is a legal formality that establishes a public record of your copyright claim. You need to have applied for a registration (for works of U.S. origin) before you can file a copyright infringement suit in court. I can sweep away the legalese with this summary: You have a copyright even if you don't register it (but you need to register before you can sue).

Going through the copyright process, step by step

You can register your copyright through the Library of Congress. To get a copyright, follow these steps:

1. **Go to** `lcweb.loc.gov/copyright`, **the Copyright Office page at the Library of Congress Web site.**

2. **Under the Publications heading, click the <u>Forms</u> link.**

You need a copy of the Adobe Acrobat Reader to view the copyright registration form. To get a free copy of the Acrobat Reader, go to the Adobe Web site at `www.adobe.com/products/acrobat/readermain.html`. Follow the instructions to download and install the reader. (If you want more detailed instructions on how to install the reader, see Chapter 1.)

3. **Scroll to the middle of the Copyright Forms page to see the list of available copyright forms.**

Most eBooks require *Form TX,* which is the form that pertains to published or unpublished non-dramatic literary works. (Your novel may be quite dramatic, but unless it's written in the form of a play, you should still use Form TX.) Even if your work is nonfiction, Form TX is the one to use when you register the copyright. You can choose from three versions of Form TX:

- **Form TX:** If you're unable to use the Short Form TX, you need to use the basic Form TX. Situations where you would use Form TX include works by multiple authors, multiple copyright owners, work done for hire, and work that contains previously published or registered material.

- **Form TX with instructions:** Both the Form TX and the Short Form TX are self explanatory, but if you're confused by a term or the information required on the form, download the Form TX with instructions.

- **Short Form TX:** You should use this form if you are the only author and copyright owner of your work, if the work wasn't done under a work for hire agreement, and if the work is completely new (doesn't contain a substantial amount of content that has been previously published, registered, or is in the public domain).

When you click the link for one of these forms, Acrobat Reader launches and displays the form that's downloaded from the Copyright Office site.

4. **After you review the contents, print a copy of the form.**

Print the form on a white, 8.5- x-11-inch piece of paper. The Short Form TX takes up one side of the paper, but if you use one of the other TX forms, you need to print the form using both sides of the paper.

The Copyright Office doesn't accept forms printed by dot-matrix printers. If you use an inkjet printer and use the Shrink to Fit Page option, you need to enlarge copies of the forms. For best results, the Copyright Office recommends using a laser printer.

5. **After you fill out the form, sign it and include the following:**

- **Two copies of the work:** If the work is unpublished, you only need to include a single copy.

- **A check or money order for $30:** Make checks payable to the Register of Copyrights.

6. **Mail the package to: Library of Congress, Copyright Office, 101 Independence Avenue S.E., Washington, DC 20559-6000.**

Several months may pass before you get the certificate, but it arrives in the mail to the address you indicate on the form.

Updating your copyrighted material

Whenever you update your eBook (by adding new content, illustrations, or anything else that can be considered a substantial change), you should remember to update your copyright registration by using Form TX. You won't be able to use the Short Form because you previously copyrighted the material.

Applying for an ISBN

Do you want to sell your eBook through a major bookseller like Amazon.com? If so, you need an *ISBN*. ISBN stands for the International Standard Book Number system. The ISBN is a ten-digit number that uniquely identifies books published throughout the world. With an ISBN, it's possible to identify a title unique to a specific publisher. Because a common numbering scheme is used, retailers are able to track the marketing and inventory of titles on a worldwide basis. ISBN numbers can usually be seen in conjunction with a bar code shown on the back cover of printed books.

eBook publishers don't need to worry about getting the bar code (unless you're required to distribute your eBooks on a physical medium like a CD-ROM), but you may want to apply for an ISBN number. For example, if I decide to ePublish a title in the public domain (for example, *Alice in Wonderland*) and your ePublishing company decides to publish an *Alice in Wonderland* title too, my ISBN helps online bookstores determine which title is which.

To publish printed books and eBooks in the United States, you can fill out the online application found on the R.R. Bowker Web site (www.bowker.com/standards/home/isbn/us/application.html). R.R. Bowker is the Agency of Record for the ISBN Agency (the International Agency that drives the standard). Any company that publishes a title in the United States must apply to R.R. Bowker for an ISBN.

Selling the Backlist

The way to make money from ePublishing is to develop a strong *backlist* (a collection of titles that can be sold year after year). If you spend the necessary money to develop an eBook in your first year of business, any money you make beyond the real cost of the eBook is profit. And if you keep selling that title in the second year of your business, all the money you bring in is profit (unless you invest in new marketing for the eBook). If you have a large number of backlist titles that bring in revenue, you have the freedom to invest more money in new titles. That's why you want to develop a good backlist as soon as possible.

Building your backlist

Generally, the more eBooks you sell, the more profitable your ePublishing venture is for you. Yet, with the exception of Stephen King's eBook (which sold close to 500,000 copies in just a few days), most eBook bestsellers have sold only a few hundred copies. Maybe you were hoping to sell a few million copies of your eBook and retire to Maui? I hate to burst your bubble, but you have a better chance of winning the lottery. (However, if you do manage to sell a few million copies, contact me so I can find out how you did it.)

Instead of hoping that one title sells many copies, focus on selling some copies of many titles. Having a backlist of titles is valuable because you can sell more, and because you can combine several titles into a packaged bundle and sell them as a set. I discuss more about bundling at the end of this chapter — here I show you how to sell multiple titles.

Selling multiple titles may sound great in theory, but if it took you months to produce *The Teen Girl's Guide to Dating,* you may wonder how you can get several titles out in a calendar year. It's pretty easy if you plagiarize yourself. Plagiarizing other people's work is *wrong,* but because you own the copyright on your own work, nothing can stop you from "serving leftovers" packaged for a different market. Look at the material you wrote for *Girl's Guide.* Chances are that most of it is pretty generic (or can be, with a little judicious editing). If you rehash some of this material and add some new content, in a short amount of time you can create the following titles:

- *What Girls Think about Dating: A Guide for High School Guys*
- *Help Your Teenager Daughter Learn about Dating*
- *The Parent's Guide to Teen Dating*
- *What to Avoid on a Date*
- *How to Get Asked for a Second Date*

These titles sound like different books, but the content is actually pulled from the same source. If you publish these titles, you'll notice that some sell many more copies than others. This means that you've done a good job of targeting a specific market (for example, if *The Parent's Guide to Teen Dating* sells well, you should write a few more books focused on parents and move away from the teen market).

Don't lower prices on backlist titles

If it ain't broke, don't fix it (and if your backlist titles are still selling well, don't change the prices on them). Unlike pBooks, you don't need to worry about the costs of holding on to physical inventory (warehouse costs, shipping costs, and so on). If you find that sales from your backlist are starting to drop, figure out why — don't just drop the prices. Is the content a bit dated? Is the topic no longer hot? If you can change the content to make it appealing again, do so and keep the higher price. If nothing seems to help, you can try lowering your prices, although you'll probably bring in more revenue by bundling slow-selling titles with better-selling titles.

Another easy way to build your backlist is to create sequels and revised editions. You can take some of the material you used in the first version and add some new content. The end result takes you less time than the first version did. For the eagerly anticipated sequel to *The Teen Girl's Guide to Dating*, I can write these titles:

- *More Teen Dating Secrets*
- *Girl's Guide: What to Wear on That Important Date*
- *Girl's Guide: Dating Etiquette*

Another point to remember when creating a new title is that eBooks don't need to have hundreds of pages. If you're not up for writing a full-length sequel, then write and publish some *eMatter* documents. (eMatter refers to electronic documents that are longer than an article, but shorter than a full book.) You can then update the first eBook with a reference to the new, shorter documents. If people like your first eBook, they'll see the advertising for your eMatter and be more likely to buy the follow-up document.

Finding other authors to ePublish

If you're serious about building up a good backlist, you can solicit work from other authors. Most ePublishers currently don't pay *advances* (money which is given to an author when a book contract is signed, before the book is written). If you don't pay an advance, you need to pay the author a higher percentage of the royalties. The standard rate is 50 percent of each eBook sold.

The real cost in finding other authors is the time that you must take to review query letters and read through manuscripts — trying to find quality eBooks to publish. Most print publishers have teams of editors who work with agents to find marketable titles. But because you're a team of one, it may be difficult to find time to do it all. If you're generating enough profits from the titles that you currently publish, you may want to hire some part-time help.

An inexpensive source of editorial help can come from your local college. Solicit the assistance of students majoring in English to do a first pass through your *slush pile* (the collection of manuscripts you must dig through to find publishable work). You can pay these students by the hour — or if you're strapped for cash, offer to pay a percentage of the royalties for each eBook that they "discover."

Updating backlist titles

You should review your backlist titles at least once a year to determine whether the content can be updated and sold to existing customers as a revised edition. You may want to review the titles more than once a year if the information that you sell changes frequently (such as titles focused on technology or medicine). When you update a title, in addition to making sure that the facts are updated, also see whether any of the following can be revised:

- ✔ Anecdotes and examples
- ✔ Lists and references
- ✔ Web addresses (URLs)
- ✔ Step-by-step instructions
- ✔ Information presented in the appendixes
- ✔ New terms to be added to an updated glossary

Don't forget to update your copyright notice.

Licensing to create derivative works

You can contact other publishers (especially small press publishers who aren't ready to tackle eBooks on their own) and offer to co-publish eBook titles based on printed titles in their backlist. The ideal arrangement would be you licensing the content without paying, in exchange for converting the title to eBook format and then distributing the eBooks through the channel that you set up for your own titles. Under this arrangement, the print publisher expects to take most of the profits because they paid all the expenses to produce the title in the first place. But this can be a good way for you to bring in revenue and build a list of quality eBook titles to sell from your site.

You can produce an eBook that's an exact version of the printed text (but in digital format). You can provide more value (and negotiate a greater share of the revenue) if you add additional interest to the title in the form of interactivity and added media. See Chapter 6 for information on how to incorporate more than just text in your eBooks.

Bundling for Greater Profit

You've done everything you can think of, and you still have only five titles to sell this year on your Web site. Is it time to give up and start planning for next year's eBook list? Not just yet . . . you, the ePublisher, still have a couple more tricks up your sleeve. You can bundle two or three of your titles together in a single package that you can sell for less than the list price of the titles if sold separately. Everybody loves the idea of a bargain, and folks are more inclined to buy if they feel they're getting a terrific value.

Microsoft made a huge success in the Office application software market when they bundled Word, Excel, Access, and PowerPoint into Microsoft Office. Microsoft sold the Office bundle for far less than the cost of the individual applications and sales were incredible.

You can do the same thing with your eBook titles. Here are some tricks to help make your bundling a success:

✔ Although you may want to include one or two *front list* (new) titles, most of the titles in your bundle should be from your backlist.

✔ Include a dog or two. Every backlist has some titles that stopped selling well (or never sold well to begin with). Make sure to include these as a part of a bundle. Although you don't have to worry about getting rid of inventory, they make the size of the bundle seem more impressive.

✔ Make sure that your bundle has a common theme so it doesn't look like it came from the $1 bin of the second-hand bookstore. Focus all the titles around a business theme, a romance theme, reference works, and so on.

✔ Give your bundle a catchy name. The *Complete Online Business Kit* will sell much better than the *Web Book Bundle*.

✔ Although you want to offer a lot of value, be sensitive to the amount of time it takes a customer to download multiple eBooks. You may want to compress all the files into a single zip file (see Chapter 12 to find out how to zip files) or send each file attached to a separate e-mail.

✔ Make sure that you provide the customer with some real value. No one wants to get obvious garbage. If none of your titles sell well, you won't increase sales by bundling them together. Your efforts would be better spent figuring out what needs to be improved.

✔ Don't think that eBooks are the only items that can be bundled. You can bundle an eBook with several eMatter articles. You can bundle a couple of eBooks with a monthly subscription to an e-mail newsletter. The possibilities are only limited by your imagination.

✔ Use bundling as a way to stand out from the competition. If the competition is selling a single eBook and you're selling a bundle with five times the amount of information at a similar price point, which offer appeals more to potential customers?

✔ If you can't beat 'em, join 'em. If a competitor wrote a title that you think is great, offer to bundle the title with complimentary ones you have on your list. You can share the profits according to the size of each company's contribution and each of you will have a chance to find new customers for the rest of your list.

✔ If you work with a print publisher, you can offer a print-eBook bundle. Include the URL where the eBook can be downloaded, printed into a copy of the bound book. Every customer who buys the printed book gets a bonus eBook.

Part V
The Part of Tens

The 5th Wave   By Rich Tennant

DENISE AND JERRY LEVIN — AUTHORS OF "LOST IN THE MALL PARKING LOT", "THE MISPLACED GALLERY INVITATION", AND, "THE BAD HAIRCUT — WHY ME?"

Truthfully? If it weren't for ePublishing, many of these stories would have remained untold.

In this part . . .

*I*f you're ready to publish your eBook, Part V gives you advice on how to market and promote your work.

Chapter 15 shows you ten ways to eMarket your work in order to increase sales.

Chapter 16 gives you ten things to try to get publicity and promotion for your eBook.

Chapter 17 describes ten other types of ePublishing if you want to branch out from eBooks.

Chapter 18 gives you ten blunders to avoid if you don't want your eBook to look amateurish.

Chapter 19 shows you ten ways that eBooks are changing the publishing industry.

Chapter 15

Ten Ways to eMarket Your Work

*Y*ou wrote your eBook, formatted and published it, and now you want to take a well-earned break before moving on to your next project. Whoa! Not just yet — no matter how much the beach beckons you. All your work is wasted unless you market your book. This chapter gives you tips on how to market your eBook and get recognition for your work.

Getting Great Online Reviews

Online reader reviews at bookstores such as Amazon.com and BN.com are critical to the success of your book sales on these sites. If someone's interest lies in a specific topic, that person will conduct a search on these Web sites. The search results return multiple books. A way to differentiate yourself from the competition is to make sure that your eBook gets great reviews. Amazon. com displays stars next to books that include reviews. The more stars a book displays, the better the book is, according to its reviewers. BN.com doesn't show any ratings next to each book that a search returns, but it ranks the books in best-selling order as it returns the search results.

Any time that someone compliments your work, say "Thank you," and ask whether he's willing to post an online review for your eBook. In time, you build up an impressive list of reviews that can help new readers decide to purchase your book instead of the competition. If your book gets a large number of reviews, one or two bad ones don't matter.

If you never get compliments on your work, however, or if your work is racking up a number of negative reviews, pay attention to what people are saying. If your book isn't satisfying your customers, rewrite it and send the revised copy to each of the negative reviewers, asking whether they're willing to critique the new version's improvements. People love seeing you take their comments seriously and using them to improve your product. If you address your reviewers' criticisms, you can often turn some of your biggest critics into your biggest fans.

Mentioning Your eBook on Everything You Do

Make sure that you mention the name of your eBook on every e-mail you send, in every letter you mail out, and every time that you introduce yourself to someone. I'm no longer just Victoria Rosenborg; I'm now Victoria Rosenborg, author of *ePublishing For Dummies*. Without even realizing it, you come in contact with dozens of people each day. Each person may become a potential client if he or she knows about your eBook.

 A simple way to make sure that your eBook is everywhere is to change the *signature* on your e-mail. A signature is a standardized message that you can automatically add to the end of every e-mail. Check to see whether your e-mail package supports signatures and update yours if it does.

Building a Web Site to Market Your Work

Even if you don't plan to sell your eBooks through your own Web site, you want to create a site specifically to market your work. You want your Web site to list every eBook you publish right on the home page, along with some biographical information about you, the author. Link each book title to a page providing information about that eBook. Make sure that these pages contain a link to a site that enables the user to purchase the eBook. You don't want to leave an interested customer with his credit card out and no way to buy.

After you build your site, add the Web address to your e-mail signature and include the URL on every piece of paper that you create. Anyone who's curious about your eBook can then go to the Web site for more information.

If you don't know how to build a Web site, see Chapter 12. The chapter explains how to create a Web site to sell your eBooks, but you can also use the information to create a marketing Web site. For detailed info on how to build a Web site, look also at *Building a Web Site For Dummies,* by David Crowder and Rhonda Crowder (published by IDG Books Worldwide).

Attracting Traffic to Your Web Site

A Web site is useless unless you get people to visit it. To promote your Web site, participate in newsgroups and chats as an active participant, write articles, and publish newsletters. (Strangely enough, these are the same activities you should do to promote your eBooks.) To spell out the obvious . . . promote your eBooks on your Web site and promote your Web site (so you can promote your eBooks). If you really want to cross-market your work, mention your Web site in every eBook that you publish.

Linking to an Affiliate Program

If you're trying to sell eBooks on your Web site, you can set up an *affiliate program* so that other Web sites drive traffic to your site. An affiliate program enables other Web-site owners to add links to your eBooks from its Web page. If a user clicks one of these links and winds up buying an eBook, you pay a small commission to the owner of the site that sent the user to you. Amazon.com uses its affiliate program with great success to drive up the sales of its books and other products.

If setting up an affiliate program sounds difficult, some Web sites manage the entire process for you. One site to check out is bCentral's ClickTrade service at http://clicktrade.bcentral.com/.

Establishing Credibility through Newsgroups

Newsgroups give you a chance to "meet" on a regular basis with people interested in your area of expertise. In addition to establishing credibility as an expert, you can see exactly what interests these people (which can then form the basis for your next eBook). As with any e-mail you send, make sure that you mention your eBook and Web site in your signature whenever you post an item to the newsgroup thread. If people like what you say, they may check out your Web site or buy your eBook.

Because newsgroups present an opportunity to impress an interested audience, take the time to spell-check and edit your responses before clicking the Submit button. You may be the greatest expert on hummingbirds the world has ever known, but you're going to look like an idiot if your post is full of grammatical errors and typos.

Chatting with Potential eBook Buyers

To bring attention to your work and establish yourself as an expert, offer to participate as the guest in online chats. Contact the moderators or online producers of Web sites devoted to your topic and offer to participate in any chats they may be planning. Ask the moderator to mention your eBook as the moderator introduces you at the start of the chat and to mention it again at the end of the chat. Don't plug your eBook during the course of the chat; just respond to questions participants present to you.

If you participate in a chat, don't let an obnoxious heckler throw you and don't let anyone draw you into pointless arguments — unless you hope to generate controversy. Ask the moderator for help if something comes up that you can't handle. That's the moderator's job, and he has probably had experience with the same participant in previous chats!

Contributing to Periodicals

After you write an eBook, you establish a credential as an author. Use this credential to contact publishers of print and digital periodicals and offer to write articles about your area of expertise. Most publishers (especially small publishers) are eager to get new contributors for their publications. Don't expect to receive payment for your efforts, but offer to write in exchange for mentioning your eBook and Web site as a part of your byline. If people value the article, they may decide to purchase your eBook for more information. If the publisher likes the content you provide, you may even become a regular contributor. Anything that brings you attention and credibility helps the sales of your work.

Publishing a Newsletter

Although becoming the publisher of a free e-mail newsletter is hard work, it's one of the best ways to build a market for your eBook. As the subscription list for your newsletter grows, you can place ads for your eBook and increase sales.

If becoming a publisher interests you, the following tips can help get you going:

✔ Decide how often you want to publish your periodical. If you distribute an e-mail newsletter, daily publication is best but is often impractical unless you have a team of people working on the content. Start with a weekly publication schedule.

✔ Don't spam (ever!). Send your newsletter only to people who subscribe. Otherwise, you risk annoying potential buyers of your eBook, getting a bad reputation, and possibly losing Internet access. (Internet Service Providers may stop service to people who use their networks to spam.)

✔ Give subscribers a way to opt in and opt out of subscribing. Doing so is easy if you work with a ListBot service. These services manage your subscription list for you. Many free or inexpensive ListBot services are available. Do a search on the word *ListBot* at your favorite search engine Web site or check out the ListBot service at www.listbot.com.

✔ Make sure that you provide valuable information to your audience. If your newsletter's nothing more than advertising for your eBook, people often cancel their subscriptions after one issue.

✔ If you don't have the time to write all the content, ask others to contribute. Look for authors who want to promote their own eBooks (especially if their books complement and don't compete with yours) and ask them to write articles in exchange for some free promotion.

✔ Make sure that the content of your newsletter mirrors the content of the eBook you're trying to promote. Otherwise, you build an audience with no interest in buying your book. If your eBook is about existential philosophy and your newsletter is about home-plumbing secrets, you're probably not going to sell many books — except to existential plumbers.

- ✔ Put a form on your Web site to enable people to sign up for your newsletter. Many ListBot services provide you with the HTML code to add such a form to a Web page after you start working with their service.

- ✔ Put the name of your newsletter on everything you create. With luck, people ask about it and you can send them a sample copy. If they like what they read, you get additional subscribers.

- ✔ If your newsletter takes off and you build a large or very targeted list of subscribers, consider selling advertisements as a way of bringing in revenue.

Becoming a Public Speaker

Do you have the gift of gab? Becoming a speaker is a great way to attract attention for your eBook.

Many ways are available for you to become a speaker. You can offer your services to local groups (by contacting your local Chamber of Commerce for more information) or phone the coordinators of conferences devoted to your eBook's topic. Mention that you're the author of a book on the topic and you'd be happy to participate as a speaker or panelist.

If someone asks you to speak, make sure that the person who introduces you mentions that you're the author of an eBook. You also want to find a way to refer to your eBook in the context of your speech. With luck, the media may even quote you!

If you're uncomfortable speaking in public, don't squander a potentially great marketing opportunity. Look up Toastmasters in your local phone book to gain experience speaking in front of a group or sign up for a public-speaking course at your local community college. Speaking in front of a group becomes easier with practice and, after a while, you may even find that you enjoy it!

Chapter 16

Ten Ways to Publicize and Promote Your eBook

- -

In This Chapter

▶ Creating press releases

▶ Putting together a media kit

▶ Building a list of media contacts

▶ Writing cover letters that get noticed

▶ Submitting press releases to wire services

▶ Interviewing tips

▶ Getting favorable reviews

▶ Sending opinion letters

▶ Holding contests related to your topic

▶ Attracting attention

- -

*U*nless you have connections with one of the large eBook publishers, you probably don't have an advertising budget dedicated to your title. If you publish your eBook independently and your last name isn't Rockefeller or Gates, I'm guessing you don't have the finances to mount a national ad campaign. (Even if your last name is Rockefeller or Gates, don't waste your money on ads; your resources are better spent on publicity.)

Publicity is the art of getting other writers to write about you and your eBook. If you can get an editor interested enough to write about you, it's like free advertising. One well-placed article can have a huge impact on the sales of your eBook. Unless you have a topic worthy of national interest, don't try to get the attention of the large periodicals (such as *Time, Newsweek, USA Today,* and so on). These journalists get inundated with press releases. Chances are that your information will wind up at the bottom of the trash bin. Instead, focus your efforts on periodicals devoted to your area of interest, such as Web-based periodicals and local newspapers and magazines. If you get these editors interested in your work, it may have a chance to be picked up by the national press.

Writing Effective Press Releases

A *press release* is a one-page document (200 words or less) that should interest an editor or journalist enough to contact you for more information. When writing a press release, focus on what your eBook does for the reader. Your eBook is not news, but how it helps readers solve problems may be newsworthy. This is especially true if your eBook is the first to cover a specific topic or if it covers a topic in a unique way.

Start your press release with a catchy headline — something humorous or controversial is always good. Focus on a single idea (for example, don't try to cover every angle — take your strongest point and hone in on it). In your press release, answer the five *W* questions: who, what, when, where, and why. Use quotes or a short anecdote to draw the editor into the story behind your eBook. Finally, don't forget to include your contact information (including the URL of your Web site).

Creating a Media Kit

A *media kit* is a package of information about your eBook that you assemble to send out to the press. At a minimum, your media kit should contain a press release and a review copy of your eBook, but it helps to include additional material to catch the eye of an editor because you want your media kit to stand out from the rest. Successful media kits include the following:

- ✔ **An attractive cover or folder:** This can be a standard folder with your eBook cover image pasted on the front. If your eBook is seasonal, experiment with images that reflect the holiday (for example, a valentine pasted to the front of a folder for an eBook describing romantic things to do on Valentine's Day).

- ✔ **Cover letter:** This is one of the most important items in the media kit. A good cover letter gets an editor to look at your press release, eBook review copy, and remaining material.

- ✔ **Press release:** See the preceding section of this chapter for tips on how to write a good press release.

- ✔ **A review copy of your eBook:** This can be provided on a floppy disk. Although it may seem expensive to include a floppy disk instead of pointing the editor to a Web site where the file can be obtained, you want to make it easy for a reviewer to see your work. If your eBook requires specific reading software (like the Acrobat Reader), don't assume that the editor has it installed. Contact the company that owns the reader to see whether you can distribute a copy with your media kit.

✔ **Author biography:** This is a one-page summary of your personal history, and should include why you're qualified to have written the book. A bio shouldn't read like your resume — feel free to personalize it by including fun facts about yourself, your interests, and hobbies. If you're unsure what to write, look at the author bios of books that you currently own. (The author's bio is often on the back of the book jacket.)

✔ **Photos:** At a minimum, include the cover image of your eBook. You can also include a photo of yourself (have this shot taken by a professional; this is not the time to ask Mom to take your picture!). You can also add photos that may be included in the eBook's content.

✔ **Media clips:** If you include sound or video clips in your eBook, consider providing these on a floppy disk in the media kit. Anything that sparks an editor's attention makes your kit stand out from the rest.

✔ **Copies of articles that already mention your eBook:** These articles can be valuable if you've gotten favorable publicity at the local level and are trying to interest the national periodicals in covering your eBook.

✔ **Testimonials from reviewers:** If you sent your eBook to a group of reviewers and got good feedback, don't be shy. Include these on a separate sheet and slip it into your media kit.

✔ **Fact sheet:** This one-pager contains a high-level overview of your eBook: the title, author, publisher, ISBN, price, publication date, eBook formats supported, and price.

Finding Media Contacts

As you do research for your eBook by reading periodicals, take a moment to write down the editor, e-mail name (if provided), periodical name, and date whenever you read an article that relates to your topic. Over time, these notes can become a valuable list of media contacts. When you're ready to promote your eBook, these editors should be the first people that you contact because they've already shown an interest in writing about your topic. Remember to save contact information not only for the print periodicals that you read, but for the Web-based news sites and e-mail newsletters as well. Also save information about chat moderators because you may want to participate in a chat as a way to promote your work.

Two print resources to help you find more media contacts include the Literary Market Place and the Standard Periodical Directory. These directories are issued annually and you can borrow a copy from your local library.

A good resource for getting contact information (such as the editor's name and address) for print and electronic publications is PubList.com. See the tips for how to conduct advanced searches through the database at www. publist.com/search.html.

Writing a Strong Cover Letter

The cover letter that you include with your media kit should be personalized for the publication or the media type that you're writing to. (Yes, this is a lot of work, but you don't want to waste your money and effort in putting together a spiffy media kit, only to blow it because you didn't want to customize the cover letter.) In the cover letter, which should be short, suggest a story idea for the editor. The cover letter should tease the editor a little, and invite him or her to review the materials in the media kit to find out more about your eBook.

Submitting to Wire Services

Many Web sites let you submit your press release to the wire services. Many local newspapers and Web sites rely on wire services like Reuters or Associated Press to provide their readers with national news and feature stories. A story picked up by the AP wire can be carried in hundreds of newspapers. The following Web sites let you submit your press release to the wire services (but this is no guarantee that your story will be covered anywhere):

- **BizWire.com:** BizWire (www.bizwire.com) structures rates by how many circuits you choose to distribute your press release to. See about.businesswire.com/ for more information about its rate card.

- **DigitalWork.com:** DigitalWork (www.digitalwork.com) submits your press release to the PR Newswire, the leading source of immediate news worldwide. The starting price for many releases is under $100, depending on how widely you want the press release to be distributed.

- **InternetWire.com:** The price for a single, unlimited-length news release on InternetWire (www.internetwire.com) is $275.

- **XpressPress.com:** XpressPress.com also charges by how many circuits your release covers; prices start at $225 per press release. See www.xpresspress.com/ for additional information.

Getting Interviews

If the rest of your media kit does its job, you will start getting requests for interviews from the press or radio. You may even get requests for television interviews, although this won't happen unless you or your eBook is particularly newsworthy. Before being interviewed by anyone, take some time to write down the four or five key points you want to get across to the audience. Review and re-review this list before the interview, so you can concentrate on these points while you answer questions. Make sure you let the audience know where to go to get more information about your eBook. Finally, take the time to send a thank-you note to the person doing the interview. The interviewer may decide to contact you again in the future, so you want to leave a favorable impression.

Getting Good Book Reviews

A good review can dramatically increase the sales of your eBook. To get good reviews, first create a great eBook, then send out as many media kits as you can to every periodical that you think may have an interest in your eBook. Make sure to include Web-based reviewers in this list of contacts because they may be more inclined to review eBooks (as compared to their counterparts in the print world). Also send review copies to key people in the field covered by your eBook. Most of the time, you won't get a response, but if you capture someone's interest, you could get a great quote to help market your eBook.

Sending Letters to the Editor

Another way to bring attention to your work is to write a letter to the editor in response to an article about your area of interest. Try to make your letter somewhat provocative and make sure that you mention your eBook within the letter. For example, "As the author of *Everything You Ever Wanted to Know About Snorkeling But Were Afraid to Ask,* I was surprised to read that Bob Smith prefers the *xyz* brand of flipper." If it's published, a well-crafted letter to the editor can bring you national news exposure that you may not be able to get any other way.

Sponsoring a Contest

One way to promote your eBook is to sponsor a contest, and alert the media to your efforts. If your eBook is about gourmet cooking, hold a contest and offer to fly to the winner's home to cook a gourmet meal for eight people. The prize that you offer is less important than trying to create interest around you and your eBook. A simple way to hold a contest is to create a Web page that explains the contest and the rules. Invite participants to submit entries via e-mail. At the contest's end, print each entry out, put each entry into a large bowl, and pull out the name of the winner.

Some states have restrictions on the type of contests that can be held and how contests should be conducted. It's a good idea to check with your lawyer before holding a contest to make sure you're in compliance with all state laws.

Getting Noticed

The point of publicity and promotion is to get attention for you and your work. Bring the same creativity to your promotional efforts that you brought to your writing.

One of my friends at Microsoft wanted to invite record executives to a technical briefing. She had invitations to the event printed on a pair of men's briefs (for a briefing, get it?). Unfortunately, our group V.P. found out about the promotion and vetoed the idea. (There are still 300 boxes of men's briefs sitting in a storage room somewhere on the Microsoft campus.) Although this idea was never fully launched, I hope it inspires your efforts. Have fun and try to get noticed — that's the whole point! With a little ingenuity, you can attract attention for yourself and your eBook, and this increases your sales.

Chapter 17

Ten Forms of ePublishing

*Y*ou can make money from your ePublishing efforts in ways other than publishing eBooks. The ideas listed in this chapter may not make you rich, but they can provide some supplemental revenue while you wait for your eBook to become the twenty-first century's *Gone with the Wind*. As you experiment with new forms of ePublishing, you may find that they trigger ideas for new eBooks.

Any ePublishing that you do can serve as a promotional vehicle for your eBook efforts. Make sure to put the name of your eBook on everything you do. A link to your Web site should be prominently featured under the title of your eBook so people know where to go to get more information — and order a copy.

Becoming a Web Journalist

After you establish yourself as an author, contact online publications that cover your area of expertise. Offer to become a regular contributor. M.J. Rose, whose eBook *Lip Service* launched her to fame, often writes articles about eBooks and the publishing industry for *Wired* magazine. Because she's well-known as a journalist, her articles help increase her eBook sales.

If you're interested in writing articles for both online and print publications, subscribe to the *Writer's Weekly* newsletter, which sends an e-mail with a weekly summary of freelance job listings and new paying markets for writers. You can subscribe to the newsletter at www.writersweekly.com/.

Publishing an E-Mail Newsletter

If you want to publish your own newsletter, Chapter 15 offers tips that can help you get started. You can make direct income from a newsletter in two ways: You can charge a subscription fee, or you can sell advertising. If you have a very successful publication, you can do both.

If you want to charge subscribers, your newsletter should provide one or more of the following:

- ✔ **Exclusive information:** If your newsletter is one of the only places where subscribers can get certain information, they'll pay a premium to get the information. Although the newsletter is free, I pay to subscribe to Inside.com (www.inside.com) because they give gossip and insider information about the book, television, media, and recording industries that I can't get anywhere else.

- ✔ **Valuable information:** A top-ranked financial analyst, Michael Murphy, is an expert in the Internet and technology industries. He can charge a premium for his newsletter because his stock recommendations help readers make money.

- ✔ **Timely information:** If you provide information before others do, you can charge a premium for the data that you distribute. Clipping services that send subscribers an alert whenever a selected company is mentioned in the press can charge a premium for this service.

- ✔ **Information that's gathered and compiled in a unique way:** Before buying our current house, my husband spent many hours on the Web, researching and comparing scores for different schools in the towns we were thinking about living in. We would have paid for a report that presented this data in a clear, easy-to-compare format. If you research and compile data, you have a publishing opportunity to sell this information to others. If you compile information regularly, your data can become the basis for a profitable newsletter.

Selling Your Expertise

If you have expertise in a particular area, offer your services as a guru on several expert Web sites like InfoRocket.com (www.inforocket.com) or Epinions.com (www.epinions.com). Registered members of InfoRocket.com post questions about different subjects. Other site members "bid" to provide the answer. When you offer to answer a question, you fill out a form that describes your qualifications for providing the answer and how much you would charge for the answer (InfoRocket.com takes 20 percent of the fee). If you're selected to answer the question, the person who posted the original question provides a rating on whether your answer was satisfactory.

Epinions.com works a little differently. After you become a member of the site, you can post an opinion on any of the 100,000 or more products listed on the site. (If you've ever dreamed of being a movie reviewer or a critic, this site is for you!) As other members read and rate your opinions, you get paid a royalty. Although the royalties are small ($0.01 to $0.03 per reading), if you build a following of readers who check your opinion on a variety of products, the royalties can start to add up!

Selling eMatter on MightyWords.com

Most of the content of this book is focused on how to create and distribute full-length eBooks, but a market is emerging for content that is shorter than book-length text. Fatbrain.com (www.fatbrain.com), an online retailer that specializes in computer and business books, has created a secondary site called MightyWords.com (www.mightywords.com). MightyWords.com offers writers the opportunity to sell *eMatter* — electronic texts that are typically longer than an article (but shorter than a full eBook). You pay $1 per file per month to list your eMatter on the site. MightyWords.com pays authors a 50 percent royalty, which means that if you sell your product for $10, MightyWords.com will send you a check for $5 for every copy sold from the site. MightyWords.com accepts files submitted in Adobe PDF format, Microsoft Word 97 or 2000 DOC file format, Adobe Postscript format, and plain ASCII text files.

Keeping an eJournal

If you're not the shy type, publish an *eJournal*. Also called Web logs, these are Web-based diaries that are published on a regular basis (daily is best). Unlike the diary I kept under lock and key as a kid, anyone on the Web can read the innermost thoughts of someone keeping an eJournal. You can publish anonymously, but some people, like exhibitionists, don't bother to mask their identities. Some eJournals are soul-searching affairs (more like my pre-teen ramblings), while others are witty commentaries on current affairs.

According to Web lore, Netscape creator Marc Andreessen started keeping the first Web log in 1993. A copy of his journal can still be seen at `www.ncsa.uiuc.edu/SDG/Software/Mosaic/Docs/old-whats-new/whats-new-0693.html`. Marc's writing style is pretty dry and very focused on technology. A different style of eJournal is Jim Romenesko's The Obscure Store and Reading Room (`www.obscurestore.com/`). Jim's eJournal is so popular that he has been able to add advertising to help support his Web site.

If you create an eJournal site that gets a lot of traffic, you can banner ads on your site or become an affiliate (see the section "Click Here to Make Me Rich" for more information about becoming an affiliate). You may not make a lot of money from your Web site, but it can be used to help promote your eBooks and newsletters.

Writing Articles for Themestream.com

If your writing is distinctive, along with your personality, you may be able to make some money writing for Themestream (`www.themestream.com`). Themestream caters to enthusiasts — people who are passionate about their hobbies, sports, and interests. When you write and publish to Themestream, you get paid every time someone views your article. Themestream has more than 1,700 topics to write about; you're likely to find a topic in your area of expertise. Themestream is currently paying authors 10 cents every time an article is viewed (although they reserve the right to change their fee structure at any time). As an author, you have the opportunity to get your article in front of millions of potential readers, and to start building a portfolio of your work.

Themestream also has a Publisher Alliance program that is offered for free to qualified participants. You can provide Themestream with articles on your area of interest. These articles are included in free, personalized newsletters that are e-mailed to Themestream members expressing an interest in specific topics. If your article is included in the newsletter, your brand and logo are featured at the beginning of the article and act as a link to your Web site.

Themestream also includes a Subscribe Now button to let the online readers begin subscribing to your newsletter. If you are trying to build a subscriber list, submitting articles to Themestream can help publicize your newsletter.

Click Here to Make Me Rich

If you attract a lot of traffic to your Web site, you can benefit by becoming an affiliate — providing links to other Web site's products for sale. If someone clicks on the link and completes the sale, you get a commission. Amazon.com (www.amazon.com) has a highly popular affiliate program (they call it an associates program). After signing up, you can link to specific books, CDs, DVDs, videos, electronics, software, video games, toys, or home improvement items. You can also place an Amazon.com search box somewhere on your site, or just link to the Amazon.com home page. When someone clicks one of the links and makes an order, Amazon.com handles the customer service, fulfillment, shipping, and tracking of sales generated from your site, plus they send you a check.

Most affiliate programs work in a similar fashion. If you want to become an affiliate for multiple sites, check out the Affiliate Program Directory at Microsoft's bCentral.com (http://revenue.bcentral.com/). This service lets you sign up for many affiliate programs quickly and easily. However, other companies offer similar services. You can do a search on the term "affiliate programs" in your favorite search engine to find more information.

Holding a Contest

You can hold a contest for other aspiring writers and publish the winning entries in an anthology eBook or on a Web site. I know of one eBook author who holds a quarterly short-story contest. She charges $5 per story entered. The author of the best short story wins $100, publication of the story on a Web site, and copies of the author's eBook products.

The cost of running a contest like this is inexpensive (you can promote the contest on your eBooks, Web site, and newsletters), and the contest can become a source of revenue in two ways. First, each entry brings in some cash. And second, you can also profit from sales of the anthology (even after paying royalties to the contributing authors).

Before holding a contest of any type, check with your lawyer to find out whether any contest restrictions exist in your state, or any specialized laws that you need to comply with.

Selling College Notes for Cash

Although it's not popular with professors and universities, online services pay students to take notes during classroom lectures. These notes are posted to a Web site where they're available for people who didn't attend the class. Students can make hundreds of dollars per month, depending on the quality of the notes that they take. If you are attending classes and are a diligent note-taker, why not profit from what you are doing anyway? If you're interested, the three largest note-publishing companies are Versity.com (which pays about $300 per course), Study24-7.com (which shares a percentage of the site's advertising revenue to note-takers), and StudentU.com (which pays about $300 a course).

It's unclear whether note-taking services violate copyright law. The good news is that in 1996, a court ruled against the University of Florida; the University claimed that selling notes violated copyright law. The court determined that although lectures and handouts belong to the professor or university, notes belong to the students who could sell them, if they wish. Similar cases will probably be heard, as online note distribution increases.

Becoming a Biographer

I admit it. I've often dreamed of being famous enough to have someone write my biography. As it turns out, I'm not the only one with grandiose dreams. A new Web site called the BioRegistry (`http://bioregistry.com/`) offers ordinary people the chance to have an author write his or her life story. BioRegistry creates memorial biographies that can be posted to a Web site or privately printed. Although the price for a work commissioned from a known biographer is $4,000 for 2,000 words, fees are lower for well-trained but unpublished writers. If you are interested in becoming one of the writers, or you want to find out more about the service, send an e-mail to `portraits@ bioregistry.com` for more information.

Chapter 18

Ten Common Blunders

*I*f you write an eBook for a publisher, you get help in preparing a professional product. Editors review the text to make sure that the text contains no grammatical errors or typos. Technical reviewers go through the content to make sure that everything's accurate. A production team gets the text ready for the printer, crops and prepares images, and makes sure that the book uses the correct fonts. The end result looks polished — as if a team of people worked on it. (That's because a team of people *did* work on it!)

If you write and publish an eBook yourself, however, you're in charge of everything. You may be the next Shakespeare, but unless you take the time to create a package that's polished and professional, people are unlikely to take your work seriously. This chapter helps you avoid ten blunders that can hurt your work and your reputation as an ePublisher.

Not Testing Your eBook's Marketability

Respectable companies don't bring a new product into the market without testing its marketability, and neither should you. Take the time to test whether your eBook idea is marketable by researching the following questions:

- ✔ How many other books on the topic are currently on the market?
- ✔ How many articles are available?
- ✔ How many questions about the topic do you find on expert-opinion Web sites?
- ✔ How often are people asking about the topic in online forums?

If your idea seems hot, it's probably worth the time to research and write about. If no one seems interested in the topic, it's either a dud or it's so new that it isn't on anyone's radar screen yet. If you're still passionate about the topic, write about it — but prepare yourself to accept the fact that you may not sell many copies of your eBook. If that's okay with you, go for it.

Editing Your Document in a Hurry

No matter how brilliant your ideas, people can't take your work seriously if your eBook contains spelling errors and grammatical gaffes. After you finish writing, put the document aside for at least 24 hours. Then read it again and expect to correct errors that you missed the first time through.

Take the time to review your document with a fresh eye. Doing so is especially important if you're rushing to meet a deadline. You tend to make the most mistakes if you're in a hurry. Schedule the time for someone else to review the document after you finish proofing it. Your editor's certain to find new typos to fix, no matter how thorough you think you are — especially if you're in a rush. (I guarantee it.)

People give you money for permission to download and read your work, so providing them with a professional product is vital. You always want to take the time to edit and proofread your work carefully.

Using Too Many Fonts in Your Document

When I worked on the team that created Microsoft Publisher, we invited users of the software to submit work samples so that we could see what they were doing with the program. I remember one five-page newsletter that used 15 different fonts! Nothing screams "amateur" more than the overuse of different fonts. If you're unsure about how many to use in an eBook, take a look at printed books and magazines for guidance. Notice how most of those documents use only a few fonts.

Refrain from using more than three fonts in your eBook. Instead, you can use different sizes of the same font to add variety.

Assuming Your eBook Looks Good on All Screens

When I bought my PC, I splurged and bought a 21-inch monitor to go with it. Because the monitor is so huge, I set my screen resolution to 1,024 x 768 pixels. This setting makes things on my screen look smaller so that I can view more windows at a single time. Designing an eBook that looks terrific on my screen, therefore, is easy for me. But someone with a smaller monitor, who keeps the resolution set to 640 x 480 pixels, must scroll vertically and horizontally to view all the text and images that I can easily see on my bigger screen.

Unless you design an eBook for an eBook Reader, such as the SoftBook Reader, customers read your text on different monitors, with different resolutions, and at different color settings. Always test your eBook on as many screens as possible, which is easy if you conduct a *beta test*. Invite a variety of people, including people you "meet" through online forums and newsgroups, to try your eBook free of charge. Follow up with everyone to discover what problems anyone may experience in reading your eBook — and then work to correct those problems.

If any of your beta testers compliments your work, invite that person to post a reader review in online bookshops like Amazon.com, after you publish your eBook.

Writing Text That Belongs in an Infomercial

Before you first decided to purchase and read this book, you probably picked up a copy and leafed through its pages. If you purchased a copy online, maybe you looked through the table of contents and read an overview about the book before buying it. Something, at least, convinced you that you wanted this book and that I, as the author, have some credibility in writing about the subject. You may have doubted my credibility, however, if you'd read the following headline: "Buy this book and you need never worry about money again!!! Make $100,000 . . . $200,000 . . . even up to *$300,000* working in your spare time!!!"

Don't write text that reads as if you're lifting it from an infomercial. Your role as an author is to teach, entertain, inform, or cause the reader to feel something (depending on your type of writing). Although marketing how-to books may encourage you to add these types of teasers to help sell your content, don't make this mistake. You lose credibility in the eyes of potential readers, sound like an amateur, and irritate everyone who does buy your work.

Leaving Stale Content on Your Web Site

Building a Web site to market or sell your work is a great idea — but only if you commit to updating your site's content on a regular basis. Daily is best, but at a minimum, you need to update the material on your front page every week. A reader who comes to your site on a regular basis is hoping to find new information. If the page looks the same the second time he visits your site, that reader's unlikely to come back a third time, and you lose the opportunity to market your work to a potential customer.

If you don't have time to keep your Web content fresh, consider licensing a *newsfeed* that ties into the topics that you write about. The newsfeed providers give you a few lines of JavaScript that are added to the HTML of a Web page on your site. The script from the newsfeed displays headlines on your Web page and gets updated every day. You can even acquire such headlines for free, as long as you're willing to show the logo of the company providing the feed. Two sites to visit if this option interests you are ScreamingMedia.com (www.screamingmedia.com) and iSyndicate.com (www.isyndicate.com). You can sign up at these sites to put headlines on your Web site's home page, along with links to information about your eBooks. Readers come back for the headlines and encounter your marketing while they surf.

Spending Too Much Time Writing but Not Enough Time Promoting

You spend years writing the best novel since *Gone with the Wind*. You type **The End** on the last page and save it in an eBook format. You upload the book to MightyWords.com (www.mightywords.com) so that readers can buy a copy. You wait for orders to come in, and . . . nothing happens.

Of *course* nothing happens — no one knows that your gem of a novel exists. To get the recognition and movie contracts that you deserve, you need to start *promoting* your eBook. Promoting means putting together a media kit and a marketing plan. Review the ten suggestions that I give you in Chapter 15 on how to market your work and prepare yourself to spend at least three to six months promoting your eBook. Marketing takes a great deal of effort, but without this effort, you're wasting the time that you spend writing because no one's ever going to read your eBook.

Charging Too Little for Your Content

Ironically, if you charge too little for your work, people assume that it's not of much value, and you're unlikely to sell as many copies as you could have if you charged more. Determining how much to charge for an eBook can often prove difficult, but you always want to charge the higher price if you're not sure which of two prices is likely to work. Lowering the price later on is easy (as buyers always like a sale), but raising the price without giving buyers more for their money is much harder to pull off.

Charging Too Much for Your Content

Would you pay $175.95 for the book that you're reading right now? (If you did pay that much, I strongly suggest that you comparison shop at other book-stores in the future.) As an eBook publisher, you may make more profit per book at a higher price point, but you're unlikely to sell as many copies and your overall profits generally aren't as good as if you were to sell the same book at a lower price. To determine how to price your work, compare yours against a number of competitive books (both eBooks and pBooks). If your work costs significantly more than its competitors without providing better value (more information, new information, bonus material, and so on), you're charging too much. Anyone who comparison shops is more likely to buy from your competition. You can make your book a *little* more pricey than similar titles (which can make your product seem more exclusive), but you need to stay in the same general price range.

Thinking Only about Your Current eBook

Wearing the dual hats of an eBook author and publisher is hard work — don't kid yourself. You're constantly busy researching, writing, editing, formatting, getting permission for media and quotes to use in the book, testing your eBook, marketing it, and promoting it. Who can spend any time thinking about the next book? You'd better — at least if you hope to end up successful.

No matter what stage you're at with your current eBook, always try to think about what you want to work on next. Keep a notebook to jot down ideas or send an e-mail to yourself whenever inspiration strikes. You don't need to actively work on the next book right now — unless you're one of those people who thrive by working on five projects at once. But you do need to keep it in mind.

You need to keep your mind open to new ideas so that you're ready to move into your next eBook the second that you finish this one. I already know the topics of my next three books (although I have no idea when I may find the time to work on them).

Chapter 19

Ten Ways eBooks Are Changing the Publishing Industry

As eBooks evolve, our notion of what books are will change. In this chapter, I peer into my crystal ball and predict how eBooks will change certain genres. Some of my predictions fall into the Well, Duh! category, but others make you think about the future. If any of these ideas excite your imagination, feel free to run with them, add your own, and start writing.

ePublishing's Impact on Business Books

Business professionals are often in a hurry to get information. Rather than reading 200 to 300 pages, they prefer to read a summary of relevant concepts presented in a 10- to 50-page format. For this reason, much business-oriented information will be published as eMatter in the future. *eMatter documents* are longer than an article, but shorter than a full-length book. All it will take for eMatter to become popular is a few eMatter bestsellers; then many authors will start publishing in a shorter format. If you're interested in writing and publishing eMatter, go to MightyWords.com (www.mightywords.com). The Web site pays authors a 50 percent royalty for every eMatter document sold from the site.

In addition to new document lengths, business eBooks will be marketed in new ways. Seth Godin, an author known for his innovative approach to consumer marketing, is launching a new eBook called *Unleashing the Ideavirus*. Seth tests the theories in his book by giving away a free PDF version of the eBook from his Web site (www.ideavirus.com/). If enough people download the free version, he will offer a printed version. His theory is that people will prefer to pay for a hardcover version, even if they can get the digital version for free.

ePublishing's Impact on Cookbooks

Although the basic nature of cookbooks won't change as more are converted to eBook format, the recipes can be enhanced by the addition of the following elements:

- **Recipe calculators:** Calculators let the cook quickly convert the amounts needed for each recipe when the number of servings changes. If you like a recipe that serves four, but you need to feed six people, the calculator automatically converts the recipe to meet your needs.

- **Searching for specific ingredients:** If you have chicken, peas, and carrots in the fridge, and noodles in the pantry, you can enter these items into a search engine and see all the recipes that use these ingredients, such as chicken-noodle soup.

- **Save your own variations of a recipe:** Because eBooks let you annotate the content, you can customize recipes and save your notes with the original cookbook.

- **Audio:** You won't need to look at the cookbook every two minutes if the instructions are read aloud to you.

- **Video:** I'm no Julia Child, so my cooking efforts could be improved if I saw a short video of how she whips egg whites into soft peaks.

ePublishing's Impact on Educational Textbooks

eBooks and are made for each other. In the future, students won't have to lug heavy book bags or wait in long lines at the college bookstore worrying whether the last copy of *Introduction to Psychology* was already sold. Instead, it will seem natural to store all textbooks on a single reading device. Students will be able to download textbooks from the college-bookstore Web site, and the funds will be debited from Mom and Dad's bank account. Professors will save lecture notes and syllabi to eBook format, so these can be installed on the eBook reader along with the textbooks. Finally, because the student can take notes on the eBook reader's screen instead of on paper, students will only need to carry their eBook device. I sprained my right shoulder from carrying a knapsack with too much jetsam. . . . If I had an eBook, I could've avoided a lot of pain.

ePublishing's Impact on Erotic Books

The video industry got its start through the sale of erotic videotapes. Many people bought VCRs so they could view the tapes in the privacy of their homes. As more homes had VCRs, family-oriented entertainment was also released on videotapes because there was enough of a market to make production profitable.

Although the model hasn't worked in exactly the same way for the growing eBook industry, there's a large market for erotic eBooks. Many of the same eBook techniques that will become prevalent in trade fiction (interactivity and the use of alternate media) will also be used in erotic work. (I could go into greater detail, but I should stop before I begin to blush. . . .)

ePublishing's Impact on Mysteries

Mysteries will become more like interactive games where readers can click clues to get more information. Some clues will be more relevant than others, but the audience won't know this until the end of the story. At the end of a Whodunit, the audience can click one of several characters (like Colonel Mustard in the library) to determine whether they guessed correctly. For mysteries and thrillers based on real life, the audience will be able to click and read supplemental information (like police reports, eyewitness accounts, and so on).

ePublishing's Impact on Reference Books

When I bought a PocketPC, it came with a copy of the Microsoft Reader and the Encarta Pocket Dictionary, so I spent some time playing with the dictionary. I have to admit, I wasn't very impressed. As much as I like eBooks, I prefer using my printed dictionary.

It wasn't until I clicked the word *brigandes* in my eBook version of Michael Crichton's *Timeline* that I discovered the dictionary was cool. After I clicked the word, the Microsoft Reader displayed a small menu of choices on top of the eBook's text (add bookmark, add highlight, add note, add drawing, find, copy text, and look up). Clicking the Lookup option showed the definition *(bandit)* in the window that previously displayed the menu. Now edified, I was able to click the text outside of the window to return to the novel.

As eBooks become more prevalent, you'll become less aware of reference books as separate entities. When you need information, it will be there whenever you request it. After getting the data you desire, you'll be able to return to whatever you were reading.

ePublishing's Impact on Romance Books

Many romance authors have already produced eBooks. The current crop of these are similar to their printed counterparts (Boy meets Girl, some obstacle prevents Boy from being with Girl, but love conquers all, and Boy gets Girl in the end). As more writers experiment with what eBooks can offer, romance novels will include some of the following interactive benefits:

- ✔ Historical novels can feature a timeline to set the story within the context of a period in time.

- ✔ In addition to reading the dialogue, the audience can click a link to find out what the main characters are really thinking or feeling at different points in the story.

- ✔ The full text of love letters from one character to another can be accessed from a link without detracting from the flow of the story.

- ✔ As with other novels, multiple endings can be presented, or the story can be told from multiple points of view.

ePublishing's Impact on Science Fiction and Fantasy Books

Many science fiction and fantasy authors have already published in eBook format, and many publishers exist that focus exclusively on these genres. Because Sci Fi and Fantasy authors create other worlds, they can experiment with creative interfaces to present the story to the audience.

Instead of starting on page one of a text, the reader could see an image of a spaceship's control panel. Clicking any one of the buttons takes the reader to a different starting point for the story. Schematics for shuttles and other equipment can be included in the story, and can act as an interface to take the audience to different sections of the story. Detailed descriptions and histories can be provided for each character.

Clicking the name of an alien shows what its native language looks like — assuming aliens can write. If sound clips are included, the audience can hear what an alien sounds like — assuming aliens can make sounds. Because of the nature of the genre, Sci Fi and Fantasy authors have the most freedom to experiment with the eBook format and help develop eBooks as a new media.

ePublishing's Impact on Self-Help Books

Although the text of self-help eBooks will stay similar to printed books, authors can offer interactive extras that can add to the value of the eBook. Some of these extras include:

- Links to online support groups where the audience can go to participate in chats and leave messages for others.

- When a person purchases a self-help eBook from a publisher, he or she can be added to a subscriber list to receive daily affirmations (or other messages) through e-mail.

- Self-help books that include worksheets can leave blank areas for the audience to write in; this can be useful for tracking progress or keeping a daily log.

- Links can take the audience to a Web site for updated information or to find a calendar which shows where and when the author will be speaking.

ePublishing's Impact on Travel Books

When my husband and I went on our honeymoon in the Cayman Islands, we packed multiple guidebooks about where to go for sightseeing, things to do, and places to snorkel and dive. Our bags would have been lighter if we had access to eBooks.

Soon, you'll be able to purchase and download the text of any travel book you want to bring on your trip. This can be especially useful if you travel to multiple destinations. Print a copy of your itinerary to eBook format, download an English-French/French-English dictionary, and you're ready for any adventure.

Part VI
Appendix

The 5th Wave   By Rich Tennant

"Exactly whose idea was it to try and download all of the Harry Potter books?"

In this part . . .

Last, but not least, Part VI contains the information about the CD-ROM that's bundled with this book. Although it may not make for the most enjoyable reading, it's definitely useful when you're trying to install the CD!

Appendix

About the CD

●●●

*Y*ou can find the following on the *ePublishing For Dummies* CD-ROM:

- ✔ Acrobat Reader 4.0, an evaluation version of the program
- ✔ Author Files mentioned in the book
- ✔ Glassbook Reader, a freeware version of the program
- ✔ Night Kitchen TK3 Reader, a beta version of the program
- ✔ Open eBook Structure Specification, a freeware version of the specification
- ✔ OverDrive ReaderWorks Standard, an evaluation version of the program
- ✔ Software Personal Publisher, a freeware version of the program

System Requirements

Make sure that your computer meets the following minimum system requirements. If your computer doesn't match most of these requirements, you may
have problems using the contents of the CD:

- ✔ A PC with an Intel Pentium II or faster processor.
- ✔ Microsoft Windows 95 or later.
- ✔ Word 2000.
- ✔ At least 32MB of total RAM installed on your computer. (For best
  performance, we recommend at least 64MB of RAM installed.)
- ✔ At least 100MB of hard-drive space available to install all the software
  on this CD. (You'll need less space if you don't install every program.)
- ✔ A CD-ROM drive — double-speed (2x) or faster.
- ✔ A monitor capable of displaying at least 16-bit color.

Need more information on the basics? Check out *PCs For Dummies,* 7th Edition, by Dan Gookin; *Windows 95 For Dummies,* 2nd Edition, or *Windows 98 For Dummies* both by Andy Rathbone (all published by IDG Books Worldwide, Inc.).

Using the CD with Microsoft Windows

1. **Insert the CD into your computer's CD-ROM drive.**

2. **Open your browser.**

   If you don't have a browser, Microsoft Internet Explorer and Netscape Communicator are included on the CD-ROM. They can be found in the Programs folders at the root of the CD.

3. **Choose Start⇨Run.**

4. **In the dialog box that appears, type** D:\START.HTM.

   Replace *D* with the proper drive letter if your CD-ROM drive uses a different letter. (If you don't know the letter, see how your CD-ROM drive is listed under My Computer.)

5. **Read through the license agreement, nod your head and smile, and click the Accept button if you want to use the CD.**

   After you click Accept, you jump to the Main Menu.

   This action displays the file that walks you through the content of the CD.

6. **To navigate within the interface, simply click any topic of interest to be taken to an explanation of the files on the CD and how to use or install them.**

7. **To install the software from the CD, simply click the software name.**

   You see two options — the option to run or open the file from the current location or the option to save the file to your hard drive. Choose to run or open the file from its current location and the installation procedure continues. After you're done with the interface, simply close your browser as usual.

To run some of the programs, you may need to keep the CD inside your CD-ROM drive. This is a Good Thing. Otherwise, the installed program would require you to install a very large chunk of the program to your hard-drive space, which would keep you from installing other software.

What's on the CD

Shareware programs are fully functional, free trial versions of copyrighted programs. If you like particular programs, register with their authors for a nominal fee and receive licenses, enhanced versions, and technical support. Freeware programs are free copyrighted games, applications, and utilities. You can copy them to as many PCs as you like — free — but they have no technical support. GNU software is governed by its own license, which is included inside the folder of the GNU software. There are no restrictions on distribution of this software. See the GNU license for more details. Trial, demo, or evaluation versions are usually limited either by time or functionality (such as being unable to save projects).

Here's a summary of the software on this CD.

Acrobat Reader 4.0

This evaluation version of the Adobe Acrobat Reader lets you view eBooks formatted as PDF files. For more information on the Acrobat Reader, visit the Adobe Web site at `www.adobe.com/products/acrobat/readermain.html`.

Author files mentioned in the book

Sample files mentioned in *ePublishing For Dummies* are included on the CD-ROM in the **\Samples** directory. This is **D:\Samples**. (Replace *D* with the proper drive letter if your CD-ROM drive uses a different letter. If you don't know the letter, see how your CD-ROM drive is listed under My Computer.)

The following sample files are included in this directory:

- ✔ A copy of Chapter 1 formatted as an Adobe Acrobat file (C1.PDF), for the Rocket eBook (C1.RB), for the Softbook Reader (C1.IMP), for the Microsoft Reader (C1.LIT), as an article (A1.PDF), as a booklet (B1.PDF), as a manual (M1.PDF), and as a chapter from an eBook (C1.PDF)

- ✔ A copy of the sample Hello Wonderland document file mentioned in Chapter 10 (Hello.doc)

- ✔ A copy of the sample Alice image mentioned in Chapter 10 (Alice.jpg)

- ✔ A copy of the OPF file created in Chapter 10 (Wonder.opf)

- ✔ A sample permission letter to use other people's work (permis.doc)
- ✔ A copy of Chapter 18 formatted with ten second-level headings (C18.doc)
- ✔ A copy of the ImageMap document mentioned in Chapter 7 (IM.doc)
- ✔ The ePublishing costs spreadsheet mentioned in Chapter 14 (EC.XLS)
- ✔ Templates to help you create articles, booklets, manuals, and eBooks (A.DOT, B.DOT, M.DOT, and e.DOT)

Glassbook Reader

This freeware version of the Glassbook Reader lets you view Acrobat (PDF files) with an eBook-like interface. The Glassbook Reader lets you organize your eBooks in a Library view and lets you purchase and download new eBooks. For more information on Glassbook, go to the Web site at bookstore.glassbook.com/store/getreader.asp.

Night Kitchen's TK3 Reader

This beta version of the TK3 Reader lets you view files created with Night Kitchen's TK3 authoring software. eBooks created with the software allow an author to incorporate media elements like animation, video, and sound. You should install *both* the TK3 Reader and the TK3 tools *before* you open any of the TK3 documents. For the latest version of the reader, visit the Night Kitchen Web site at www.nightkitchen.com/downloadreader.

Open eBook Structure Specification

This freeware version of the specification describes how Open eBook (OEB) files should be formatted and describes how to use metadata tags to describe the eBook's content. To get more information about the specification, go to the Open eBook Web site at www.openebook.org/. You can see formatted eBook samples at www.openebook.org/samples.htm.

Note: This product went through revisions after this book went to print. For the most up-to-date info, go to www.openebook.org.

OverDrive ReaderWorks Standard

This evaluation version of ReaderWorks Standard lets you create eBooks formatted for the Microsoft Reader. The Publisher program is more comprehensive than the Microsoft Reader Word Add-in tool. The Publisher program lets you add custom eBook covers and metadata information to the eBook that you create. For more information about OverDrive Systems and its eBook Publishing solutions, visit the Web site at `www.overdrive.com/`.

SoftBook Personal Publisher

This freeware program works with Microsoft Word 2000 to create eBooks formatted for the SoftBook Reader. The program converts Word documents into eBooks and lets you save ORB files as a by-product of the conversion process. For more information about the Personal Publisher software, visit SoftBook's Web site at `www.softbook.com/enterprise/personal.asp`.

If You've Got Problems (Of the CD Kind)

I tried my best to compile programs that work on most computers with the minimum system requirements. Alas, your computer may differ, and some programs may not work properly for some reason.

The two likeliest problems are that you don't have enough memory (RAM) for the programs you want to use, or you have other programs running that are affecting installation or running of a program. If you get error messages like `Not enough memory` or `Setup cannot continue`, try one or more of these methods and then try using the software again:

- ✔ **Turn off any anti-virus software that you have on your computer:** Installers sometimes mimic virus activity and may make your computer incorrectly believe that it's being infected by a virus.

- ✔ **Close all running programs:** The more programs you run, the less memory is available to other programs. Installers also typically update files and programs. So if you keep other programs running, installation may not work properly.

- ✔ **Have your local computer store add more RAM to your computer:** This is, admittedly, a drastic and somewhat expensive step. However, if you have a Windows 95 PC, adding more memory can really help the speed of your computer and allow more programs to run at the same time. This may include closing the CD interface and running a product's installation program from Windows Explorer.

If you still have trouble installing the items from the CD, please call the IDG Books Worldwide Customer Service phone number: 800-762-2974 (outside the U.S.: 317-572-3993).

Index

Notes

Notes

IDG Books Worldwide, Inc., End-User License Agreement

READ THIS. You should carefully read these terms and conditions before opening the software packet(s) included with this book ("Book"). This is a license agreement ("Agreement") between you and IDG Books Worldwide, Inc. ("IDGB"). By opening the accompanying software packet(s), you acknowledge that you have read and accept the following terms and conditions. If you do not agree and do not want to be bound by such terms and conditions, promptly return the Book and the unopened software packet(s) to the place you obtained them for a full refund.

1. **License Grant.** IDGB grants to you (either an individual or entity) a nonexclusive license to use one copy of the enclosed software program(s) (collectively, the "Software") solely for your own personal or business purposes on a single computer (whether a standard computer or a workstation component of a multiuser network). The Software is in use on a computer when it is loaded into temporary memory (RAM) or installed into permanent memory (hard disk, CD-ROM, or other storage device). IDGB reserves all rights not expressly granted herein.

2. **Ownership.** IDGB is the owner of all right, title, and interest, including copyright, in and to the compilation of the Software recorded on the disk(s) or CD-ROM ("Software Media"). Copyright to the individual programs recorded on the Software Media is owned by the author or other authorized copyright owner of each program. Ownership of the Software and all proprietary rights relating thereto remain with IDGB and its licensers.

3. **Restrictions on Use and Transfer.**

   (a) You may only (i) make one copy of the Software for backup or archival purposes, or (ii) transfer the Software to a single hard disk, provided that you keep the original for backup or archival purposes. You may not (i) rent or lease the Software, (ii) copy or reproduce the Software through a LAN or other network system or through any computer subscriber system or bulletin-board system, or (iii) modify, adapt, or create derivative works based on the Software.

   (b) You may not reverse engineer, decompile, or disassemble the Software. You may transfer the Software and user documentation on a permanent basis, provided that the transferee agrees to accept the terms and conditions of this Agreement and you retain no copies. If the Software is an update or has been updated, any transfer must include the most recent update and all prior versions.

4. **Restrictions on Use of Individual Programs.** You must follow the individual requirements and restrictions detailed for each individual program in Appendix A of this Book. These limitations are also contained in the individual license agreements recorded on the Software Media. These limitations may include a requirement that after using the program for a specified period of time, the user must pay a registration fee or discontinue use. By opening the Software packet(s), you will be agreeing to abide by the licenses and restrictions for these individual programs that are detailed in Appendix A and on the Software Media. None of the material on this Software Media or listed in this Book may ever be redistributed, in original or modified form, for commercial purposes.

5. **Limited Warranty.**

IDGB warrants that the Software and Software Media are free from defects in materials and workmanship under normal use for a period of sixty (60) days from the date of purchase of this Book. If IDGB receives notification within the warranty period of defects in materials or workmanship, IDGB will replace the defective Software Media.

(b) **IDGB AND THE AUTHOR OF THE BOOK DISCLAIM ALL OTHER WARRANTIES, EXPRESS OR IMPLIED, INCLUDING WITHOUT LIMITATION IMPLIED WARRANTIES OF MERCHANTABILITY AND FITNESS FOR A PARTICULAR PURPOSE, WITH RESPECT TO THE SOFTWARE, THE PROGRAMS, THE SOURCE CODE CONTAINED THEREIN, AND/OR THE TECHNIQUES DESCRIBED IN THIS BOOK. IDGB DOES NOT WARRANT THAT THE FUNCTIONS CONTAINED IN THE SOFTWARE WILL MEET YOUR REQUIREMENTS OR THAT THE OPERATION OF THE SOFTWARE WILL BE ERROR FREE.**

(c) This limited warranty gives you specific legal rights, and you may have other rights that vary from jurisdiction to jurisdiction.

6. **Remedies.**

(a) IDGB's entire liability and your exclusive remedy for defects in materials and workmanship shall be limited to replacement of the Software Media, which may be returned to IDGB with a copy of your receipt at the following address: Software Media Fulfillment Department, Attn.: *ePublishing For Dummies,* IDG Books Worldwide, Inc., 10475 Crosspoint Blvd., Indianapolis, IN 46256, or call 800-762-2974. Please allow three to four weeks for delivery. This Limited Warranty is void if failure of the Software Media has resulted from accident, abuse, or misapplication. Any replacement Software Media will be warranted for the remainder of the original warranty period or thirty (30) days, whichever is longer.

(b) In no event shall IDGB or the author be liable for any damages whatsoever (including without limitation damages for loss of business profits, business interruption, loss of business information, or any other pecuniary loss) arising from the use of or inability to use the Book or the Software, even if IDGB has been advised of the possibility of such damages.

(c) Because some jurisdictions do not allow the exclusion or limitation of liability for consequential or incidental damages, the above limitation or exclusion may not apply to you.

7. **U.S. Government Restricted Rights.** Use, duplication, or disclosure of the Software for or on behalf of the United States of America, its agencies and/or instrumentalities (the "U.S. Government") is subject to restrictions stated in paragraph (c)(1)(ii) of the Rights in Technical Data and Computer Software clause of DFARS 252.227-7013, or subparagraphs (c) (1) and (2) of the Commerical Computer Software – Restricted Rights clause at FAR 52.227-19, and in similar clauses in the NASA FAR supplement, as applicable.

8. **General.** This Agreement constitutes the entire understanding of the parties and revokes and supersedes all prior agreements, oral or written, between them and may not be modified or amended except in a writing signed by both parties hereto that specifically refers to this Agreement. This Agreement shall take precedence over any other documents that may be in conflict herewith. If any one or more provisions contained in this Agreement are held by any court or tribunal to be invalid, illegal, or otherwise unenforceable, each and every other provision shall remain in full force and effect.

Installation Instructions

The *ePublishing For Dummies* CD-ROM offers valuable information that you don't wanna miss. To install the items from the CD to your hard drive, follow these steps:

1. **Insert the CD into your computer's CD-ROM drive.**

2. **Open your browser.**

   If you don't have a browser, Microsoft Internet Explorer and Netscape Communicator are included on the CD-ROM. They can be found in the Programs folders at the root of the CD.

3. **Click Start⇨Run.**

4. **In the dialog box that appears, type** D:\START.HTM.

   Replace *D* with the proper drive letter if your CD-ROM drive uses a different letter. (If you don't know the letter, see how your CD-ROM drive is listed under My Computer.)

5. **Read through the license agreement, nod your head and smile, and click the Accept button if you want to use the CD.**

   After you click Accept, you jump to the Main Menu.

   This action displays the file that walks you through the content of the CD.

6. **To navigate within the interface, simply click any topic of interest to be taken to an explanation of the files on the CD and how to use or install them.**

7. **To install the software from the CD, simply click the software name.**

   You see two options — the option to run or open the file from the current location or the option to save the file to your hard drive. Choose to run or open the file from its current location and the installation procedure continues. After you're done with the interface, simply close your browser as usual.

For more complete information, please see the Appendix, "About the CD."

IDG BOOKS WORLDWIDE
BOOK REGISTRATION

Register
This Book
and Win!

We want to hear from you!

Visit **http://my2cents.dummies.com** to register this book and tell us how you liked it!

- ✔ Get entered in our monthly prize giveaway.

- ✔ Give us feedback about this book — tell us what you like best, what you like least, or maybe what you'd like to ask the author and us to change!

- ✔ Let us know any other *For Dummies®* topics that interest you.

Your feedback helps us determine what books to publish, tells us what coverage to add as we revise our books, and lets us know whether we're meeting your needs as a *For Dummies* reader. You're our most valuable resource, and what you have to say is important to us!

Not on the Web yet? It's easy to get started with *Dummies 101®: The Internet For Windows® 98* or *The Internet For Dummies®* at local retailers everywhere.

Or let us know what you think by sending us a letter at the following address:

For Dummies Book Registration
Dummies Press
10475 Crosspoint Blvd.
Indianapolis, IN 46256

BESTSELLING
BOOK SERIES